## Praise for *Crucial Collaborations: A Framework to Enhance Inclusion for Students With Disabilities*

"Through scholarly research and personal narrative, the contributors to *Crucial Collaborations* open an essential conversation about cross-functional approaches to processes and cultures that prioritize an accessibility mindset. Theoretically based, the groundbreaking framework is immediately applicable and ultimately beneficial to all stakeholders involved. *Crucial Collaborations* is an important contribution to all those who support students and their educational goals."

—**Michele C. Murray**, Senior Vice President for Student Development and Mission, College of the Holy Cross

"*Crucial Collaborations* provides an invaluable tool for realizing equality for students with disabilities in higher education. It seamlessly integrates the knowledge garnered by years of practical application by its editors with the lived experiences of successful college graduates with disabilities."

—**Michael Ashley Stein**, Executive Director, Harvard Law School Project on Disability

"This book is ideal for experienced practitioners who have been yearning for a premiere resource to guide the delivery of optimal learning experiences for students in a post-ableist framework. The distinctive operational focus of this compilation is complemented by helpful first-person narratives that will resonate with professionals committed to inclusion and success for all students with varying and often complex exceptionalities."

—**Peter F. Lake**, Professor of Law, Stetson University College of Law

"Too often when equity, social justice, and inclusion are front and center issues on college and university campuses, those with disabilities do not consistently come to mind and can be some of the most marginalized members. This book and the Collaborative Framework are valuable resources in addressing this shortcoming. They are much needed tools for improving services and support to students who offer much to our campuses but continue to encounter too many institutional and individual barriers to their success."

—**Mike Segawa**, Vice President for Student Affairs, University of Puget Sound and Pitzer College (retired)

"*Crucial Collaborations* takes a layered, systematic approach to solving accommodations conundrums. The Collaborative Framework is a practical way of working to share information across educators and service providers with the goal of ensuring equitable, inclusive practices without sacrificing academic rigor."

—**Kristie Proctor**, Director of Student Accessibility Services, Quinsigamond Community College

"People with disabilities constitute a critical and integral part of higher education. To guarantee students' success in pursuing educational goals, we must rely on best practices and tools that will help them succeed. The Collaborative Framework is based on years of experience by the authors. It is a practical visual road map to success! The Collaborative Framework, best practices, and student narratives make this book a must-read for stakeholders invested in the long-term success of students with disabilities."

—**Ruth M. Molina**, Director of the New England Higher Education Recruitment Consortium, Harvard University

"At once practical and aspirational, *Crucial Collaborations* invites readers to rethink current methods of facilitating inclusion and belonging in higher education, and to demonstrate that accessibility for all benefits all. This book is a thoughtful celebration of difference; it should be required reading for optimizing success of students with disabilities."

—**H'Sien Hayward**, Licensed Clinical Psychologist

"*Crucial Collaborations* is a necessary and critical resource at a time when the dialogue around disability and neurodiversity is greatly improving on campus, but institutions are challenged in navigating ever more complex issues, including digital accessibility, increasing technology in the classroom, changed expectations following a pandemic, and a range of other issues. The editors bring their own expertise to the fore in setting the structure, but also provide ample room for their stellar contributors to provide their own view of where disability rights are now and where they have the potential to move in the future."

—**Phil Catanzano**, Faculty, Harvard Graduate School of Education

# CRUCIAL COLLABORATIONS

*A Practical Framework to Ensure Access, Equity, and Inclusion for Students With Disabilities*

# CRUCIAL COLLABORATIONS

*A Practical Framework to Ensure Access, Equity, and Inclusion for Students With Disabilities*

Neal E. Lipsitz
Michael Berger
Eileen Connell **Berger**
*Editors*

Student Affairs Administrators
in Higher Education

Copyright © 2024 by the National Association of Student Personnel Administrators (NASPA), Inc. All rights reserved.

Published by
NASPA–Student Affairs Administrators in Higher Education
111 K Street, NE
10th Floor
Washington, DC 20002
www.naspa.org

No part of this publication may be reproduced, stored in a retrieval system, or transmitted in any form or by any means, now known or hereafter invented, including electronic, mechanical, photocopying, recording, scanning, information storage and retrieval, or otherwise, except as permitted under Section 107 of the 1976 United States Copyright Act, without the prior written permission of the Publisher.

Additional copies may be purchased by contacting the NASPA publications department at 202-265-7500 or visiting http://bookstore.naspa.org.

NASPA does not discriminate on the basis of race; color; national origin; religion; sex; age; gender identity or expression; affectional or sexual orientation; veteran status; disability; marital status; personal appearance; family responsibilities; genetic information; educational status; political affiliation; place of residence or business; source of income; caste; matriculation; credit information; status as a survivor or family member of a survivor of domestic violence, a sexual offense, or stalking; reproductive health decision making; or any other basis protected by law in any of its policies, programs, publications, and services. NASPA prohibits discrimination and harassment at any time, including during its events or within publications and online learning communities.

**Library of Congress Cataloging-in-Publication Data**

Names: Lipsitz, Neal E., editor. | Berger, Michael (Chemistry professor), editor. | Berger, Eileen Connell, editor.

Title: Crucial collaborations : a practical framework to ensure access, equity, and inclusion for students with disabilities / Neal E. Lipsitz, Michael Berger, Eileen Connell Berger, editors.

Description: First edition. | Washington, DC : NASPA–Student Affairs Administrators in Higher Education, [2024] | Includes bibliographical references and index.

Identifiers: ISBN: 978-1-948213-44-8 (paperback) | 978-1-948213-45-5 (ebook)

Subjects: LCSH: Students with disabilities--Education (Higher)--United States. | Students with disabilities--Services for--United States. | Students with disabilities--Legal status, laws, etc.--United States. | Student affairs services. | Inclusive education. | BISAC: EDUCATION / Administration / Higher. | EDUCATION / Schools / Levels / Higher. | EDUCATION / Inclusive Education. | EDUCATION / Student Life & Student Affairs.

Printed and bound in the United States of America

FIRST EDITION

# Contents

| | |
|---|---|
| *Glossary of Abbreviations and Acronyms* | ix |
| *List of Figures and Tables* | xiii |
| *Preface* | xv |
| *Acknowledgments* | xxi |
| *Editors and Contributors* | xxiii |

## Part I
## The Collaborative Framework

Chapter 1   Structure and Function of the Collaborative Framework     3
*Neal E. Lipsitz, Michael Berger, and Eileen Connell Berger*

## Part II
## Self-Advocacy and Inclusion/Socialization

Chapter 2   Relationships Matter: Self-Advocacy, Mentorship, and the Transformative Power of Disability Services     45
*Kevin T. Mintz and Eileen Connell Berger*

Chapter 3   The Importance of Feeling Included: Perceived Belonging Among Students With Disabilities in Higher Education     61
*Katherine C. Aquino*

# Part III
# Individual Differences, Life Transitions, and Attitudes

| | | |
|---|---|---|
| Chapter 4 | My Search for Access and Accommodations in Higher Education<br>*Valerie Piro* | 89 |
| Chapter 5 | Disability Rights Are Civil Rights<br>*Mary Lee Vance* | 105 |
| Chapter 6 | Neurodiversity<br>*Neal E. Lipsitz* | 121 |

# Part IV
# Academic Rigor, New Pedagogies, Disability Law, and Technology

| | | |
|---|---|---|
| Chapter 7 | New Pedagogy With Academic Rigor: Universal Design for Learning<br>*Lyman L. Dukes III and Joseph W. Madaus* | 141 |
| Chapter 8 | A Conversation About Disability Law With Paul Grossman and Jamie Axelrod<br>*Michael Berger* | 159 |
| Chapter 9 | College Experiences of Students With Disabilities Viewed Through a Technology Lens<br>*Sheryl Burgstahler* | 189 |

# Part V
# Implementation and Best Practices

Chapter 10  How to Use the Collaborative Framework          215
          *Neal E. Lipsitz, Michael Berger, and*
          *Eileen Connell Berger*

*Appendix: The Collaborative Framework*                     *237*
*Index*                                                     *239*

# Glossary of Abbreviations and Acronyms

Many acronyms are used in higher education and the disability community, and readers may not be readily familiar with all of them. This glossary provides a quick reference to acronyms and abbreviations used in this book.

| ADA | Americans with Disabilities Act of 1990 |
| --- | --- |
| ADAAA | Americans with Disabilities Act Amendments Act of 2008 |
| ADD | attention-deficit disorder |
| ADHD | attention-deficit/hyperactivity disorder |
| ADS | access and disability services |
| AEO | access to education office |
| AHEAD | Association on Higher Education and Disability |
| AT | assistive technology; refers to technology that is accessible to, usable by, and inclusive of students with disabilities |
| ATS | accessible technology services |
| CAST | Center for Applied Special Technology |
| DEI | diversity, equity, and inclusion |
| DO-IT | Disabilities, Opportunities, Internetworking, and Technology Center |
| DOJ | U.S. Department of Justice; prosecutes civil rights violations |

| | |
|---|---|
| **DRC** | disability resource center |
| **DSO** | disability services office |
| **DSS** | disability support services |
| **EEOC** | U.S. Equal Employment Opportunity Commission; wrote the regulations for the **ADAAA** |
| **FERPA** | Family Educational Rights and Privacy Act |
| **HIPAA** | Health Insurance Portability and Accountability Act |
| **IDEA** | Individuals with Disabilities Education Act of 1976; pertains to K–12 and ensures a free and appropriate public education for students with disabilities |
| **IEP** | individualized education programs |
| **IT** | information technology; refers to computer and data systems |
| **NCES** | National Center for Education Statistics |
| **NCSA** | National Council on Severe Autism |
| **NIH** | National Institutes of Health |
| **OCD** | obsessive-compulsive disorder |
| **OCR** | U.S. Department of Education Office for Civil Rights; processes civil rights complaints |
| **ODS** | office of disability services |
| **OSA** | office for student access |
| **SAS** | student accessibility services |
| **Section 504** | Section 504 of the Vocational Rehabilitation Act of 1973; an anti-discrimination federal law |
| **STEM** | science, technology, engineering, and math |
| **SWD** | students with disabilities |
| **UD** | universal design; general principles to ensure accessibility, usability, and inclusivity in all environments for all users |

| UDHE | universal design in higher education; includes all aspects of technology procurement, development, and use to ensure that everyone in postsecondary education has access to information, courses, media, and physical spaces |
|---|---|
| UDI | universal design of instruction; another term for **UDL** |
| UDL | universal design for learning; refers to the design of curriculum and instruction based on **UD** principles |
| UID | universal instructional design; another term for **UDL** |

# List of Figures and Tables

## Figures

| | | |
|---|---|---|
| 1.1 | Areas of Interest and Influence for Major Stakeholders | 30 |
| 7.1 | The UDL Circle | 146 |
| 7.2 | Lesson Orientation Process | 150 |
| 9.1 | Sheryl and Rodney With His Magic Switch Box | 191 |
| 9.2 | Characteristics of Any UD Strategy: Is It Accessible, Usable, and Inclusive? | 196 |
| 9.3 | Components of the UDHE Framework | 199 |
| 9.4 | DO-IT's Student-Centered Stakeholder Model | 201 |

## Tables

| | | |
|---|---|---|
| 1.1 | Description of Nine Lenses Mapped to the Most Relevant Stakeholders | 29 |
| 1.2 | The Collaborative Framework Architecture | 32 |
| 1.3 | The Collaborative Framework for Mapping Varying Degree of Significance of the Lenses for Each Stakeholder | 33 |
| 1.4 | Examples of Stakeholder Roles and Responsibilities for the Lenses of Self-Advocacy, Individual Differences, and Life Transition | 35 |
| 1.5 | Examples of Stakeholder Roles and Responsibilities for the Lenses of Academic Rigor, New Pedagogies, and Technology | 36 |

| | | |
|---|---|---|
| 1.6 | Examples of Stakeholder Roles and Responsibilities for the Lenses of Disability Law, Attitudes, and Inclusion/Socialization | 37 |
| 3.1 | Characteristic Comparison of Students With and Without Self-Identified Disabilities, Percentage ($N = 18,990$) | 69 |
| 3.2 | Identified Disability Characteristics of Students With Disabilities, 2011–2012 Academic Year, Percentage ($N = 2,120$) | 70 |
| 3.3 | Perceived Positive Socioacademic Experiences by Disability Self-Disclosure Status, Percentage ($N = 18,990$) | 72 |
| 3.4 | Differences in Socioacademic Postsecondary Experiences by Disability Self-Disclosure Status ($N = 18,990$) | 73 |
| 7.1 | CAST UDL Guidelines Applied to Higher Education | 153 |
| 10.1 | The Collaborative Framework Considering Self-Advocacy, Individual Differences, and Life Transition | 218 |
| 10.2 | The Collaborative Framework Considering Academic Rigor, New Pedagogies, and Technology | 220 |
| 10.3 | The Collaborative Framework Considering Disability Law, Attitudes, and Inclusion/Socialization | 223 |
| 10.4 | Completed Collaborative Framework for *Grabin v. Marymount Manhattan College* Case | 233 |

# Preface

As authors and colleagues, we have explored, over 15 years, every aspect of providing services in access and disability services (ADS). We have surveyed, researched, studied, written articles, presented workshops, conducted trainings, and created events on our campuses to bring together all stakeholders in our work. We have also sought a deeper understanding of individual differences among our students and colleagues—one that resonates with the cultural changes encouraging the conversations and shifts around the acceptance and celebration of differences in all our campus communities. Our varied experiences in institutions of higher education—as a director of an accessibility and disability services office, as an associate dean for student well-being, and as a faculty member—have shown us that ensuring appropriate access and a sense of belonging for students with disabilities can be a complex and difficult process. Each student with a disability can have their own unique physical or mental health requirements, and every institution has its own unique organizational structure, culture, faculty, staff, and students. Compliance with disability law is an important component often not correctly or completely considered when institutions attempt to untangle myriad issues involving those stakeholders—all of whom have different priorities or responsibilities on campus.

In this book, we introduce and explain the Collaborative Framework—a tool that helps stakeholders see the big picture and best allocate resources, while minimizing misunderstandings, gaps in service, and duplicative efforts. ADS providers will find the framework useful for meetings with students, faculty, administrators, and parents/guardians when participants seek to discuss a collaborative approach to student success, assessment of access/disability services, and training access/disability service providers, among other uses.

The framework is based on lenses and stakeholders. Each stakeholder views a student's college experience through a unique set of lenses—defined by that stakeholder's specific role, responsibilities, and priorities—which influences their assessment of that student's college experience. We have selected lenses frequently addressed in the higher education and disability studies literature for significantly affecting the educational experience: self-advocacy or self-determination, individual differences, life transition, academic rigor, new pedagogies, technology, disability law, attitudes, and inclusion/socialization. The framework provides a structure for an analytical review of the current roles and responsibilities of stakeholders who can affect the collegiate experience of students with disabilities—specifically, faculty, disability service providers, senior administration, and parents/guardians, along with the students themselves.

There is a considerable body of literature, especially in the area of disability studies, that describes different models or frameworks for understanding disability, such as the medical model (focus on the student), the social model (focus on the institution and society), and the minority model (focus on students with disabilities as a subgroup). Critical disability theory and the disability-diversity (dis)connect model are recent theoretical frameworks that contextualize students with disabilities in the social–political environment, including human rights and diversity. Rather than taking a theoretical approach, the Collaborative Framework is a practical tool for stakeholders.

Focusing on the work of an ADS office, we demonstrate how student affairs professionals can use the framework to evaluate whether their processes and systems are effectively and efficiently delivering services to students. The framework considers the complexities of laws, policies, and practices, as well as the roles and responsibilities of the stakeholders, to ensure institutional compliance with civil rights and disability law. It can identify where opportunities exist to create a foundation for a more collaborative effort. The framework is also laid out in a clear format that is accessible to all stakeholders, providing a visual schema clearly assigning stakeholder roles and responsibilities.

## Organization of the Book

**Part I** lays the foundation for the Collaborative Framework. Chapter 1 describes how the framework is put together, identifying the stakeholders and the lenses they may use to view a particular request or resolve an issue with a student with a disability. Each lens is described in detail with extensive references, and we discuss which stakeholder is more likely to use which lenses in understanding or interpreting an issue with a student with a disability. Those using the framework clearly see that different stakeholders may be looking at a case quite differently, thus impeding an efficient and optimal solution to what at first may appear to be an unsurmountable problem.

**Part II** takes an in-depth look at the college experience of students with disabilities through various lenses. Stakeholders bring their own personal experiences and expertise to the table. Through a variety of exposition formats—conversations, reflections, and analysis—students with disabilities describe best practices to improve collaboration, optimize the delivery of access and disability services, and enhance their educational experience. We hear from former students with disabilities about their journey beyond college, and we hear from faculty, administrators, and staff responsible for providing access for them.

Chapter 2, a conversation between Kevin T. Mintz and Eileen Connell Berger, focuses on the lenses of self-advocacy and self-determination. In this chapter, Mintz describes his incredible journey through undergraduate and graduate schools. Despite his severe physical handicaps, he has succeeded thanks to the transformative power that mentorship and robust disability services can provide. The dialogue focuses on the following lenses through postsecondary education for a particular student with significant disabilities: campus attitudes, inclusion and socialization, individual differences, and self-advocacy/self-determination.

In Chapter 3, Katherine C. Aquino examines the lens of inclusion/socialization and finds that various sociocademic experiences can contribute to the perceived sense of belonging for students with self-disclosed disabilities. Stakeholders within the campus community who can support students with disabilities, including faculty members, disability resource professionals, and other institutional administrators, are important actors in a student's overall sense of belonging.

**Part III** presents three contributions that examine the lenses of individual differences and life transitions. In Chapter 4, Valerie Piro, a current doctoral student with physical disabilities, describes her search for access and accommodations in higher education. In Chapter 5, Mary Lee Vance, an experienced director of accessibility services, describes her academic and professional experiences as a Korean-born adoptee with muscular, visual, and auditory disabilities. She discusses the concept of disability rights as civil rights. In Chapter 6, Neal E. Lipsitz discusses the shift of neurodiversity from a pathology to a natural and valuable variation in neurology. There are personal narratives from two neurodiverse undergraduates, Clara Gibson and Terrence Smith.

**Part IV** details how to implement the framework and discusses best practices for its use. In Chapter 7, Lyman L. Dukes III and Joseph W. Madaus present an overview of universal design for learning (UDL). The authors describe instructional techniques and strategies they have used that both reflect UDL and maintain typical academic expectations for students. UDL is a pedagogical approach that can be employed in college settings to meet the learning needs of an array of students more effectively—without compromising the academic rigor of a university course. This chapter provides an outline—from design and planning to course delivery, instruction, and assessment—to implement UDL in your work.

In Chapter 8, Paul Grossman and Jamie Axelrod engage in a frank discussion that focuses on the status of disability law, its relationship to the Civil Rights Movement, and some of the major challenges to inclusion for students with disabilities in higher education. Grossman, a civil rights lawyer for nearly 50 years, is an active member of the California bar and the Disability Rights Bar Association. Axelrod is the director of disability resources at Northern Arizona University and a former president of the Association on Higher Education and Disability.

In Chapter 9, Sheryl Burgstahler points out that technology solutions and practices are becoming increasingly important for higher education institutions as they search for ways to provide, across degree programs, fluid access to materials and pedagogy with UD principles. This access will facilitate broader inclusion for all students and, consequently, lessen the need for individualized technology accommodations through ADA compliance.

**Part V** consists of Chapter 10, in which the editors review the many uses of the framework and offer guidance for implementation. Uses include facilitating inclusion and socialization, empowering through shared knowledge, and conducting assessment and analysis. This chapter maps two legal cases involving students with disabilities onto the framework to clarify stakeholders' roles and responsibilities, shedding light on stakeholder priorities and biases via a visual schema that can be used to think through more efficient—and more effective—solutions to complex issues that can arise in the real world. The framework can also be used to analyze a decision or process in the past: what went wrong, what went right, and what was learned.

Other uses of the framework described in this chapter are training, onboarding, internal and external reviews, assessment of campus attitudes toward students with disabilities (including disability as diversity), assessment of liability risk, and gap analysis.

The appendix includes a blank framework for your use.

Neal E. Lipsitz<br>
Michael Berger<br>
Eileen Connell Berger<br>
*September 2023*

# Acknowledgments

We express our gratitude to NASPA–Student Affairs Administrators in Higher Education and appreciate its support for the opportunity to address the topic of optimizing the educational experience of students with disabilities. We are grateful for the generosity of our authors and contributors, who have shared their expertise, scholarship, insights, and personal experiences. They have created an authentic and accessible narrative—giving readers a special way to understand the breadth and richness of diverse individuals in higher education. We have learned much from our authors; they have shown us how they have navigated the complex landscape of higher education from a disability perspective. We hope readers will also benefit from the knowledge and insights shared by the authors.

# Editors and Contributors

## Editors

**Eileen Connell Berger**, MSEd, has a unique set of professional experiences and a commitment to equal access and opportunity for students with disabilities as a speech–language and hearing educator, consultant, and administrator in public and private K–12 schools for two decades prior to her 28 years as an access and disability administrator in higher education. Now retired, she served as assistant director of the Office of Student Affairs and head of access and disability services at the Harvard Graduate School of Education (GSE), and director of the Office for Students with Disabilities at Salem State University and at Bunker Hill Community College. Berger regularly consults, writes, and presents with colleagues on aspects of disability, diversity policy, and practice. In 2015 she received the Excellence in Inclusive Leadership Award from the Harvard GSE Alumnae of Color Association, and while serving as the NASPA–Student Affairs Administrators in Higher Education Disability Knowledge Community cochair, she coproduced the webinar "Beyond the Americans with Disabilities Act." Berger holds an MS in education; worked toward an EdD in special education; has New York State, New York City, and Massachusetts speech, language, and hearing teacher certification; and has certification in assistive technology. She holds leadership roles as a consultant to nonprofit boards and organizations and maintains a private disability consultation practice.

**Michael Berger**, MBA, PhD, formerly senior scientist at Polaroid Corporation, is professor of chemistry at Simmons University, where he has taught chemistry, climate change, and sustainability for nearly 20 years. He has served as the director of the Colleges of the Fenway Center for Sustainability and the Environment and was awarded a National Science Foundation STEM (science, technology, engineering, and math) grant to promote disadvantaged and capable students into STEM professions. Berger uses a variety of high-impact methods to engage students in chemistry, including research, learning communities, service-learning, mentoring, technology, and study abroad programming. He is a coauthor of "World Challenge: Engaging Sophomores in an Intensive, Interdisciplinary Course," published in the *International Journal of Teaching and Learning in Higher Education* (2014). He advocates for the inclusion of women in science—and for equal access for all students. He coedited *Environmental Research Literacy: Classroom, Laboratory, and Beyond* (American Chemical Society, 2020). Berger has presented the framework at the Postsecondary Disability Training Institute, AHEAD, and NASPA national meetings and has served as the faculty representative on a Simmons task force that developed guidelines for enhanced ADA compliance at the university.

**Neal E. Lipsitz**, PhD, is associate dean for student well-being and director of student accessibility services at the College of the Holy Cross. He oversees counseling and psychological services, health services, student wellness education, and student accessibility services. He currently coordinates services for students with disabilities along with his other administrative responsibilities. Lipsitz has been a licensed psychologist and has worked in the field of college health, wellness, and student development since 1986. He presents frequently at local and national conferences on various aspects of service provision to students with disabilities. In addition to teaching at the postsecondary level for many years, he maintains a small private practice in Newton Centre, Massachusetts. He coedited *Beyond the Americans with Disabilities Act: Inclusive Policy and Practice for Students With Disabilities in Higher Education* (NASPA, 2014).

## Contributors

**Katherine C. Aquino**, PhD, is an assistant professor in the Department of Administrative and Instructional Leadership for the School of Education at St. John's University. Aquino's research interests include the socio-academic transitioning into and within the higher education environment for students with disabilities and post-traditional students. She is dedicated to investigating the complexity of disability in the postsecondary setting. Her work has been published in the *Journal of Diversity in Higher Education*, *Journal of College Student Development*, and *Journal of Postsecondary Education and Disability*, among others. She coauthored *Disability as Diversity in Higher Education: Policies and Practices to Enhance Student Success* and *Improving Postsecondary Choice and Pathways: Student Access and College Match*. Aquino holds a BS in psychology; an MA in school psychology; a PhD in higher education leadership, management, and policy; and an advanced certificate in instructional design and delivery.

**Jamie Axelrod**, MS, is the director of disability resources at Northern Arizona University and a former president of the Association on Higher Education and Disability (AHEAD). Due to his expertise in disability law and policy, communication and information technology access, and the reasonable accommodation process, Axelrod is a sought-after speaker on topics related to disability access and higher education. A go-to consultant on complex issues, he is a respected contributor to professional listservs, having received the Fink-Ryan Award for the quality of his guidance. Axelrod has worked for the University of Wisconsin–Madison's athletic department as a mental health therapist and for Protection and Advocacy Systems, Inc., a disability rights advocacy law firm where he served as an advocate for individuals with disabilities who were claiming civil rights violations. He has served as cochair of Northern Arizona University's Commission on Disability Access and Design and AHEAD's board of directors, as well as on the board of directors for the Coalition for Disability Access in Health Science Education. Axelrod is a contributing author to the recently published *Two Key Analytic Tools for Addressing Postsecondary Disability Law Questions* (AHEAD, 2023).

**Sheryl Burgstahler**, PhD, founded and currently directs Accessible Technology Services—which includes the DO-IT (Disabilities, Opportunities, Internetworking, and Technology) Center and the IT Accessibility Team (ITAT)—at the University of Washington. These groups offer mentoring and other interventions to support the success of students with disabilities in postsecondary education and careers. These groups also promote UDL opportunities, facilities, websites, media, documents, other IT, and services to ensure that all are accessible to, usable by, and inclusive of individuals with disabilities. She is author of *Creating Inclusive Learning Opportunities in Higher Education: A Universal Design Toolkit* (Harvard Education Press, 2020).

**Lyman L. Dukes III**, PhD, is a professor of special education in the College of Education at the University of South Florida. With more than 25 years of experience in education, Dukes has served in higher education in several capacities—both academically and administratively. He has published and presented extensively on topics related to secondary and postsecondary education for students with disabilities and has an extensive grant-funding record. He recently received the AHEAD Ronald E. Blosser Dedicated Service Award. Dukes serves on the editorial boards of several professional journals. His current research interests include transition from school to adult life for students with disabilities, universal design in higher education, and inclusive postsecondary education for students with intellectual disabilities.

**Clara Joy Gibson**, MA, is a doctoral candidate in the cultural studies program at George Mason University. Her most recent project was an analysis of the connection between concept albums and their historical and political contexts. Since being diagnosed with autism spectrum disorder at age 13, she has been involved in autism self-advocacy and disability rights causes. She holds a BA in English literature from the College of the Holy Cross and an MA in English from Concordia University.

**Paul Grossman**, JD, graduated from the University of Wisconsin–Madison Law School. He is an active member of the State Bar of California and the Disability Rights Bar Association. Currently, Grossman is executive counsel for AHEAD. He has been a civil rights lawyer for nearly 50 years, participating in the development and growth of civil rights protections based on race, national origin, disability, sex, and sexual orientation. Grossman taught disability law at Hastings College of Law for more than 20 years and remains a guest lecturer and legal advisor on postsecondary student disability law across the country. His clients include Stanford University and all three of the University of California higher education systems. Grossman has several published scholarly works, including a disability law textbook. His work was most recently included in *Laws, Policies, and Processes* (AHEAD, 2023). His favorite topics include intersectionality in disability law and the application of universal design to legal education.

**Joseph W. Madaus**, PhD, is the director of the Collaborative on Postsecondary Education and Disability and a professor in the Department of Educational Psychology in the Neag School of Education at the University of Connecticut. His research and publication interests include postsecondary education, transition, assessment, and postschool outcomes of adults with disabilities. He is a former president of the Division on Career Development and Transition (DCDT) of the Council for Exceptional Children and was awarded the Oliver P. Kolstoe Award by DCDT for significant contributions to the field of career development and transition. Madaus is on the editorial board of numerous professional journals related to special education, secondary transition, and postsecondary education and disability. He is the co-principal investigator on a 5-year federal grant related to promoting access to college for gifted students with autism spectrum disorder.

**Kevin T. Mintz**, PhD, is a postdoctoral fellow in the Stanford Training Program in Ethical, Legal, and Social Implications Research at the Stanford Center for Biomedical Ethics and the Center for Integration of Research on Genetics and Ethics. Mintz is also the first trainee with cerebral palsy at the Stanford School of Medicine. He received his PhD from the Department of Political Science at Stanford University in 2019. He also holds an AB in government from Harvard College, an MSc in political theory from the London School of Economics and Political Science, and a doctorate of human sexuality from the Institute for Advanced Study of Human Sexuality. Prior to returning to Stanford, he was a postdoctoral fellow in the Department of Bioethics at the National Institutes of Health. Mintz studies the mechanisms underlying structural ableism in medicine and biomedical research. His work has appeared in a variety of academic journals and newspapers, including *Pediatrics*, *The Hastings Center Report*, and the *Los Angeles Times*.

**Valerie Piro**, EdM, MPhil, is a doctoral candidate in the History Department at Princeton University, where her dissertation focuses on poverty in early medieval Western Europe. Prior to her matriculation at Princeton, she completed an EdM in higher education at the Harvard GSE in 2017, focusing on inclusive education for students with disabilities. There, Piro gave talks on how to prepare students with disabilities for the transition from K–12 to higher education. She received an MPhil in medieval history from the University of Cambridge in 2015; there she researched perceptions of disability in the early Middle Ages. Alongside her research, Piro has written about disability-related topics for *The New York Times*, *Inside Higher Ed*, and *Healthline*.

**Terrence Smith**, BFA, is a freelance writer and editor of *Teaching a Fish to Fly: True Stories of Autism and More* (2017). He has contributed to such publications as *Game Rant*, *MetaStellar*, and *Hypergrid Business*. He dreams of working to create comic books. Smith has also contributed his video-editing skills to Northampton Open Media. He holds a BFA from the College of the Holy Cross.

**Mary Lee Vance**, PhD, directs the Disability Access Center at California State University–Sacramento and served as interim director for the Office of Equal Opportunity; Title IX; and Discrimination, Harassment, and Retaliation. Vance has worked full-time at the University of California, Berkeley; the University of Montana; George Mason University; the University of Wisconsin–Superior; Iowa State University; and Orange Coast College, directing academic advising, career services, TRIO programs (McNair and student support services), minority recruitment and retention, enrollment management, student teaching and certification, disability services, and minority affairs. She has taught undergraduate and graduate courses, including disability studies; written federal grants; and published in referred journals, books, and periodicals. Vance served two consecutive terms on the AHEAD board of directors, edited five books, and is a reviewer for two referred journals: *Journal of Postsecondary Education and Disability* and *NACADA Journal*. Among other honors, Vance was presented AHEAD's Professional Recognition Award in 2012 and the Duraese Hall Excellence in Diversity and Inclusion Award in 2020. Her motto is "I have disabilities, but they are not disabling unless I have been disabled by poor planning."

# PART I

# The Collaborative Framework

# CHAPTER 1

# Structure and Function of the Collaborative Framework

Neal E. Lipsitz, Michael Berger, and Eileen Connell Berger

A framework is a way of relating differing—and even apparently unrelated—factors to one another based on a unifying concept or underlying idea. The *framework* in this book aims to describe the relationships among stakeholders in higher education and their roles in providing an optimal educational experience to students with disabilities. It provides a visual schema, a grid if you will, based on stakeholders and lenses. *Stakeholders* are students, faculty, access and disability services (ADS), the administration, and parents or guardians. The *lenses* are each stakeholder's role in the institution, priorities, access to resources, and biases. We, the authors, have chosen lenses that have been addressed often in the literature of higher education and disability studies; these lenses affect the educational experience of students, especially underrepresented students. Such lenses include self-advocacy, individual differences, life transition, academic rigor, new pedagogies, technology, disability law, attitudes, and inclusion/socialization.

The Collaborative Framework offers an objective analytical structure for institutions reviewing current roles and responsibilities of stakeholders who provide accommodations—for example, an analysis of who made the decision to grant (or deny) specific accommodations, whether that decision was consistent with instructional policy and best practice, and whether that action was consistent with disability law. The framework encourages all stakeholders to consider the complexities of laws, institutional policies, and practices as well as stakeholders' roles and responsibilities to ensure institutional compliance with civil rights and disability law. The framework can also identify duplicative efforts, suggest more effective responses to unexpected demands, and indicate opportunities for more collaboration. The framework has also been shown to be useful for training employees who provide access and disability services; for preparing progress and formative assessments; and for creating a "road map" for students and providers to collaboratively develop a best-practice approach for efficient and effective compliance and service delivery. Moreover, the framework is a tool to help students with disabilities understand whom to contact and how to find resources and support to have a successful college experience.

## The Lenses

### Self-Advocacy

*Self-advocacy* means that students know their rights and responsibilities, understand community expectations, and can reach out to others who can deliver the resources and access they need. Self-advocacy requires effective communication strategies and collaboration with faculty and support personnel. Note that different stakeholders may have different expectations for student self-advocacy. It is important that faculty and ADS, personnel mentors, and coaches help students to develop self-advocacy skills.

Test et al. (2005) compiled a chronology of self-advocacy definitions. Since the 1970s, the term *self-advocacy* had been used in the context of education and the civil rights movement and as a component of self-determination. Teaching self-advocacy is an example of the educational context. In civil rights, self-advocacy describes a social movement to achieve equal rights for those with disabilities. An examination of self-advocacy regards it as a skill set enabling a person to get their needs met (White & Vo, 2006); as such, it is considered a subset of self-determination. Examples of self-advocacy in this context include the effective communication of one's needs, goals, interests, desires, and rights; knowing about one's disability, strengths, and functional limitations; and having an awareness of the accommodations associated with removing barriers. In academic settings, this would include barriers to learning.

Multiple studies have shown that adults with disabilities are not as successful as those without disabilities in seeking and maintaining employment, achieving a satisfactory standard of living, developing independence, and acquiring and maintaining other quality-of-life indicators (Field et al., 2003). Self-advocacy has been shown to be a critical component for a student with disabilities to make a successful transition to adult life (Reiff, 2007). Often students come to college not knowing about their disability or how to advocate for themselves, although self-advocacy has been associated with success in higher education and beyond (Brinckerhoff, 1994; Getzel & Thoma, 2008).

In a qualitative virtual study, Yeager et al. (2022) examined the influence of social support on the development of self-advocacy for college students with disabilities. The research was modeled on the four subcategories of self-advocacy proposed by Test et al. (2005): knowledge of self, knowledge of rights, communication, and leadership. Yeager et al. found that knowledge of the disability by the individual is an important starting point in developing self-advocacy, followed by dealing with stigma about their needs. The researchers found that it was helpful for many students with disabilities to draw on social supports (family, friends) as well as counselors and ADS staff in their search for self-awareness. In coping with barriers for access and accommodations, many of these students learned about their rights by reading disability law. Subsequently knowing their rights and being self-aware encouraged them to reach out, communicate with others, broaden their resource networks, and even assume leadership roles in some organizations.

In a qualitative study, Pfeifer et al. (2020) examined how Test et al.'s conceptual framework for self-advocacy applied to students with disabilities in science, technology, engineering, and math (STEM) majors. Students with disabilities in STEM majors used fewer accommodations than did those in other disciplines, often because they were unaware of possible accommodations and how they could apply to STEM courses with specific requirements, such as labs. Students who had knowledge of their disability, rights, accommodations, and learning contexts were better able to effectively communicate with accessibility service providers and with their STEM instructors.

Bruce and Aylward (2021) documented the experiences of students with disabilities and their professors by exploring how student self-advocacy shaped the experience of both teaching and learning: "The relational dynamics involved with self-advocacy [are] . . . a complicated, nuanced, and potentially unrealistic systemic requirement that often generates concerns related to stigma and identity" (p. 17). Although self-advocacy training in high school and coaching in college was found to be useful to students with disabilities, the unequal relationship between them and their faculty was difficult to overcome. And the knowledge of disability legal rights for students with disabilities was found to be insufficient on its own. More useful was the knowledge of the specific process and the right connections/collaborations within the institution.

The student is the key stakeholder and should have the most interest in self-advocacy in the college setting; however, many students often arrive at college unaware of the specific aspects of their disability and unsure about what accommodations they may need. Parents/guardians have typically been the ones to get their students' needs met. Therefore, early on in the college experience parents/guardians will often be the students' best advocate; they too will be interested in learning about self-advocacy. Finally, ADS, faculty, and administration will need to be responsive to the advocacy being conducted for and by students. ADS and other stakeholders can help students become effective self-advocates.

## Individual Differences

The second lens is individual differences—that is, each student will differ in their own way. In a sense, this is a form of diversity, but one that is elaborated on an individual basis. Other stakeholders view the student individually rather than as a part of a group. Americans with Disabilities Act of 1990 (ADA) legislation mandates that accommodations and access must be considered specifically for each individual student, so stakeholders must consider the needs of a student on an individual basis and not part of a class or a group. The individual-differences lens is a powerful one through which to observe the personal experience of a student with disabilities and evaluate the attitudes of that student toward their abilities. How do students with disabilities consider themselves socially, academically, and culturally? What is the culture of the campus? Through the lens of individual differences, the student has responsibility for self-reflection ("What is my disability identity?") and should collaborate with other stakeholders in constructing a plan of action. ADS must provide both academic accommodations and access to the campus social network to enhance socialization/inclusion, recognizing that some students may require more support than others. Thus, academic accommodations must be tailored to the needs and personality of the individual student. Faculty must consider learning differences in selecting pedagogy, designing the course syllabus, and accommodating the student.

Hutcheon and Wolbring (2012) studied the experiences of students with disabilities and found that the ableist language and policies of institutions "while usually addressing immediate concerns such as accessibility, do not provide . . . expression, social outlets, or opportunities to embrace [students with disabilities'] identities" (p. 48). The authors recommended that "policymakers, educators, and students, both disabled and nondisabled, critically examine their own assumptions regarding difference" (p. 47). Gibson (2006) described a disability identity development model consisting of three stages. In stage 1 (passive awareness) the student denies social aspects of disability and does not associate with others with a disability; in stage 2 (realization) the student, often in early adulthood, begins to recognize their disability, develops a concern for the opinions of others, and exhibits anger; and in stage 3 (acceptance) the student shifts from seeing their difference in a negative light to embracing their full self. The student with a disability in college may be in any one of these three stages and present very differently to the administration, faculty, or other students.

In 2017, Forber-Pratt and Zape took issue with Gibson's theoretical model, claiming that identity development can go beyond coming to terms with one's own disability. They argued that Gibson's theory was too individually focused and didn't take into account one's sense of belonging within their community. These researchers suggested that institutional stakeholders "include relationships, involvement, and community as important elements in disability identity formation" (p. 351). Forber-Pratt and Zape proposed a model of psychosocial disability identity development, suggesting it can help administrators and faculty better understand individual differences of students with disabilities. As such, the "voice" of one student might be different from that of another, even with the same disability.

## Life Transition

Another lens focuses on the changes a student undergoes when entering college and experiencing a whole new world. The life transition of a college student involves developing a personal identity and, for some, an understanding of their own disability. Students also develop patterns of interdependency and personalize a communication style. *Transition* in the academic context was defined by Kampsen (2009, p. 5) as "the process of becoming academically and socially integrated into the college environment" and referred to the "three stages of student integration into the college environment: separation, transition, and incorporation," as originally defined by Tinto (1975). Separation occurs at home and in high school before students enter college, when they disassociate, to some extent, from their past community. "The transition stage is a situation in which students have successfully separated from past norms and communities, but have not yet integrated the norms and behaviors of the new environment" (Kampsen, 2009, p. 6). Incorporation occurs when academic and social integration processes are complete.

Coburn and Treeger (2003) suggested that during this life transition, students must reestablish their identity outside of their family and high school groups. The researchers explained that some students struggle with guilt during the transition to college—wanting to remain close and loyal to their family and their values while trying to figure out who they are in their new community. Coburn and Treeger (2003) went on to state that technology has complicated this process. And of course today, with parents checking in and family and friends texting, FaceTiming, and remaining an integral part of the student's daily life, the nature of this life transition has changed.

Student involvement on campus, a precursor to "university belonging," has been associated with successful transitioning. "Of college students, those in their 1st year who reported more peer support or higher levels of friendship quality displayed higher academic performance" (Pittman & Richmond, 2008, p. 346). Hadley (2011) stated that students cannot successfully transition and integrate if they are not socially and academically engaged and involved. If "involvement does not happen there will be a greater chance for at-risk students to feel isolated and withdraw" (p. 79). Hadley noted these "at-risk" students include those with disabilities who are stigmatized or do not fully understand how their disability will affect them in their new environment, which has new rules, new types of testing, new methods of classroom instruction, challenging social interactions, and a heavier workload. Thus, integration into college environments for students with disabilities requires knowing what their issues are, knowing what they need, and advocating for themselves. Many college students have not practiced these behaviors in their past because parents or guardians have done it for them. These students need to learn these skills in college. Without these skills, these students may face challenges in accessing accommodations and academic and cultural resources; these elements can affect their academic success and retention in college.

Preparation, self-identity, and self-advocacy are key factors in a successful transition for students with disabilities. First, they must become aware of the services available and how to access them. Then, they must understand their disability fully and how it affects them, and then articulate what they need to make academic progress (Hadley, 2011). Kampsen (2009) noted, "Perhaps the most essential aspect of navigating the transition to college and the change in laws is that if college students with disabilities want access to support services for their disability, they are required to self-disclose and advocate for themselves" (p. 47). Reed (2009) also stated that self-determination is the most important issue to address during the transition to college.

More recent literature related to the transition to college is offered with respect to how this transition manifests for specific identity groups categorized, for example, by ethnicity or race (Ramirez et al.,

2023; Sasser et al., 2023; Sladek et al., 2023); mental health (Martel et al., 2018; Sabaner & Arnold, 2020); neurodiversity (Madaus et al., 2023); first-generation status (Jackson et al., 2022); and by specific issues such as belonging (Offidani-Bertrand et al., 2022) and substance abuse/recovery (Boyadjian et al., 2023; Trager et al., 2023). Of course, the danger here is the possibility of losing sight of the individual differences experienced by students in their transition, regardless of their affiliation with others.

Life transition, then, is an important lens because student success can so forcefully hinge on a successful transition to college life. The degree of academic and social integration can help predict student success; therefore, life transition can be used as a metric for student success. As Light (2001) pointed out, engagement with faculty and with cocurricular activities enhances the college experience for all students.

The strong interest in life transition as a lens is shared by both students and ADS. In college, students are responsible for their success; hence, students must negotiate a successful transition to college to succeed. ADS can help students with disabilities by discussing their recommended accommodations and why these accommodations are important. This conversation can enhance student self-awareness, student self-advocacy, and successful transition to college life. Cawthon and Cole (2010) further suggested that participation and careful planning are key components of a successful transition for students with disabilities. Students must be active participants in the formation of their accommodation plan. This type of involvement makes the student more aware and helps to develop self-advocacy skills.

Parents and guardians should have an interest in this lens as well. They can help their students' transition to college by relaying information about any past educational planning/needs and by encouraging the student to seek support at the college. This kind of participation can enhance the student's life transition because they will integrate further into the college environment by taking their needs seriously—and getting these needs met.

## Academic Rigor

The fourth lens, academic rigor, focuses on the institution's embedded academic culture. Some faculty might define *rigor* as how "tough" courses are for students or how many hours students are expected to spend on assignments; some might include the toughness of the grading policy. Today, the term *academic rigor* not only describes the meaningful learning outcome expectations but also includes the institutional support to help students achieve those learning outcomes and an assessment program with a variety of tools to measure student achievements.

Wraga (2010) noted the archaic and negative connotations of the terms *academic* and *rigor*, as associated in the past, with a fixed curriculum stressing mental discipline. Other authors, however, emphasized the broader scope of academic rigor that goes beyond grades and course content—one that presents a holistic view of education advancing practical skills, human cultures, the natural world, and personal responsibility (Savitz-Romer & Jager-Hyman, 2009). Effective ongoing communication about academic rigor between faculty and administration as well as among the faculty is also an important pursuit that sets appropriate and consistent levels of expectations and student support throughout the institution.

While ongoing formative assessments are valuable for the student, adequate support structures are also essential for student success. "Conversations about rigor often miss the crucial importance of providing adequate support for students to meet such standards. A network of academic and social supports is critical to ensure that all students—regardless of their socio-economic background or previous educational experience—have the opportunity to succeed at high levels" (Savitz-Romer & Jager-Hyman, 2009, p. 1). For students with disabilities, ADS becomes an important facilitator to ensure that the student has the appropriate network of academic and social support that affords them the opportunity to meet the expected academic rigor.

Faculty members are often seen as the "owners" of the academic-rigor lens, as they have the responsibility for grading and for designing curricular content. They are responsible for preparing and delivering course material that forces students to address increasingly complex problems in a specific subject area; however, academic rigor can present a challenge for faculty who are simultaneously balancing those factors that influence their tenure and promotion (i.e., student evaluations strongly linked to anticipated grades versus department and administrative goals for academic excellence that eschew "grade inflation"; Bart, 2011). The student also has a vital interest in academic rigor. A student's success in graduate school, in professional programs, or in future careers is built on the foundation of specific knowledge and processes developed during undergraduate education (Wagner, 2008).

Culver et al. (2021) studied two components of academic rigor: workload and cognitive challenge. The authors concluded that "students' cognitive development is best fostered through constructively challenging coursework rather than strenuous workloads" (p. 1158). They urged institutional leaders and administration to consider how to better assess the level of cognitive challenge that students experience, rather than workload, especially in light of the changes in content delivery brought on by the COVID-19 pandemic, hybrid and blended modalities, and new pedagogies.

Rigorous courses develop students' ability to deal effectively with complexity and to recognize multiple perspectives—key skills that facilitate deep engagement in course material that supports self-motivated learning, especially for at-risk students. Culver et al. (2019) recommended that administrators support rigorous coursework;

advisors encourage students to take rigorous courses; and faculty be supported institutionally to develop and learn best practices in the teaching of rigorous courses.

**New Pedagogies**

Any change in higher education must consider the lens of new pedagogies, the knot linking students and faculty. Pedagogy is currently undergoing a marked change. Why? Changes in society, student expectations, and technology are motivating universities and colleges to rethink the methods and goals of academia. The sheer quantity and fine detail of new knowledge are increasing at an ever-accelerating rate. The increasing numbers of diverse and nontraditional students require new educational approaches. Also, a more complex and global society calls for new skills, such as entrepreneurship, interdisciplinarity, and competency with technology. A distinctive element of the new pedagogies often includes various forms of learner empowerment that also challenge the model of the conventional classroom.

Fullan and Langworthy (2014) defined the new pedagogies as a "new model of learning partnerships between students and teachers, aiming towards deep learning goals and enabled by pervasive digital technology" (p. 2). The authors suggested that new pedagogies will change the instructor's role in the educational process, requiring new teacher skills across several disciplines, including digital and social fluency, as well as the ability to access content required for lifelong learning.

Recent innovations in specific chemistry classrooms have been effective in helping students develop lifelong learning skills by incorporating tools such as metacognition (or "learning how to learn"), articulated study skills, planned time management, and self-assessment directly into course pedagogy (Cook et al., 2013). Service-learning, in which students provide a service to a specific community in the context of an academic course, has been shown to create an authentic learning experience, engaging the student through outreach on one hand and self-reflection on the other. Student research is another "high-impact practice" traditionally available only to postgraduate students. A recent trend in many colleges is to engage students earlier in their undergraduate career, even as freshmen, in authentic research projects that offer them opportunities to tackle real-life applications and report their results in presentations and publications. This activity also allows faculty and upper-level students to collaborate and presents opportunities for mentoring (Kuh, 2008).

Technology, an integral part of new pedagogies, offers not only a wealth of content but also synchronous assessment, feedback, and communication between students and faculty. Online learning has been a key contributing factor, and blended learning combines the traditional classroom with an online presence. The use of smartphones and other student response technologies has increased student participation in the classroom, while blogs and discussion boards allow for asynchronous collaboration. However, technology alone cannot adequately satisfy the new requirements for today's students—unless employed as part of an appropriate holistic pedagogy. A report by the Higher Education Academy argued that "the proliferation of new technologies in higher education teaching and learning, coupled with a diversification of learner profiles and pathways through higher education, has triggered developments to extend flexible learning at several levels" (Ryan & Tilbury, 2013, p. 4).

Such "flexible learning" was realized in the design of Berger et al.'s (2013) unique 2-week, group-based, reflective course for sophomores that incorporated several new pedagogies. Students directed their own learning to develop creative solutions to the problem of "health, hunger, and humanity." Scaffolding provided by several faculty members from multiple disciplines allowed students to direct "their own learning in small groups to research this global problem and develop local solutions" (p. 333). During this experimental course, several assessment tools, such as pretest/post-test, rubrics, questionnaires, focus groups, peer assessments, and self-reflections, were used to document increases in content knowledge, student engagement, and other outcomes. Student comments at the end of the course suggested that the intensive experience was indeed transformative.

The transition from high school to college can be a challenge for many students, and the introduction of a new pedagogy—one not seen in high school—can present even more difficulties. Students with disabilities may experience yet additional stress, as the new pedagogies can require nontraditional relationships with faculty and the use of unfamiliar learning accommodations. It is important that all students have access to new pedagogies that have had considerable forethought and planning by faculty, student cooperation, and support by administrators. The design of curricula usable by all students is the basis for universal design of instruction (UDI). Burgstahler (2015) noted that UDI provides opportunities for students with diverse abilities to participate in "all aspects of instruction (e.g., delivery methods, physical spaces, information resources, technology, personal interactions, assessments)" (p. 1).

Massive open online courses (MOOCs) have been especially popular since the COVID-19 pandemic. A study of the effectiveness of MOOCs (Ogunyemi et al., 2022) focused on learner engagement, a prerequisite for effective learning. By analyzing the recent literature, the researchers found that there were several factors that fostered engagement and that many of these factors involved real-time interaction and feedback. While this study found a hybrid approach to be the most successful, the researchers found it difficult to quantify engagement.

Clearly, faculty members have the major responsibility for introducing new pedagogy into the educational program. From the faculty's perspective, there has been a shift in focus from content delivery to student engagement to develop student self-efficacy in learning. The "sage on the stage" model has given way to a new pedagogy that is learner centered. The classroom structure has been evolving from hierarchical in a fixed location to collaborative interactions in class or online and community-based learning. Some faculty members have not had experience with these new teaching and learning environments, prompting an often-anxious reconsideration of their role in the educational process, as they share the responsibility with students for learning, authority, and assessment.

The administration can play a supportive role to help faculty introduce new pedagogy. For example, in R1 (research intensive) institutions, where quality and quantity of research and scholarship are key elements that contribute to the success of the faculty's academic careers, the prioritization of teaching at the expense of research can become an issue. University administrators can provide an incentive for pedagogical innovation.

**Technology**

Technology has been a major disruptor of traditional higher education, opening new avenues of learning. Technology has forced all stakeholders to reevaluate their presumptive modes of operation in the college setting. The term *technology* encompasses the digital hardware, software, social media, auxiliary aids, and services related to the educational experience. It includes personal devices and systems used by students and faculty in addition to those owned and supported by the institution. Likewise included is the infrastructure associated with information technology (IT) used to support academic management and pedagogy. The increasing use of technology in all aspects of education has presented students and teachers alike with a double-edged sword: On the one hand, new technology places demands for mastery of new content and cutting-edge tools, but on the other hand it offers avenues for facile student access to many useful resources (Martin, 2006).

There has been a broad recognition of the importance of technology in education since the 1980s, especially for students with disabilities. The Assistive Technology Act provides funding for assistive technology (AT) to serve all people with all types of disabilities, of all ages, in all environments (e.g., early intervention, K–12, postsecondary, vocational rehabilitation, community living, aging services). Accessible AT has also been mandated by landmark federal legislation, including the ADA (with the 2008 amendments) and Section 504 of the Rehabilitation Act of 1973. For more detail, see the "Disability Law" section and visit the Assistive Technology Act website (http://www.ataporg.org/history.html).

Technology also affords significantly greater access to socialization and academic material, especially for students with disabilities—and this may be a key factor in the success of these students in college. By providing accessibility, technology can be an especially important part of curricular design. Courses and educational activities that are constructed to present content, engagement, and assessment in many alternative modalities to be accessible to all learners, despite their learning style or disability, are considered to have a universal design.

Technology is a lens because the availability of adequate, accessible, and appropriate technologies can significantly affect academic and social experiences for students with disabilities. ADS must be familiar with any new technology used in a course to ensure that it is appropriate for these students; this effort may require additional training and staff development because it is important that students with disabilities can use these technologies and that faculty be aware of their degree of accessibility for these students.

For short-term planning, such as providing accommodations that involve technology, ADS should keep the administration and IT apprised of new technology introduced by students with disabilities or faculty. For long-term planning, administrators and IT should evaluate the accessibility and ease of use of software; they should also apprise ADS of potential changes that may affect access for students with disabilities. Communication among stakeholders is essential for the proper acquisition and use of accessible academic technology.

A comprehensive literature review from 2009 to 2020 on the use of AT for students with disabilities indicated that although AT was successful in bettering inclusion and access, instructors' lack of awareness of the technology and a lack of faculty training inhibited greater adoption (Fernández-Batanero et al., 2022). The authors found that AT imparts to students more successful inclusion and accessibility to school and that it enhances the development of autonomy and independence, social skills, participation, and motivation.

A South African study by de Klerk & Palmer (2022) of open distance learning (ODL) during and after the COVID-19 pandemic found that the creation of inclusive spaces equipped with appropriate technology enabled students with disabilities to participate in a collaborative online international learning program that facilitated remote interactions between students with disabilities and others. The authors concluded, "By transforming their experiences, students living with disabilities may be positioned to transform their communication skills, as well as expand their knowledge and abilities" (p. 89).

In addition to offering enhanced access to academic content, digital technologies have been found to lead to greater social engagement. A study in Canadian secondary schools showed that digital technology facilitated interactions of students with disabilities with both their peers and their teachers by conferring on students with disabilities credibility and status through their expertise with digital devices and software (Rizk & Hillier, 2022).

The access provider is a key facilitator for the appropriate use of technology for students with disabilities in both academic and cocurricular activities. In this role, the access provider must communicate with faculty and students with disabilities as well as encourage IT and administration to maintain an adequate budget for needed technology. It is important for ADS to be current on ever-changing technology; this effort will require training with consequent budgetary demands. The administration is also a key stakeholder in planning appropriately for new software and upgrades, new hardware, and training. In addition, the administration has a longer term responsibility to work with IT to provide up-to-date, secure, and accessible networks that satisfy the needs of the institution's overall educational strategy. It is important for the administration, IT, and ADS to be current with the evolving area of disability law, since failure to provide appropriate, accessible AT to students with disabilities can result in noncompliance and may result in significant fines and other actions against the institution.

### Disability Law

The term *disability law* refers to the body of federal civil rights legislation in the United States prohibiting discrimination against individuals with disabilities in education, employment, housing, and access to public services. Disability law includes regulations that specify the implementation of and compliance with the enabling legislation as well as the enforcement actions by the executive branches of the federal government, carried out by the Department of Justice and the Office for Civil Rights. The U.S. Equal Employment Opportunity Commission is a federal agency that administers and enforces civil rights laws against many forms of discrimination in the workplace, including higher education institutions. The judicial branch also plays an important role through federal court decisions that interpret the extent of the laws and their accordant regulations. Thus, the field of disability law is complex and ever evolving.

Although the ADA along with Section 504 (Rehabilitation Act, 1973) give civil rights protections to disabled persons (Burgstahler,

2015), the protections provided under the Individuals with Disabilities Education Act (2004) for identifying students with disabilities is not embedded in ADA or Section 504; therefore, those students in higher education face the added burden of self-disclosing their disability. Thus, the nature of these federal legislations leads to an individualized approach to each case in higher education, with an emphasis on compliance to the detriment of social and cultural inclusion of the disabled community (Walstra & Chukwuma, 2023).

Cook et al. (2009) surveyed faculty members about students with disabilities at an eight-campus university system in the Midwest. The authors examined the following areas: legal, accommodations in terms of willingness, accommodations in terms of policy, UDI, disability characteristics, and disability etiquette. The survey showed that accommodation policy and disability etiquette were being addressed satisfactorily, but issues with the law, UDI, and special or specific disability issues were not.

In general, research indicates that the administration in colleges and universities must clearly support faculty development and training for student support services to keep abreast of the changing demographics of students with disabilities. Burgstahler (1994) described practical measures to ameliorate on-campus attitudes at University of Washington's DO-IT program (Disabilities, Opportunities, Internetworking, and Technology), which increases faculty awareness of disability law, disability types, and use of technology for better inclusion of students with disabilities. This National Science Foundation–funded program has the goal of enhancing the campus climate for students with disabilities to increase their successful participation. One focus of the DO-IT program is to improve faculty attitudes using printed and electronic resources as well as workshops for faculty.

Other authors found that faculty need more written information about disability law and access services (Baker et al., 2012; Cook et al., 2009). Such written material includes brochures, pamphlets, faculty handbooks, or one-page sheets prepared by ADS. More information about universal design for learning (UDL) would also be helpful to faculty (Burgstahler & Moore, 2009) in creating more welcoming classroom environments. Online training for faculty and student services offices has also been beneficial (Upton & Harper, 2002). A model of social justice challenges faculty to "have a moral commitment and courage to make changes that will transform education for all students" (Chardin & Novak, 2021, p. 11). UDL seeks to proactively eliminate inequities that are inherent in a diverse student population (Walstra and Chukwuma, 2023).

## Attitudes

The next lens, attitudes, refers to campus culture and embedded expectations as well as assumed standards of behavior. Gething and Wheeler (1992) observed that "most theorists regard prevalent community attitudes towards people with disabilities as negative and devaluing, with non-accepting attitudes associated with a view as these people as separate and different . . . [implying] deficiency or inferiority" (p. 75). Attitudes usually bring about predictable reactions toward certain types of individuals and can form the basis of a group culture when many people in the group share certain attitudes. A distinct campus culture has great value for the institution and the students. "The campus culture is a powerful source of socialization through students' perception of the institution's norms, including peer norms, and their habitual participation in routine practices and communal events" (Colby et al., 2015, para. 1). Campus culture often reflects the institution's vision or mission, which underpins the activities on campus and guides interactions among students and between students and faculty. Students' interactions with staff and the administration also influence campus culture. Of course, many cultures might coexist on one campus as the various groups coalesce around particular identities, interests, or activities.

Diversity and celebration of differences on campus not only provide a source of strength and resilience for the institution, but they also act as learning opportunities for students as they interact with different cultures. However, students with disabilities often sense a prejudicial climate on campus due to their "difference." Since the passage of Section 504 of the Rehabilitation Act of 1973 and subsequent legislation (see earlier discussion of disability law), colleges and universities have seen a significant increase in the number of students with disabilities. Institutions have continued to modify their physical plant and provide mandated accommodations to them.

However, as Teresa Danso-Danquash, former president of the Cornell Union for Disabilities Awareness, pointed out in the *Cornell Daily Sun*, disability is complex and continues to evolve: "When you think of diversity, many people think of racial or ethnic diversity. We are trying to change that to make people also consider neurodiversity. That encompasses a lot of different disabilities that are more than just a person in a wheelchair, which is what people think of as a disability" (Ferguson, 2015, para. 44). Danso-Danquash reported that the attitudes on campus toward students with disabilities are mixed.

In the 1990s, several investigators evaluated the implementation of Section 504 of the Rehabilitation Act of 1973 in higher education and examined factors that were either assisting or impeding achievement of students with disabilities in college. Some reported that success in large part depended on the attitudes of the faculty and student affairs administrators. Leyser et al. (1998) investigated changes in the knowledge, attitudes, and practices of university faculty regarding students with disabilities since the passage of the federal legislation. They found that although faculty had a supportive attitude toward students with disabilities and were willing to provide accommodations in their courses, they were unfamiliar with available services provided by the university. Faculty were willing to accommodate students with disabilities but not to the extent of what faculty members perceived as lowering course standards or requiring extra work on their own part.

Faculty attitudes and the classroom environment are key factors in the success of students with disabilities (Hehir, 2005; Hehir et al., 2016; Hehir & Schifter, 2015). "The prevailing characteristics of the environment (climate), particularly in the classroom, affect students' success, especially for students with disabilities" (Baker et al., 2012, p. 309). Thus, unless faculty establish a welcoming classroom environment, demonstrate a knowledge of disability law, and are open to accommodating differences, students with disabilities may be reluctant to share their strengths and weaknesses to faculty and ask for accommodations (Cook et al., 2009; Nutter & Ringgenberg, 1993; Wolman et al., 2004). "The stigma of being labeled different or having to use accommodations or resources is something that impedes people. . . . According to students and administrators, there is still work to be done in encouraging a more accepting campus culture" (Ferguson, 2015, para. 2).

Clearly, faculty and the administration are largely responsible for setting the campus climate. Faculty have the most frequent and consistent interaction with students and must maintain a supportive learning environment. The administration is responsible for providing academic and physical accommodations and for setting the campuswide priorities and establishing a welcoming climate to students with differences. Cook et al. (2000) indicated that students with disabilities believe the faculty and administrators do not fully understand the issues they face in pursuing a college education.

Lombardi and Lalor (2017) reviewed the literature on disability-related knowledge and attitudes of higher education faculty and administrators. These authors reported that there continue to be no formal training requirements for faculty on teaching students with disabilities. They also reported that most universities offer no professional development or training to faculty on their legal obligations under ADA or on administration of accommodations to students with disabilities. Studies have shown that faculty generally have positive attitudes about students with disabilities and are willing to provide accommodations but often feel unprepared to provide the supports needed.

Studies have also suggested that in the administration, student services staff have not had adequate training and sufficient information to appropriately assist students with disabilities and offer a welcoming environment (Junco & Salter, 2004; Lombardi & Lalor, 2017). In a 2002 survey of students at a large Midwestern university, Upton and Harper (2002) found that the general student population viewed classroom accommodations for students with disabilities on a "continuum of accommodation deservedness" (p. 115) on which accommodations for visible disabilities were rated as most deserved and accommodations for nonvisible disabilities least deserved. This study suggested it is the responsibility of ADS to engage in outreach initiatives to educate faculty and the general student population about disabilities, disability law, and the accommodations process.

**Inclusion/Socialization**

Researchers who study inclusive education highlight the importance of social justice, democracy, and the elimination of all forms of exclusion and discrimination (Hernández-Torrano et al., 2022). According to Walstra and Chukwuma (2023), higher education globally and nationally has become increasingly diverse, along with a significant rise in the number of students with disabilities, but discussions and efforts about diversity, equity, and inclusion on college campuses frequently exclude disability. According to U.S. federal data (National Center for Education Statistics, 2018), nearly 20% of undergraduate students have reported one or more disabilities.

Hafner (2008) stated that "inclusion on a college campus requires the acceptance of students with significant disabilities (under the federal civil rights laws) into college courses, access to integrated student housing, employment opportunities, and shared college campus experiences" (p. 8). Hafner also posited that the key components of successful inclusion for students with disabilities include employment and internships, individualized learning objectives, peer mentors, community partnerships, on-campus student housing, and UDI. It is important to note that students without disabilities also benefit when those with disabilities are included. Students with disabilities are often left out of leadership and internship opportunities in higher education. By supporting students with disabilities, and helping them gain access to campus resources and opportunities along with their nondisabled peers, all students may become more supportive of one another.

Although inclusion and belonging are important components for an engaging education that involves individual stakeholders, higher education institutions have yet to effectively engage and include students with disabilities in their diversity initiatives. According to Kim and Aquino (2017), "instead, disability has been stuffed in the 'Disability Services' closet, with some obvious negative ramifications, such as a lack of disability programming or events, lack of social inclusion, 'access' being framed as an individual issue, requiring documentation and individual accommodation, and lack of information, training, or support for faculty in practices such as Universal Design for Learning (UDL)" (p. 186).

Students with disabilities have unique differences that add to their burdens and complications, and they often encounter policies and people who make them feel as if they do not belong. They are often neglected by the diversity, equity, and inclusion initiatives and personnel meant to empower them. Students with disabilities face the added challenges—from physical, medical, psychological, social, behavioral, and learning differences—to accessing academic and community belonging, and they are left without the empowerment claimed by other diverse groups on campus. Judy Heumann, renowned disability civil rights leader, advocated for equity of access. She recognized differences and believed cross-cultural and intersectional partnerships among minorities should include disability (Newnham & LeBrecht, 2020). Moreover, Aquino (2016) noted that current theoretical constructs isolate disability from other student diversity characteristics, warning that until the disconnect between disability and diversity can be reconceptualized, the equity and inclusion of persons with disabilities will not be achieved—and the disabled community will not be able to claim empowerment that has come to other diverse groups.

What can stakeholders do to increase inclusion and belonging? Families can play a critical and positive role in the inclusion and retention of students with disabilities in college life. Families collaboratively prepare, plan, and create a web of support as well as personal and health services plans, and they partner with on-campus support services (authorizing waiver of HIPAA [Health Insurance Portability and Accountability Act] and FERPA [Family Educational Rights and Privacy Act] restrictions) to continue needed feedback from and among specialists along with family coaching that may help mediate overwhelming these students' mental health challenges (Hibbs & Rostain, 2019).

Faculty play a central role in the inclusion of students with disabilities and their feelings of belonging (Aquino, 2016). Faculty employ new pedagogy with innovative inclusive practices, such as UDL, team projects, and integrating interdisciplinary and interactive modalities, and they work to meet the differing learning styles of nontraditional learners. Collaboration among faculty, ADS, and students with disabilities is needed to meet the challenges of changing student demographics (Berger et al., 2014). Educators who embrace UDL employ a process that uses inclusive teaching approaches to address the expected learning differences of their students. As Burgstahler (2015) has shown, the application of UDL can be effective when educators employ multiple modes for delivering content, several methods to promote student interaction, and different ways for students to demonstrate what they have learned.

The day-to-day work of ADS staff involves communicating with relevant stakeholders to provide appropriate access for students with disabilities on campus. ADS can also enhance inclusion of these students by creating cocurricular programming that involves them and their allies in leadership roles that promote disability rights, advocacy, education, mentoring, and diversity. ADS plays a central role in fostering collaboration among all stakeholders.

Overall, stakeholders in higher education should collaborate to reconceptualize the understanding of diversity as a way to promote a more inclusive environment in which students with disability feel welcomed and engaged (Walstra & Chukwuma, 2023).

## Stakeholders

To more completely measure the quality of the educational experience of the student, it is important to evaluate the effectiveness and appropriateness of the roles of stakeholders in forming that experience. In this chapter, we propose a framework that can inform the educational experience of the student with a disability. This framework involves various stakeholders: the student, faculty, administration, ADS, and parents/guardians. However, all these stakeholders view the college experience through their own unique "lenses" that shape their expectations and, eventually, their assessments. The stakeholders and their lenses form the framework for viewing the educational experience. This framework is used to facilitate an analysis of the strengths and weaknesses of disability services delivery, institutional response, and student success.

Table 1.1 summarizes the description of each lens discussed earlier and aligns the lens with those stakeholders who would most likely use it.

*Structure and Function of the Collaborative Framework*  29

Table 1.1
*Description of Nine Lenses Mapped to the Most Relevant Stakeholders*

| Stakeholder | Lens | Description of lens |
|---|---|---|
| Student with disability | Self-advocacy | Self-determination; students have knowledge of their own rights, responsibilities, and community expectations; effective communication strategies; collaboration with faculty and support personnel |
| | Individual differences | Dealing with diversity; policy, peers, faculty, staff, specific program development |
| | Life transition | Students develop a personal identity, understanding their own disability, patterns of interdependency, and communication style |
| Faculty | Academic rigor | Culture and embedded expectations for all students; level of scholarship and engagement |
| | New pedagogies | Online and blended courses, "flipped" classes, student-centered learning, service-learning, student research |
| Administration and disability services | Technology | Software, hardware, social media, auxiliary aids, and services |
| | Disability law | Student rights and responsibilities, eligibility for services, understanding compliance with laws and mandates |
| Administration and faculty | Attitudes | Culture and embedded expectations, assumed standards of behavior |
| All | Inclusion/ socialization | Routes of accessibility to peers, facilities, events, resources |

From the viewpoint of the student with a disability, the major points of contact with the academic institution are the faculty and the administration. To shed light on the complexity of interactions among the major stakeholders, Figure 1.1 maps the degree of ownership and responsibility for a particular lens into a space defined by the relative amount of interest and influence of the student, the administration, and the faculty. The closer the lens is to a point of the triangle, the greater the interest, influence, or responsibility of that stakeholder. Thus, self-advocacy is brought about mainly by the student. New pedagogy is the main concern of the faculty, and technology is planned and implemented by the administration. Some lenses are shared by only two of the stakeholders. For example, keeping current with the requirements of disability law usually falls to ADS, it must work with faculty to ensure compliance and successful implementation. Academic rigor is largely the responsibility and concern of faculty, who must work with students with disabilities to ensure appropriate accommodations are in place. Both administration and faculty are both responsible for the culture of the institution (attitudes of the faculty and staff toward students). Some lenses, such as socialization/inclusion, require the cooperation effort of all major stakeholders (Hehir & Katzman, 2012; Nguyen & Phuong, 2016; Phuong et al., 2017a, 2017b).

Figure 1.1
*Areas of Interest and Influence for Major Stakeholders*

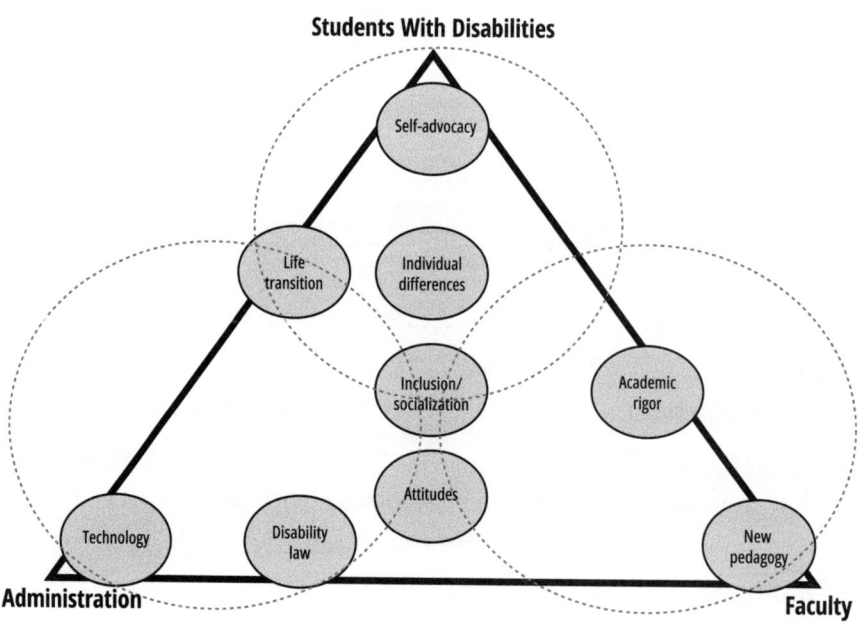

## The Collaborative Framework

We propose a framework based on this collaborative and interactive model. This framework includes five major stakeholders. For the administration category, we differentiate accessibility services from the upper administration; the concerns of senior administrators must be broader (considering the needs of the entire institution often with a longer time horizon) than those of accessibility services. We also include parents or guardians, who can sometimes be critical for the success of students with disabilities, especially undergraduates. This grid of lenses and stakeholders, as shown in Table 1.2, allows us to understand through which lenses each stakeholder views the student's experience. Moreover, it shows which stakeholders might provide specific support to students most efficiently and most effectively. Thus, this grid can be used to identify primary and supportive roles of each stakeholder in some aspect of the student experience.

As described previously, each stakeholder views certain aspects of the college experience through different lenses. In addition, each stakeholder assumes varying degrees of responsibility for each aspect of the college experience. Table 1.3 indicates typical stakeholder roles and responsibilities for a fictional college. The darkest boxes suggest that a stakeholder has a major role in providing initiatives that address one aspect of the college; the lighter boxes suggest the stakeholder has a more supportive role; and white boxes indicate that the stakeholder has little or no role in the college experience as viewed through that particular lens. Thus, Table 1.3 indicates (for a typical institution of higher learning) that the student has a major role and responsibility in developing self-advocacy and coping with personal life transitions and individual differences while agreeing to standards of academic rigor as laid out by the faculty and dealing with attitudes on campus. Faculty members play a major role in setting standards of academic rigor and introducing new pedagogy, and they play a supportive role by knowing disability law and providing appropriate accommodations. Tables 1.4 through 1.6 give a detailed look at specific roles and responsibilities of various stakeholders.

## Table 1.2
*The Collaborative Framework Architecture*

| Lens | Stakeholder | | | | |
| --- | --- | --- | --- | --- | --- |
| | Student | Faculty | Accessibility services | Senior administrators | Parent/ guardian |
| Self-advocacy | | | | | |
| Individual differences | | | | | |
| Life transition | | | | | |
| Academic rigor | | | | | |
| New pedagogies | | | | | |
| Technology | | | | | |
| Disability law | | | | | |
| Attitudes | | | | | |
| Inclusion/ socialization | | | | | |

*Note.* Copyright © 2023 by Neal E. Lipsitz, Michael Berger, and Eileen Connell Berger.

## Table 1.3
*The Collaborative Framework for Mapping Varying Degree of Significance of the Lenses for Each Stakeholder*

| Lens | Stakeholder | | | | |
|---|---|---|---|---|---|
| | Student | Faculty | Accessibility services | Senior administrators | Parent/guardian |
| Self-advocacy | Major | | | | Minor |
| Individual differences | Major | Minor | Minor | | Minor |
| Life transition | Major | | Minor | | Minor |
| Academic rigor | Minor | Major | Minor | Minor | |
| New pedagogies | Minor | Major | Minor | Minor | |
| Technology | Minor | Minor | Major | Minor | |
| Disability law | Minor | Minor | Major | Major | Minor |
| Attitudes | Minor | Major | Major | Major | Minor |
| Inclusion/socialization | Major | Major | Major | Major | Minor |

| | | |
|---|---|---|
| ■ (dark) | Major role | Initiates/provides/leads |
| ▨ (light) | Minor role | Uses/supports/understands |
| □ (white) | Often no direct role | |

*Note.* Stakeholder roles and responsibilities vary with different aspects of a student's college experience. The darkest boxes indicate that a stakeholder has a major role in providing initiatives that address one aspect of the college experience as viewed through a particular lens. The lighter boxes indicate more supportive roles, and white boxes indicate little or no role in the college experience as viewed through a particular lens.

## Stakeholder Roles and Responsibilities Defined by the Lenses

Although typical stakeholder roles and responsibilities for a college or university are shown in Table 1.3, they will undoubtedly vary by type of circumstance at an institution. Indeed, stakeholders at every institution should discuss and then agree on their roles and responsibilities. The advantages of such meetings and discussions among stakeholders include transparency of the process and responsibilities; inclusiveness and the resulting buy-in of outcomes; and the identification of any potential problems, such as a lack of resources or conflicts with existing policies. Tables 1.4 through 1.6 represent one example of possible assignments of roles and responsibilities that could result from a meeting of stakeholders at a typical institution of higher education. ADS providers include coordinators and offices that interface directly with students with disabilities, organizing with faculty and facilities to provide accommodations and access to academic and cocurricular activities. The term *senior administrators* refers to vice presidents, deans, directors, or members of legal counsel who may not interact directly with the student with a disability but who are involved in decisions about resources and access for that student.

## Table 1.4
*Examples of Stakeholder Roles and Responsibilities for the Lenses of Self-Advocacy, Individual Differences, and Life Transition*

| Lens | Student | Faculty | Accessibility services | Senior administrators | Parent/ guardian |
|---|---|---|---|---|---|
| Self-advocacy | Knows their rights and responsibilities, recognizes community expectations, employs effective communication strategies. | Often no direct role | Provides counseling and support services, is an intermediary with faculty, teaches self-advocacy. | Often no direct role | Allows student to advocate for self (stays "out of the way"). |
| Individual differences | Recognizes communication styles of others; seeks out mentors and advisors; uses accommodations. | Recognizes that different students can require a spectrum of accommodations, and uses inclusive pedagogy. | Assists students in finding mentors and peer support; acts as a resource for faculty on assistive technology; recommends accommodations. | Often no direct role | Often no direct role |
| Life transition | Recognizes that they are developing their personal identity with their specific functional limitations. | Provides career and other advising | Provides counseling and support services. | Often no direct role | Prohibited from advocating directly (FERPA). |

*Note.* While the student is responsible for initiatives in these aspects of the college experience, support from other stakeholders is also necessary.

## Table 1.5
*Examples of Stakeholder Roles and Responsibilities for the Lenses of Academic Rigor, New Pedagogies, and Technology*

| Lens | Stakeholder | | | | |
| --- | --- | --- | --- | --- | --- |
| | Student | Faculty | Accessibility services | Senior administrators | Parent/ guardian |
| Academic rigor | Actively engages in course content and works with faculty to meet agreed-upon learning outcomes. | Defines *academic rigor*, works with students to clarify expectations and expected behavior, and uses inclusive pedagogy; maintains academic integrity. | Works with faculty and students to provide reasonable accommodations. | Supports academic integrity. | Often no direct role |
| New pedagogies | Works with faculty and DSO to ensure new pedagogies are accessible. | Ensures that new pedagogy such as online or flipped classes, student-centered learning, and service-learning are accessible by working with the student and DSO. | Works with faculty and student to ensure that new pedagogy is accessible. | Often no direct role | Often no direct role |
| Technology | Works with faculty and DSO to implement appropriate technology. | Works with student to integrate technology into the learning experience. | Determines appropriate software, hardware, auxiliary aids and services; coordinates delivery and training. | Provides technology resources and training for DSO, faculty, and students; ensures an accessible technology infrastructure. | Often no direct role |

*Note.* Stakeholder roles and responsibilities for the lenses of academic rigor and new pedagogies are largely the responsibility of the faculty, while the use of technology is often driven by senior administration and the disability services office.

# Structure and Function of the Collaborative Framework

## Table 1.6
*Examples of Stakeholder Roles and Responsibilities for the Lenses of Disability Law, Attitudes, and Inclusion/Socialization*

| Lens | Stakeholder | | | | |
|---|---|---|---|---|---|
| | Student | Faculty | Accessibility services | Senior administrators | Parent/guardian |
| Disability law | Understands rights and responsibilities and limits of the law; understands definition of *disability*. | Works with students and DSO to provide services consistent with disability law; understands definition of *disability*. | Informs students of rights and responsibilities under the law; apprises administration and faculty | Responsible for collegewide policy and compliance under the law. | Often no direct role |
| Attitudes | Understands the culture and embedded expectations, assumed standards of behavior. | Works with students to clarify expectations and expected behavior, and uses inclusive pedagogy. | Helps the student balance service needs with contributions to the class and school community. | Promotes a culture of inclusiveness with policy, programs, and outreach. | Supports the student emotionally, and lets the student develop self-advocacy. |
| Inclusion/socialization | Communicates frequently with DSO and faculty on expectations and experiences. | Provides an inclusive atmosphere and pedagogy. | Ensures appropriate routes of accessibility to peers, facilities, events, and resources. | Provides resources for accessibility and socialization: buildings, events, and classrooms. | Sees their student as a student rather than disabled. |

*Note.* Senior administration and ADS are primarily responsible for overseeing compliance with disability law, but faculty must be trained and students informed of their rights and responsibilities under the law. Attitudes and inclusion/socialization are important underpinnings of campus culture, and all stakeholders share responsibility for these lenses.

In the following chapters, various stakeholders reflect on their experiences in higher education and describe how specific lenses have shaped their understanding of their roles and responsibilities with regard to students with disabilities.

## References

Americans with Disabilities Act of 1990, 42 U.S.C. § 12101 *et seq.* (1990). https://www.ada.gov/pubs/adastatute08.htm

Aquino, K. (2016). A new theoretical approach to postsecondary student disability: Disability-diversity (dis)connect model. *Journal of Postsecondary Education and Disability, 29*(4), 317–330. https://www.ahead.org/professional-resources/publications/jped/archived-jped/jped-volume-29

Bart, M. (2011, April 11). What can be done to boost academic rigor? *Faculty Focus.* http://www.facultyfocus.com/articles/teaching-and-learning/what-can-be-done-to-boost-academic-rigor

Baker, K. Q., Boland, K., & Nowik, C. M. (2012). A campus survey of faculty and student perceptions of persons with disabilities. *Journal of Postsecondary Education and Disability, 25*(4), 309–329. https://www.ahead.org/professional-resources/publications/jped/archived-jped/jped-volume-25

Berger, M., Scott, E., Axe, J., & Hawkins, I. (2013). World challenge: Engaging sophomores in an intensive, interdisciplinary course. *International Journal of Teaching and Learning in Higher Education, 25*(3), 333–345.

Berger, M., Lipsitz, N., & Berger, E. (2014). Identifying the challenges for disability services in an increasingly complex higher education environment. *Excellence in Practice: Knowledge Communities,* 21–22.

Boyadjian, T., Sabelli, R. A., Wong, I. L., & Skeer, M. R. (2023, March 14). Perceptions on transition to college among high school students in recovery. *Contemporary School Psychology.* https://doi.org/10.1007/s40688-023-00458-4

Bruce, C., & Aylward, M. (2021). Disability and self-advocacy experiences in university learning contexts. *Scandinavian Journal of Disability Research, 23*(1), 14–26. https://doi.org/10.16993/sjdr.741

Brinckerhoff, L. C. (1994). Developing effective self-advocacy skills in college-bound students with learning disabilities. *Intervention in School & Clinic, 29*(4), 229–237.

Burgstahler, S. (1994, July 11–15). *Improving campus attitudes about students with disabilities* [Paper presentation]. Association on Higher Education and Disability, Annual Conference, Columbus, OH, United States.

Burgstahler, S. (2015). *Universal design of instruction (UDI): Definition, principles, guidelines, and examples.* DO-IT, University of Washington. https://www.washington.edu/doit/sites/default/files/atoms/files/UD_Instruction_06_15_20.pdf

Burgstahler, S., & Moore, E. (2009). Making student services welcoming and accessible through accommodations and universal design. *Journal of Postsecondary Education and Disability, 21*(3), 155–174. https://www.ahead.org/professional-resources/publications/jped/archived-jped/jped-volume-21

Cawthon, S. W., & Cole, E. V. (2010). Postsecondary students who have a learning disability: Student perspectives on accommodations access and obstacles. *Journal of Postsecondary Education and Disability, 23*(2), 112–128. https://www.ahead.org/professional-resources/publications/jped/archived-jped/jped-volume-23

Chardin, M., & Novak, K. (2021). *Equity by design: Delivering on the power and promise of UDL.* Corwin Press.

Coburn, K. L., & Treeger, M. L. (2003). *Letting go: A parents' guide to understanding the college years.* Quill.

Colby, A., Ehrlich, T., Beaumont, E., & Stephens, J. (2015). Campus culture or climate. *The New York Times.* http://www.nytimes.com/ref/college/collegespecial2/coll_aascu_ecculture.html

Cook, B. G., Gerber, M. M., & Murphy, J. (2000). Backlash against inclusion of students with learning disabilities in higher education: Implications for transitions to post-secondary environments. *Work: A Journal of Prevention, Assessment, & Rehabilitation, 14*(1) 31–40.

Cook, E., Kennedy, E., & McGuire, S. (2013). Effect of teaching metacognitive learning strategies on performance in general chemistry courses. *Journal of Chemical Education, 90*(8), 961–967.

Cook, L., Rumrill, P. D., & Tankersley, M. (2009). Priorities and understanding of faculty members regarding college students with disabilities. *International Journal of Teaching and Learning Higher Education, 21*(1), 84–96.

Culver, K. C., Braxton, J., & Pascarella, E. (2019). Does teaching rigorously really enhance undergraduates' intellectual development? The relationship of academic rigor with critical thinking skills and lifelong learning motivations. *Higher Education, 78*(4), 611–627. https://doi.org/10.1007/s10734-019-00361-z

Culver, K. C., Braxton, J. M., & Pascarella, E. T. (2021). What we talk about when we talk about rigor: Examining conceptions of academic rigor. *Journal of Higher Education, 92*(7), 1140–1163. https://doi.org/10.1080/00221546.2021.1920825

de Klerk, E. D., & Palmer, J. M. (2022). Technology inclusion for students living with disabilities through collaborative online learning during and beyond a pandemic. *Perspectives in Education, 40*(1), 80–95. https://doi.org/10.18820/2519593X/PIE.V40.I1.5

Ferguson, Z. (2015, February 5). Access and stigma key issues for disabled students. *The Cornell Daily Sun*. https://issuu.com/cornellsun/docs/02-05-14_entire_issue_lo_res_016df071fcfd14

Fernández-Batanero, J. M., Montenegro-Rueda, M., Fernández-Cerero, J., & García-Martínez, I. (2022). Assistive technology for the inclusion of students with disabilities: A systematic review. *Educational Technology Research and Development, 70*(5), 1911–1930. https://doi.org/10.1007/s11423-022-10127-7

Field, S., Sarver, M. D., & Shaw, S. F. (2003). Self-determination: A key to success in postsecondary education for students with learning disabilities. *Remedial and Special Education, 24*(6), 339–349.

Forber-Pratt, A. J., & Zape, M. P. (2017). Disability identity development model: Voices from the ADA-generation. *Disability and Health Journal, 10*(2), 350–355. https://doi.org/10.1016/j.dhjo.2016.12.013

Fullan, M., & Langworthy, M. (2014, January). *A rich seam: How new pedagogies find deep learning*. Pearson. http://www.michaelfullan.ca/wp-content/uploads/2014/01/3897.Rich_Seam_web.pdf

Gething, L., & Wheeler, B. (1992). The Interaction with Disabled Person Scale: A new Australian instrument to measure attitudes towards people with disabilities. *Australian Journal of Psychology, 44*(2), 75–82.

Getzel, E. E., & Thoma, C. A. (2008). Experiences of college students with disabilities and the importance of self-determination in higher education settings. *Career Development for Exceptional Individuals, 31*, 77–84.

Gibson, J. (2006, November/December). Disability and clinical competency: An introduction. *The California Psychologist, 39*, 6–10.

Hadley, W. M. (2011). College students with disabilities: A student development perspective. In W. S. Harbour & J. W. Madaus (Eds.), *Disability services and campus dynamics* (New Directions for Higher Education, No. 154, 77–81). http://dx.doi.org/10.1002/he.436

Hafner, D. (2008). *Inclusion in postsecondary education: Phenomenological study on identifying and addressing barriers to inclusion of individuals with significant disabilities at a four-year liberal arts college* (Publication No. 3337318) [Doctoral dissertation, Edgewood College]. ProQuest Dissertations and Theses Global.

Hehir, T. (2005). *New directions in special education: Eliminating ableism in policy and practice*. Harvard Education Press.

Hehir, T., Grindal, T., Freeman, B., Lamoreau, R., Borquaye, Y., & Burke, S. (2016). *A summary of the evidence on inclusive education* [Unpublished manuscript]. Harvard Graduate School of Education, Harvard University.

Hehir, T., & Katzman, L. (2012). *Effective inclusive schools: Designing successful schoolwide programs*. Jossey-Bass.

Hehir, T., & Schifter, L. (2015). *How did you get here? Students with disabilities and their journeys to Harvard*. Harvard Education Press.

Hernández-Torrano, D., Somerton, M., & Helmer, J. (2022). Mapping research on inclusive education since Salamanca Statement: A bibliometric review of the literature over 25 years. *International Journal of Inclusive Education, 26*(9), 893–912. https://doi.org/10.1080/13603116.2020.1747555

Hibbs, J., & Rostain, A. (2019). *The stressed years of their lives: Helping your kid survive and thrive during their college years*. St. Martin's Press.

Hutcheon, E. J., & Wolbring, G. (2012). Voices of "disabled" post secondary students: Examining higher education "disability" policy using an ableism lens. *Journal of Diversity in Higher Education, 5*(1), 39–49. https://doi.org/10.1037/a0027002

Individuals with Disabilities Education Act, 20 U.S.C. § 1400 *et seq*. (2004).

Jackson, A., Colson-Fearon, B., & Versey, H. S. (2022). Managing intersectional invisibility and hypervisibility during the transition to college among first-generation women of color. *Psychology of Women Quarterly, 46*(3), 354–371.

Junco, R., & Salter, D. W. (2004). Improving the campus climate for students with disabilities through the use of online training. *NASPA Journal, 41*(2), 263–276. https://doi.org/10.2202/1949-6605.1333

Kampsen, A. (2009). *Personal, social, and institutional factors influencing college transition and adaptation experiences for students with psychiatric disabilities* [Doctoral dissertation, University of Minnesota]. University of Minnesota Digital Conservancy. http://conservancy.umn.edu/bitstream/handle/11299/58441/Kampsen_umn_0130E_10858.pdf?sequence=1&isAllowed=y

Kim, E., & Aquino, K. C. (2017). *Disability as diversity in higher education: Policies and practices to enhance student success*. Routledge.

Kuh, G. D. (2008). *High-impact educational practices: What they are, who has access to them, and why they matter*. American Association of Colleges and Universities.

Leyser, Y., Vogel, S. Wyland, S., & Brulle, A. (1998). Faculty attitudes and practices regarding students with disabilities: Two decades after the implementation of Section 504. *Journal of Postsecondary Education and Disability, 13*(3), 5–19. https://www.ahead.org/professional-resources/publications/jped/archived-jped/jped-volume-13

Light, R. J. (2001). *Making the most of college: Students speak their minds*. Harvard University Press.

Lombardi, A. R., & Lalor, A. R. (2017). Faculty and administrator knowledge and attitudes regarding disability. In E. Kim & K. C. Aquino (Eds.), *Disability as diversity in higher education: Policies and practices to enhance student success* (pp. 107–121). Routledge.

Madaus, J., Cascio, A., Delgado, J., Gelbar, N., Reis, S., & Tarconish, E. (2023). Improving the transition to college for twice-exceptional students with ASD: Perspectives from college service providers. *Career Development and Transition for Exceptional Individuals, 46*(1), 40–51. https://doi.org/10.1177/21651434221091230

Martel, A., Derenne, J., & Leebens, P. K. (2018). *Promoting safe and effective transitions to college for youth with mental health conditions: A case-based guide to best practices*. Springer.

Martin, S. (2006). *Special education, technology, and teacher education*. http://citeseerx.ist.psu.edu/viewdoc/download?doi=10.1.1.113.1310&rep=rep1&type=pdf

National Center for Education Statistics. (2018, May). Table 311.10: Number and percentage distribution of students enrolled in postsecondary institutions, by level, disability status, and selected student characteristics: 2015–16 [Data table]. In *Digest of Education Statistics*. U.S. Department of Education, Institute of Education Sciences. https://nces.ed.gov/programs/digest/d18/tables/dt18_311.10.asp

Newnham, N., & LeBrecht, J. (Directors). (2020) *Crip camp: A disability revolution* [Film]. Netflix; Higher Ground; Rusted Spoke Productions. https://w.youtube.com/watch?v=OFS8SpwioZ4

Nguyen, J., & Phuong, A. E. (2016). The impacts of a democratic-gamified pedagogy on equity in higher education. *The Berkeley McNair Research Journal, 23*, 89–105.

Nutter, K. J., & Ringgenberg, L. J. (1993). Creating positive outcomes for students with disabilities. In S. Kroeger & J. Schuck (Eds.), *Responding to disability issues in student affairs* (pp. 45–58). Jossey-Bass.

Offidani-Bertrand, C., Velez, G., Benz, C., & Keels, M. (2022). "I wasn't expecting it": High school experiences and navigating belonging in the transition to college. *Emerging Adulthood, 10*(1), 212–224. https://doi.org/10.1177/2167696819882117

Ogunyemi, A. A., Quaicoe, J. S., & Bauters, M. (2022). Indicators for enhancing learners' engagement in massive open online courses: A systematic review. *Computers and Education Open, 3*, Article 100088. https://doi.org/10.1016/j.caeo.2022.100088

Pfeifer, M. A., Reiter, E. M., Hendrickson, M., & Stanton, J. D. (2020). Speaking up: A model of self-advocacy for STEM undergraduates with ADHD and/or specific learning disabilities. *International Journal of STEM Education, 7*, Article 33. https://doi.org/10.1186/s40594-020-00233-4

Phuong, A. E., Nguyen, J., & Marie, D. (2017a). Conceptualizing an adaptive and data-driven equity-oriented pedagogy. *Transformative Dialogues: Teaching and Learning Journal, 10*(2), 1–20.

Phuong, A. E., Nguyen, J., & Marie, D. (2017b). Evaluating an adaptive equity-oriented pedagogy: A study of its impacts in higher education. *The Journal of Effective Teaching, 17*(2), 5–22.

Pittman, L. D., & Richmond, A. (2008). University belonging, friendship quality, psychological adjustment during the transition to college. *The Journal of Experimental Education, 76*(4), 343–362.

Ramirez, B. R., Puente, M., & Contreras, F. (2023, January 12). Navigating the university as nepantleras: The college transition experiences of Chicana/Latina undergraduate students. *Journal of Diversity in Higher Education.* Advance online publication. https://dx.doi.org/10.1037/dhe0000463

Reed, D. S. (2009). *College students with bipolar disorder and their personal transition from high school to college* (Publication No. 337425) [Doctoral dissertation, University of North Florida]. ProQuest Dissertations and Theses Global.

Rehabilitation Act of 1973 § 504, 29 U.S.C. § 794 *et seq.* (2012).

Reiff, H. B. (2007). *Self-advocacy skills for students with learning disabilities: Making it happen in college and beyond.* Dude.

Rizk, J., & Hillier, C. (2022). Digital technology and increasing engagement among students with disabilities: Interaction rituals and digital capital. *Computers and Education Open, 3*, Article 100099. https://doi.org/10.1016/j.caeo.2022.100099

Ryan, A., & Tilbury, D. (2013). *Flexible pedagogies: New pedagogical ideas.* Higher Education Academy.

Sabaner, C., & Arnold, K. D. (2020). Mental health in the transition to college: Experiences of six low-income, high-achieving students. *Journal of College Counseling, 24*(1), 18–35. https://doi.org/10.1002/jocc.12174

Sasser, J., Waddell, J. T., & Doane, L. D. (2023). Family dynamics and adjustment across Latino/a students' transition to college: Disentangling within- and between-person reciprocal associations. *Developmental Psychology, 59*(3), 487–502. https://doi.org/10.1037/dev0001474

Savitz-Romer, M., & Jager-Hyman, J. (2009). *Removing roadblocks to rigor: Linking academic and social supports to ensure college readiness and success.* Institute for Higher Education Policy. http://www.ihep.org/assets/files/programs/pcn/Roadblocks.pdf

Sladek, M. R., Gusman, M. S., & Doane, L. D. (2023). Ethnic-racial identity developmental trajectories across the transition to college. *Journal of Youth and Adolescence, 52*(4), 880–898. https://doi.org/10.1007/s10964-022-01724-z

Test, D. W., Fowler, C. H., Wood, W. M., Brewer, D. M., & Eddy, S. (2005). A conceptual framework of self-advocacy for students with disabilities. *Remedial and Special Education, 26*(1), 43–54. https://doi.org/10.1177/07419325050260010601

Tinto, V. (1975). Dropout from higher education: A theoretical synthesis of recent research. *Review of Educational Research, 45*(1), 89–125. https://doi.org/10.2307/1170024

Trager, B. M., Morgan, R. M., Boyle, S. C., Montiel Ishino, F. A., & LaBrie, J. W. (2023). Capturing the bigger picture: A gestalt of general and alcohol-specific social media usage during the transition to college as a predictor of first-year alcohol use and consequences. *Addictive Behaviors, 136*, Article 107472. https://doi.org/10.1016/j.addbeh.2022.107472

Upton, T. D., & Harper, D. C. (2002). Multidimensional disability attitudes and equitable evaluation of educational accommodations by college students without disabilities. *Journal of Postsecondary Education and Disability, 15*(2), 115–130. https://www.ahead.org/professional-resources/publications/jped/archived-jped/jped-volume-15

Wagner, T. (2008). Rigor redefined. *Educational Leadership, 66*(2), 20–24.

Walstra, R., & Chukwuma, E. (2023). Inclusion of disability within the spectrum of diversity and the implications for accounting education. *Issues in Accounting Education, 38*(1), 149–162. https://doi.org/10.2308/issues-2021-007

White, G. W., & Vo, Y. T. (2006). Requesting accommodations to increase full participation in higher education: An analysis of self-advocacy training for postsecondary students with learning and other disabilities. *Learning Disabilities: A Multidisciplinary Journal, 14*(1), 41–56. https://js.sagamorepub.com/index.php/ldmj/article/view/5498

Wolman, C., McCrink, C. S., Rodriguez, S.F., & Harris-Looby, J. (2004). The accommodation of university students with disabilities inventory (AUSDI): Assessing American and Mexican faculty attitudes toward students with disabilities. *Journal of Hispanic Higher Education, 3*(3), 284–295. https://doi.org/10.1177/1538192704265985

Wraga, W. G. (2010, April 30–May 4). *What's the problem with a "rigorous academic curriculum"?* [Paper presentation]. Society of Professors of Education/American Educational Research Association Annual Meeting, Denver, CO, United States. https://eric.ed.gov/?id=ED509394

Yeager, K., Gandara, G. A., Martinez, C. (2022). "It's bigger than me:" Influence of social support on the development of self-advocacy for college students with disabilities. *Journal of Postsecondary Education and Disability, 35*(2), 145–159. https://www.ahead.org/professional-resources/publications/jped/archived-jped/jped-volume-35

# PART II

## Self-Advocacy and Inclusion/Socialization

# CHAPTER 2

# Relationships Matter
## Self-Advocacy, Mentorship, and the Transformative Power of Disability Services

Kevin T. Mintz and Eileen Connell Berger

In spring 2008, I became only the second person with cerebral palsy to be accepted as an undergraduate at Harvard University. Shortly after my acceptance, I googled "Disability Services" and inadvertently found a website for the Graduate School of Education's (GSE) Access and Disability Services Office. Finding that website was the beginning of a lifelong friendship with Eileen Berger, a coeditor of this volume. At that time, she was the assistant director of the Office of Student Affairs and Access and Disability Services Administrator for the GSE. Without Eileen's mentorship and love, I would have dropped out and would not be the academic professional I am today. For my contribution to this volume, Eileen and I decided to transcribe a conversation from January 2023 about our remarkable journey together at the university and beyond. I hope readers come to understand not only how profoundly our relationship has shaped both our lives but also how transformative mentorship and robust disability services can be in empowering someone with my level of disability to succeed in all levels of postsecondary education.

—*Kevin Mintz*

## Life Transitions

**EILEEN:** *Tell me about your early educational experiences before college and how they shaped your journey in postsecondary education.*

**KEVIN:** I was the first person with cerebral palsy—a quadriplegic wheelchair user and with impaired speech—ever integrated fully into general education in Miami-Dade County Public Schools back in 1995. I was able to do that because my special education prekindergarten teacher at my elementary school went with my parents on a tour of a segregated kindergarten in our district where all of the kids were in a circle doing absolutely nothing. And within 5 minutes, my teacher said, "I don't care what I have to do, Kevin is not coming here," because she knew, even when I was 4, how intelligent I was. And so she negotiated with the principal of my elementary school that in the second year of pre-K, I would spend half the day in the kindergarten class I would go into, and if the teacher felt comfortable with me, I would be allowed to stay. And the rest is history. I mention that because I learned instinctively from a very early age that I had to be proactive and nice to people. I loved my K–12 experience because I was especially close with my teachers. I had to be, because none of them had ever worked with someone like me before. My parents and I worked with them to make sure everything went well. There are a few bad examples of things going wrong, and I lived in fear that with one misstep I'd be sent back to segregated special education. But all in all, it was very positive, and my parents did most of the heavy lifting for me—to the point where my dad was even my care provider in school from 8th grade until 12th grade because the school district could neither find a paraprofessional who could help me in the restroom without creeping me out nor get scribing services. At the start, my dad scribed for me, and by 12th grade, we're talking AP calculus and, you know, art history, and lots of cool, complicated subjects.

**E:** *Given your determination, your self-advocacy, and your confidence in your academic ability, as well as your confidence in knowing what kind of accommodations you needed, did you feel prepared for what you encountered when you entered college?*

**K:** Absolutely not! I got into Harvard University knowing how to work with people but not really knowing the ways of the world as it relates to the transition from the Individualized Education Program model, under the Individuals with Disabilities Education Act, to the accommodation and modification model under Section 504 and the Americans with Disabilities Act. I didn't even know really what Section 504 was. But I think it's important for our readers to know that no one actually explains the differences to you and your parents; it's really on you to find the answers, which is very unfair because you're still both navigating the lack of support in the K–12 education system and trying to understand this whole new world of disability services while adjusting to college. I thought I was ready for the typical college stuff, but I was not prepared for the different ways that students have to navigate the undergraduate environment, disabled or not, and the attitudes of the people who are charged with providing services. I was totally out of my element; everything was overwhelming and scary. It's surreal to think back to that time, as everything is so natural and like *duh!* to me now, but it literally felt like being reborn. I didn't even realize that my university had different schools and that each school has its own disability services office.

**E:** *Your school of enrollment was one of many in the large, decentralized university where each school functioned separately and had its own model for providing services to students with disabilities. Roles and responsibilities varied widely from school to school. As an admitted undergraduate, you encountered a service model that was distinctly different from that at GSE. I remember you also petitioned* *your undergraduate dean's office to register for 10 courses in GSE over your 4 undergraduate years, where I got to know you so well.*

## Attitudes

**E:** *Remember when I first met you and your mother on that lengthy interview-type call? I thought, Wow, this is a great well informed and enthusiastic incoming student and family to work with! When I heard you were not a graduate student, I was disappointed, knowing you would have a different experience in a larger undergraduate school. I think it's important to describe some of why you were so overwhelmed at first.*

**K:** After speaking with you, we called the undergraduate accessibility office. We didn't have another welcoming or warm conversation like we had with you. The real discomfort began when I visited during their pre-orientation weekend. I remember the director of the office came out and said to me and my parents, "I told you over the phone I don't talk to parents. You can wait outside while I meet with Kevin, and if you have any quick questions at the end, I'll answer, but this is about Kevin." I was not prepared to enter that meeting myself under any circumstances, and I think I should have been allowed to sign something that let my parents be with me. I had no idea what was going on in that meeting. I felt like I was having an out-of-body experience.

**E:** *I'm so sorry you had such a painful experience and were unprepared to hear that message from them. If you had more experience or transition advice you might have asserted yourself and asked to have your parents join the meeting. Informing students early in their transition that an authorization for parental involvement is an option can be reassuring to the student and a helpful, supportive resource for ADS.*

**K:** I had gotten accepted a month prior to that meeting that was personally traumatic. I felt I wasn't in a position to be critical about what they were telling me. The one positive moment in that meeting was they told me that they had to provide digitized texts, which was revolutionary because while I was in high school, my parents would read all my books and homework assignments to me. And even without fully realizing how revolutionary a screen reader would be, I knew it would make my academic life so much easier. I thought once I was actually in the fall semester, I could ask more questions.

**E:** *It's hard to believe your public high school did not provide you with accessible digital texts! In my K–12 disability program experience as a teacher and administrator, we would have provided you with access technologies. In higher education, I provided assistive technology staff and student interns as a critical component of disability support services and appropriate accommodations.*

**K:** This is an important part of the story: I didn't realize until I read *New Directions in Special Education* (Hehir, 2005) that the reason the digitized text was in place was because a student who had cerebral palsy filed an Office for Civil Rights complaint with the Department of Education in order to get the university to do that. And, honestly, reading that story was the real start of my realization that I would be in over my head, and I did not realize how difficult life would actually be. I fantasized about withdrawing my intent to enroll and figuring out how to get Georgetown University to let me come even though I had declined.

## Stakeholders

**K:** Can I ask you a question? I think readers might find themselves in situations where they are in institutional contexts that don't support them in doing the right thing. I'd be curious to hear what advice you have for someone in that situation.

**E:** *There were times in my career when I had to deal with people who lacked empathy or were resistant to fully including students with disabilities. And some with ableist bias. The truth is I love my work! I thoroughly enjoy the challenge of solving problems that are unique to each student through mentoring, advising, organizing, and collaborating with faculty, staff, and ADS colleagues to empower students through cocurricular planning, internships, access technologies, and professional development event planning. Building optimism, forging relationships, finding allies, and collaboration are crucial elements for all stakeholders. Working with faculty and students directly created collaborative relationships and opportunities for building trust, confidence, and academic success for students.*

*My position gave me the opportunity to work with students in building community and fostering inclusion: Students were trained to work as interns in the office to provide technological and academic assistance for other students with disabilities. The office supported the creation of a unique student organization that planned and ran cocurricular events and programs that offered opportunities for students to engage with faculty and other students.*

*I remember you shared many moments when problems seemed overwhelming. With coaching sessions, we were able to put things in perspective, take appropriate actions, feel relieved, and often share a hot chocolate and good laugh, too! Many of your GSE faculty created classes designed to be accessible for all learners. Your professors were engaged, collaborative, and even enthused by the challenges of individual differences you brought them and became the best allies for you and other students with disabilities. That's one of the things that excited me about the work—forming an inclusive intersectional community of students with disabilities, with faculty and administrative allies. Providing appropriate support for your academic, physical, and social access was very challenging and complex and required the collaboration of many stakeholders. Collaboration with other professional colleagues in national and local organizations, such as NASPA–Student Affairs Administrators in Higher Education and the Association on Higher Education and Disability, is a fabulous way to share, support, and learn.*

**K:** What I just heard you say is that it's important for disability providers to know who the stakeholders are and how to find allies and build relationships. The most interesting part of that for me is I feel like that's one of the most important things you taught me how to do. Yes, I was provided with the essential access services I needed to be academically successful, to become a meaningful participant in the community, and to have the opportunity to develop my voice—my narrative as a person with a disability. For instance, academically, you gave me notetakers who were qualified in each particular class, as note-taking became quite complicated in graduate school.

I'm thinking in particular of my statistics courses, where the professors would lecture using a blackboard or an overhead projector because they would manually solve mathematical problems. In order for you to truly understand what I needed, Eileen, you observed the classes, consulted professors, hired and supervised sometimes three or four student notetakers per class who embedded the projected and written images into the notes, took photos of the faculty writing on the blackboard, and even embedded the professor's PowerPoint slides and faculty class notes in the notes file you sent from the office. And you got it all to me the next day!

I was provided with scribes on campus and in my residence hall who helped me complete written graduate-level assignments and converted texts to e-text for all my graduate classes. That was a lot of work and coordination of services. I'm so grateful. Your open-door office policy, the opportunities to participate in cocurricular programming that included my faculty and the student disability organization, and the sense of community spirit among students with disabilities made me feel it was the place I belonged.

**E:** *You taught us so much about individuality. Getting to know you and what worked for you as well as the differences in the level of services you needed in each course was quite a good learning experience for all of us administrators, faculty members, librarians, student services, and technology staff. You are right in mentioning notetaking services for your statistics classes that were especially challenging to plan and organize with you and the faculty. In some of your doctoral-level statistics courses, we assigned a head notetaker and four other notetakers; each one was responsible for each facet of a fast-moving, content-packed class with very hard class deadlines and turnover times for notes, usually by the following day in an accessible digital format. Often faculty gave us consultation time and even their own course notes before the classes so we could at least have the lecture content ahead of time. Everybody who worked with you—fellow students, technology staff, librarians, operations staff, faculty members, and myself—gained a learning experience and friendship we will always cherish and carry with us.*

## Inclusion and Socialization

**K:** I think the most valuable support you gave me was mentoring me on how to navigate all of the services, because I was a very naïve teenager in general. I think whether it's through disability services or not, all students with disabilities need individualized support in figuring out how to be their own agents and advocates so they can learn how to cultivate relationships to manage their own unique support structure. All these years later, I frankly forgot about just how complicated the statistics notes were, and the logistics of exam accommodations, but I always remember the individual coaching, the Friday lunches and coffees, and, when I turned 21, cocktails with grad students in local pubs, where we would think about the challenges of the week and how to navigate them. That's one of the most valuable things I learned how to do in college, and I don't think at the time you got enough credit for helping me figure all that out.

**E:** *You felt included! When your functional limitations required support, you learned how to reach out to different members of the community—fellow students, faculty, and ADS—with whom you shared academic achievements, social events, and friendships. Your experience as an undergraduate in graduate courses in GSE helped model a path toward your professional future. The people who got to know you learned from you and loved being with you! When students became your friends, they also became your advisors—and advocates. When faculty got to know you they became critical advisors and mentors in your scholarly work, giving you a vision and opportunities for your future career in academia.*

**K:** I think about that every time I go to one of their weddings or get to meet their children, 14 years later. But it's a blessing, and it's these kinds of relationships even more than the official college curriculum that are important for students while they're in college and beyond. They're how people get jobs and cultivate full lives, and it kind of happened organically for me because, I think, you're special, and the GSE was a special place. I think an interesting challenge for all of us as educators and scholars who work in this field to consider is how we cultivate environments of belonging where those kinds of relationships happen for students with disabilities, many of whom spent K–12 socially isolated because they're the different kids, or the special education kids, or whatever negative term a community places upon them.

## Self-Advocacy

**K:** After graduating, I had a great experience in a master's program in the United Kingdom. I then started a doctoral program and was met with a lot of resistance for my needed accommodations. The only reason I received my PhD was that I had faculty who cared about me and knew that what I was asking for was reasonable. I picked a supportive doctoral supervisor and taught her a lot of things about what I needed for scholarly research, the interdependencies in my life, and my deep enjoyment, love of, and appreciation for the people I meet. She was able to get me access to resources that other graduate students with disabilities, unfortunately, might not have gotten from ADS. I still had to advocate for my needs involving lengthy commutes to another campus, obtaining peer scribes, and negotiating with faculty about academic requirements to remain in the program. It's remarkable that I am at the same institution, in my second postdoctoral program, as a medical ethicist. Thankfully, my current mentor advocated for me to get 40 hours of scribing and 40 hours of personal care assistance, because at a medical school, I have the potential to work with patients directly, and my mentors haven't ever wanted me to have a bathroom accident in front of patients.

## Individual Differences

**E:** *Who are the people who could have been more responsive to your needs in your academic journey?*

**K:** I've thought a lot about this very carefully, particularly as I've become an early career academic. I don't think disability offices are necessarily set up for someone like me to be in doctoral-level programs doing advanced work. Disability offices have no idea what goes on in medical schools, and the accommodations they provide are often not compatible with the technical standards of the medical school curricula. And so I think part of what I realized is—and this might sound egotistical—that it's so amazing that I'm even here. As I progressed through my career, I felt like the only one like me anywhere, and not that this is an excuse, but I simply don't think the transactional model that most disability offices work from is set up for someone with my complicated level of need—and particularly post-COVID, with 20% of undergraduate students registering for disability services.

I don't think they're even set up to meet the needs of students today. Even some ADS services that traditionally used to support that model of "Here's what we give you, and good luck" don't work anymore because so many students need support, and they need individualized support. I try to do what I can in my own teaching practice, beyond what's in the accommodations letter, and meet students where they are, but that should be a practice everyone does within various offices and roles in universities. We need to break out of the mold—which comes from special education—that these students are still the responsibility of one office. They're all of our responsibility.

**E:** *Exactly! All stakeholders have some responsibility.*

**K:** And see, that's on medical schools. Now we're getting into my area of current research, but medical schools in particular need to think about what *really* are technical standards—what does a doctor *need* to be able to do versus what things have we just gotten so much into the habit of doing.

**E:** *It's important having the student be a part of the discussion with the stakeholders in problem solving, by looking with a fresh eye, mind, and heart at what is a fundamental requirement and how or if that requirement can be modified. Through the pandemic, we had to rethink many aspects of how we operate and with whom we collaborate. Using the framework [in this book], stakeholders will benefit from learning about important collaborations that are possible and often necessary to give students with disabilities an equitable higher education experience.*

*It's a whole new world for changes in educational policy and practice. We can't just continue doing the same things in the same ways when often it doesn't seem to work.*

**K:** It never worked, but especially now it's not working to the point of people across the board needing to find a new way of offering support and doing things. And I hope we have come out of the pandemic with better models and lessons for how to do things.

My current mentors wouldn't have been able to do what they did for me if my wonderful boss at the National Institutes of Health (NIH), where I did my first postdoc, hadn't worked with me and my primary mentors to figure out how to hire 40 hours of care providers and 40 hours of research and administrative support. These accommodations served as a model for my current mentors (Mintz, 2022).

**E:** *The NIH model that you mentioned could be a way for students, faculty, and administrators to reconceptualize what it means to accommodate students and employees with disabilities and complex needs who are coming into specialized graduate programs.*

**K:** My boss at NIH is a case study in cultural humility. They were open to learning what they needed to do. They are very thoughtful about how things need to get done. Nothing they did is rocket science: it's just listening, being able to learn from mistakes when things go wrong, and always having an open mind and an open heart. I think in higher education we get so ingrained in our models of how to do things and our standard operating procedures that we lose the ability at times to just reimagine things and listen to what people need.

## The Framework

**E:** *One thing the Framework shows is how to get people to think and work collaboratively. As you said, it's important to have cultural* *humility and caring and open-minded leadership as an example of the power of collaboration in an interactive process. If we get mired in standard operating procedures, we lose our ability to listen and learn from our constituents, our students with disabilities.*

**K:** You have to start with what you can and hope what you do in your corner of the world somehow gets out into other parts of the world. That's why this book is so important, because we're telling people's stories and describing collaborative practices.

## Self-Advocacy and Self-Determination Redux

**E:** *What values do you, as a professional bioethicist, think should orient the efforts that academic professionals undertake to promote disability access in postsecondary education?*

**K:** The first one is student autonomy, and I think we're not talking about the kind of autonomy where the student knows what to ask for, we give it to them, and they go away; that's transactional. That's a very individualistic take on autonomy, but particularly if we're thinking about undergraduate students. The future 18-year-old Kevins who arrive at college need to know what they're getting into. We need to take a more relational approach to students' autonomy. There is literature on relational autonomy in philosophy and bioethics, but the idea is that everyone is interdependent on other people. Autonomy is about enabling people to recognize their own self-agency and value through their interdependencies. So, I explain it as though I'm moving pieces on a chessboard that enable me to live my life and complete my work independently. Others are helping me do things, but I'm the one overseeing the board and thinking through how the pieces should fit together, recognizing that not everyone—or every piece, I should say—can do everything. My parents can't provide all my support, especially as they're getting older. A caregiver can't do the same things a research assistant can do, and vice versa, but we need to think about how to teach students like me how to think through that kind of critical planning process and put the pieces in place. The other value is equity, not equality. Equity is thinking in terms of what is necessary to give everyone the same educational benefit even if it involves having different ways of doing things for different students. I think it's OK to do different things to meet different needs, as long as you are thoughtful about what the goals are, how you individualize technical standards and the like, and justice. We need to be fair to all students, and students in turn need to treat the people who support them respectfully.

That's the other part of the puzzle that I've reckoned with as I've transitioned from student to academic professional: We have a lot on our plates, and students need to recognize that we often juggle a lot in addition to our teaching responsibilities, so it's important to teach students how to communicate with very busy, many times overextended, teaching staff, faculty, and administrators—something that you taught me because you're great at this stuff. It's something I probably wouldn't have picked up on my own at 18 to 22 because I was not in the frame of mind to fully recognize how many responsibilities professors, graduate students, and others have before they're even in front of a lecture or seminar.

**E:** *Getting coaching that teaches self-reflection is an important step in the self-advocacy process. What role do you think self-advocacy plays in disability inclusion in higher education? You just named quite a few things—the last one being justice. In your view, how does self-advocacy fit alongside the other lenses in the framework?*

**K:** I want to begin by acknowledging that some people with disabilities hate the term *self-advocacy*. I've never fully understood why, but as I understand it, it's the idea that all people, not just students with disabilities, need to be advocates for themselves. And when we use the term *self-advocacy*, we're not trying to make it sound as though individuals with disabilities live on their own planet and are expected to be their very special self-advocate. I think all students need to be advocates for themselves, disabled or not. If a student completes a higher education degree, or worse, completes it without the skills they need to self-advocate, then we have failed as educators. Whether it's helping undergraduate students figure out who they want to be in the world or supporting graduate and professional students as they proceed in their chosen careers, that's what we as higher education professionals are trying to do.

I think *self-advocacy*, as we're using it, has to be at the center of the framework because unless the student with the disability becomes proactive in knowing what they need, asking for it, and problem solving, they're doomed. I do not say that lightly. It's an ableist world out there, and we can't magically make that go away from them, unfortunately. The justice warrior in me wants the ableist biases to change. Students with disabilities need to know how to be comfortable with themselves in a world that is, most of the time, going to treat them poorly. Self-advocacy is at the core of the framework because of that expectation and reality, as unfortunate as it may be. All the other framework lenses—individual differences, life transition, academic rigor, new pedagogies, technology, disability law, attitudes, and inclusion/socialization—are pieces of what it takes for a student with a disability to be successful and to become an advocate for their dreams.

## References

Hehir, T. (2005). *New directions in special education: Eliminating ableism in policy and practice.* Harvard Education Press.

Mintz, K. T. (2022). Serendipity and social justice: How someone with a physical disability succeeds in clinical bioethics. *Narrative Inquiry in Bioethics, 12*(3), 265–273. https://doi.org/10.1353/nib.2022.0061

CHAPTER 3

# The Importance of Feeling Included

## Perceived Belonging Among Students With Disabilities in Higher Education

Katherine C. Aquino

A student's *sense of belonging*—their feeling of being included and valued in their community—is a key aspect of student persistence in the higher education setting (Pedler et al., 2022). For stakeholders in postsecondary institutions, understanding how to engage students and foster their perceived belongingness is crucial to their overall success (Hoffman et al., 2002; Museus et al., 2017). According to Strayhorn (2019), numerous elements contribute to a student's sense of belonging, including interaction with peers, active engagement in coursework, and connection to the institutional environment. Because so many elements can affect a student's retention and degree completion, it is vital to recognize the influence of belongingness on student motivation toward their postsecondary achievements (Tinto, 2015).

Any student can struggle to feel like a part of their institution's community, but certain characteristics may make it harder for them to create and maintain a positive sense of belonging; these characteristics include race, international status, and ability (Rainey et al., 2018; Rivas et al., 2019; Vaccaro et al., 2015). Students with disabilities in the higher education environment face additional challenges that may affect their overall success in the postsecondary environment (Fleming et al., 2017), including engagement in an ableist institutional environment (Dolmage, 2017) and perceived stigmatization from members of the campus community (Akin & Huang, 2019; Kimball et al., 2016). Students with disabilities have lower persistence and completion rates compared with students without disabilities, and a decreased sense of belonging is a factor in their reduced opportunity for success (Kutscher & Tuckwiller, 2019; Verdinelli & Kutner, 2016). As such, students with disabilities have additional obstacles that can affect their overall perceived belongingness and success.

This chapter explores the socioacademic experiences of students with disabilities in the postsecondary setting that may contribute to their sense of belonging. These two research questions drive this chapter:

1. What percentage of students with disabilities perceive positive socioacademic experiences in the higher education environment?
2. What are the descriptive differences in socioacademic postsecondary experiences based on disability self-identification?

Several terms must be defined to assist the reader in this work. First, the term *socioacademic* is used throughout this chapter to explore experiences students have related to both academic and social activities. Deil-Amen (2011) noted that examples of socioacademic activities in the higher education setting include in-class interactions, interactions with faculty and peers, and participation in academically related activities and clubs. Additionally, Tinto (1997) urged the use of socioacademic framing because this idea better highlights how "social and academic life are interwoven" (p. 619) in the campus setting. This chapter also incorporates the concept of sense of belonging; however, it is understood that overlap exists among terms related to one's perceived belongingness, integration, and inclusion in the higher education environment. These terms may be, at times, interchangeable in this chapter, but this project is guided by Strayhorn's (2012) definition of *sense of belonging*—"students' perceived social support on campus, a feeling or sensation of connectedness, the experience of mattering or feeling cared about, accepted, respected, valued by, and important to the group (e.g., campus community) or others on campus (e.g., faculty, peers)" (p. 3).

Although at times this chapter aggregates student disability types to highlight the potential differences in sense of belonging among individuals who do or do not disclose a disability, disability is "not a monolith and shouldn't be treated as such" (Rajkumar, 2022, para. 14). Because many types of disability are included the reader must be aware that each type can have a different impact on the individual as well as on how the individual navigates different environments and situations (Linton, 1998; Wong, 2020).

Although this chapter uses person-first language, I wish to acknowledge the use of both person-first and identity-first language when discussing disability. The choice between person-first and identity-first language can be associated with different models of disability (Ferrigon & Tucker, 2019), and specific language choice is often associated with user preference or organization recommendations (Association on Higher Education and Disability, n.d.; Dunn & Andrews, 2015).

Finally, I must address the diversity of and within the idea of disability. Scholarship continues to highlight that one's disability should be viewed as a component of diversity (similar to one's race, sexual orientation, and age), but this also applies to the higher education environment (Aquino, 2016a; Kim & Aquino, 2017). Programs and initiatives must be embedded in a campus community that views disability as a key element of student identity instead of as a medical condition or limitation that negatively affects an individual's life. This can create a positive and inclusive understanding of disability in the campus environment (Aquino, 2020; Shea et al., 2019).

## Literature Review

A student's sense of belonging can be influenced by many factors, including their involvement in the higher education setting, relationships formed in their academic and social activities, and their perceptions of their overall environment (Vaccaro & Newman, 2016). Gillen-O'Neel (2021) identified the importance of students' ongoing engagement in developing a sense of belonging in the postsecondary setting. As noted by Ahn and Davis (2019), "students' sense of belonging is known to be strongly associated with academic achievement and a successful life at university" (p. 622). Engaging in academic and social experiences, as well as in surroundings (e.g., living space, geographical location) and personal interests, contributes to the development of students' sense of belonging. Bettencourt (2021) noted that students often create their sense of belonging instead of it being "facilitated by institutions" (p. 760).

### Academic Experiences in the Higher Education Environment

When enrolled in their postsecondary studies, students have ongoing interactions with faculty members. Research suggests that these interactions with faculty may have a significant influence on their overall participation and sense of belonging. In a study exploring the responses of nearly 9,000 college seniors using the National Survey of Student Engagement, Miller et al. (2018) found that diverse interactions with faculty members, including faculty–student research opportunities and ongoing interactions between students and faculty, positively contributed to students' perceived belongingness.

For positive relationships to form between students and faculty members, faculty members must be aware of students' diverse needs and identities (Booker, 2016). Students' active participation in their coursework also contributes to their perceived belongingness (Kane et al., 2014; Vogel & Human-Vogel, 2018). Students' interactions with faculty and satisfaction with their studies can affect their commitment to their academic activities. It is therefore important for members of the higher education environment to create inclusive learning opportunities and to support student needs (Aguirre et al., 2021; Burgstahler, 2020). Students' academic commitment can not only influence their sense of belonging but also influence their retention in the postsecondary setting (Ahn & Davis, 2020).

## Social Experiences in the Higher Education Environment

In addition to students' satisfaction and active participation in their coursework, research notes the importance of establishing social networks, feeling supported, and developing friendships to aid students' sense of belonging (Jiang & Altinyelken, 2022; Wegemer & Sarsour, 2021). A student's social adjustment to the postsecondary setting is key to their overall success (Bowman et al., 2019a), and early development of friendships and social networks can predict student retention (Bowman et al., 2019b). In a study exploring the role of social integration on motivation, Noyens et al. (2019) highlighted the importance of social integration of students' success in the first year of coursework, noting that participating in informal social campus activities and creating peer networks provided strong opportunities for developing friendships and social support. When students do not create the needed social connections in their campus community, they may feel homesick, which can negatively affect their overall success and subsequent retention (Sun & Hagedorn, 2016).

Different student groups may have varying opportunities to integrate in their higher education community (Rubin & Wright, 2015).

Shepler and Woosley (2012) noted that "the earliest college transition issues for students with disabilities are similar to the issues for other students" (p. 37). However, Aquino (2016b) found that disability type may negatively affect a student's social sense of belonging. Students with disabilities may have additional challenges in perceiving their social belongingness because of potential stigmatization and isolation related to their disability (Bialka et al., 2017; Dolmage, 2017).

### Sense of Belonging and Support for Students With Disabilities

Although critical to any student's overall success, a sense of belonging for minoritized and at-risk students is much more important because of their increased chance of attrition (O'Keeffe, 2013). For students with disabilities, if their campus environment is not inclusive and does not promote an accessible and welcoming setting to support needed accommodations and diverse learning needs, obstacles in developing and maintaining a sense of belonging will occur (Collins et al., 2018). When campus environments are aware of the additional needs that students with disabilities require, it can create a more supportive environment for this student group to thrive (Brown & Broido, 2019).

Research highlights the ongoing challenges of individuals with disabilities perceiving their role, inclusion, and overall sense of belonging (Mahar et al., 2012). When compared with students without disabilities, Aquino et al. (2017) found that sense of belonging was lower and perceived bias and discrimination were higher for students with disabilities enrolled in postsecondary coursework. Additionally, when exploring the sense of belonging of students with autism, Pesonen et al. (2020) found that "students related how subjective feelings and emotional responses form a substantial part of belonging as they described the performative nature of negotiating their autistic identities at university" (p. 13). Overall, the presence of disability, and the specific aspects related to specific disability types, may influence how students with disabilities participate and perceive their belongingness in higher education (Venville et al., 2016).

## Positionality

While I understand the need to both advocate for and empirically explore the success of students with disabilities in higher education, it is essential that I explain my positionality to better place the research presented in this chapter and the overall importance of investigating the sense of belonging for this student group. My academic preparation focused on psychology and higher education leadership and policy. Throughout my postsecondary education, I have been committed to examining student experience, focusing mainly on students with disabilities. Although research notes the various challenges students with disabilities have in their academic journey, I have always been committed to exploring this student group's experiences and opportunities for success. Also, in my many roles in the higher education environment, including graduate assistant, administrator, and currently faculty member, I have had the opportunity to support students with disabilities in various positions and through various lenses. In all academic and professional experiences, I have been committed to supporting students with disabilities through asset-based approaches and to participating in projects that highlight the importance of the success of students with disabilities in higher education. For that reason, contributing to an edited volume that explores how various members of the postsecondary community support students with disabilities is aligned with my research objectives and personal commitment to this student group's success.

## Methods

Data in this chapter are from the restricted-use *2012/2017 Beginning Postsecondary Students Longitudinal Study (BPS:12/17)* data set (Bryan et al., 2019), a nationally representative sample of first-time undergraduate students in the United States (National Center for Education Statistics, n.d.). The original sample included approximately 35,540 students. The BPS:12/17 data set consists of three data collection points: 2012, 2014, and 2017. This chapter focuses on the first wave of data collection—students who began postsecondary education in the 2011–2012 academic year. All analyses were conducted in Stata 16 and were weighted to be representative of the population (Bryan et al., 2019). Variables in this chapter are from the base year of the survey, that is, those variables that occurred in students' first year enrolled in higher education. Most of the variables focus on the individual, including their demographic characteristics, as well as aspects associated with their institution (e.g., institutional level and control) and institution-going behavior (e.g., full-time enrollment, Pell eligibility). Variables related to a student's overall sense of belonging, including student interactions with faculty, interaction with other students, and satisfaction with academic and social experiences at their institution, are included in the analyses.

This project includes students with a valid weight for an analytic sample of 18,990 students. Table 3.1 shows a characteristic comparison of students who did and did not disclose a disability during the base year of the survey (their first year enrolled). In addition to the percentages in Table 3.1, the average age for students with and without a self-disclosed disability was 22.54 and 20.92, respectively, and the average first-year grade-point average for students with and without a self-disclosed disability was 2.76 and 2.99, respectively. Of the sample, 11.18% identified with a disability during the base year of the survey. Table 3.2 includes the specific disability characteristics of the students identifying with a disability during the 2011–2012 academic year.

Table 3.1

*Characteristic Comparison of Students With and Without Self-Identified Disabilities, Percentage (N = 18,990)*

| Student category | Students with disabilities (*n* = 2,120) | Students without disabilities (*n* = 16,870) |
|---|---|---|
| Dependency status | 62.9 | 75.2 |
| Four-year institution | 57.1 | 60.1 |
| Public institution | 45.2 | 48.0 |
| Ethnicity: Hispanic or Latina/o/x | 18.6 | 21.0 |
| First-generation status | 69.5 | 65.0 |
| Full-time status | 62.9 | 72.1 |
| Gender: Male | 41.0 | 41.3 |
| Lives on campus | 20.0 | 28.4 |
| Low-income status | 49.5 | 37.1 |
| Military experience | 4.8 | 2.1 |
| Pell eligibility | 64.8 | 56.3 |
| Primary language spoken: English | 85.7 | 81.9 |
| Race | | |
|     American Indian or Alaska Native | 8.1 | 5.2 |
|     Asian | 4.8 | 6.5 |
|     Black | 20.0 | 18.9 |
|     Native Hawaiian or Other Pacific Islander | 2.4 | 2.6 |
|     White | 73.8 | 72.6 |
| U.S. born | 94.3 | 91.3 |

*Note.* Sample size is rounded to the nearest 10 per Institute of Education Science restrictions. Data are from *2012/2017 Beginning Postsecondary Students Longitudinal Study (BPS:12/17),* by M. Bryan, D. Cooney, and D. Richards, 2019, U.S. Department of Education, National Center for Education Statistics, Institute of Education Sciences (https://nces.ed.gov/pubs2020/2020522.pdf). In the public domain.

Table 3.2

*Identified Disability Characteristics of Students With Disabilities, 2011–2012 Academic Year, Percentage (N = 2,120)*

| Student category | Students identifying with disability (*N* = 2,120) |
| --- | --- |
| Attention deficit disorder (ADD) | 30.1 |
| Blindness or visual impairment | 4.5 |
| Brain injury | 1.6 |
| Depression | 14.5 |
| Developmental disability | 0.9 |
| Health impairment or problem | 2.6 |
| Hearing impairment | 5.4 |
| Mental, emotional, psychiatric condition | 13.4 |
| Orthopedic or mobility impairment | 4.7 |
| Other identified disability | 16.9 |
| Specific learning disability or dyslexia | 4.8 |
| Speech or language impairment | 0.5 |

*Note.* Data include participant responses to "main type of condition or impairment" (survey language) and do not account for multiple disabilities. The survey determined disability categories. Sample size is rounded to the nearest 10 per Institute of Education Sciences restrictions. Data are from *2012/2017 Beginning Postecondary Students Longitudinal Study (BPS:12/17),* by M. Bryan, D. Cooney, and D. Richards, 2019, U.S. Department of Education, National Center for Education Statistics, Institute of Education Sciences (https://nces.ed.gov/pubs2020/2020522.pdf). In the public domain.

To address the research questions, weighted descriptive statistics were conducted to examine trends in the sense of belonging among students with and without disabilities. Also, to address the second research question, significance tests were conducted to assess whether statistically significant differences existed in socioacademic postsecondary experiences based on disability self-identification. For Likert-based questions, the variables were recoded into dichotomous variables (positive and nonpositive). For example, "strongly agree" and "somewhat agree" were recoded as "1," and "strongly disagree," "somewhat disagree," and "neither disagree nor agree" were recoded as "0."

Several limitations must be addressed in this chapter. To begin, this sample included individuals who self-identified with a disability. It is important to note that nondisclosure of one's disability does not mean an individual does not have a disability. Also, for those who identified with a disability in the BPS:12/17 base year, it does not mean that they disclosed their disability to their postsecondary institution and/or received accommodations. This chapter also includes secondary data and therefore includes variables not created specifically for this research project. The use of secondary data may create a potential limitation because it may not fully capture student attitudes and experiences related to institutional belongingness. And although several variables were included to gauge a wide range of experiences related to students' sense of belonging during their first year of higher education, as this is self-reported at a single time point, it may not necessarily be a completely accurate description of all their experiences and attitudes during their first year of higher education.

## Results

This chapter disaggregates disability self-disclosure status by identifying those with a disability during the first academic year of their postsecondary journey. Findings related to student socioacademic experiences included perceived belongingness to their institution, positive interactions with faculty and other students, and their satisfaction with their studies and social experiences at their institution. These key elements support positive socialization and successful transition throughout students' higher education experience. In all areas, students with disabilities had lower percentages of positive belongingness than did students without self-identified disabilities. Additionally, when comparing student socioacademic experiences, several statistically significant differences were noted. Statistically significant differences existed in perceived positive socioacademic experiences in the five variables between students with and without disabilities.

When investigating students' sense of belonging ("felt like a part of the institution") by disability disclosure type, 70.6% of students with a disability had a positive sense of belonging to their institution, compared with 77.1% of students without disabilities. For positive interactions with faculty, 80.8% of students with disabilities noted positive interactions, compared with 86.8% of students without disabilities. For positive interactions with other students, 79.7% of students with disabilities noted positive interactions, compared with 85.5% of students without disabilities. With regard to student satisfaction with their studies, 74.1% of students with disabilities noted positive interactions, compared with 81.7% of students without disabilities. Last, with regard to satisfaction with their social experiences at the institution, 69.5% of students with disabilities noted positive interactions, compared with 75.5% of students without disabilities. See Tables 3.3 and 3.4 for additional information.

Table 3.3

*Perceived Positive Socioacademic Experiences by Disability Self-Disclosure Status, Percentage (N = 18,990)*

| Student category | Students with disabilities (*n* = 2,120) | Students without disabilities (*n* = 16,870) |
|---|---|---|
| Felt like a part of institution | 70.6 | 77.1 |
| Interactions with faculty | 80.8 | 86.8 |
| Interactions with other students | 79.7 | 85.5 |
| Satisfaction with studies | 74.1 | 81.7 |
| Satisfaction with social experience at institution | 69.5 | 75.5 |

*Note.* Sample size is rounded to the nearest 10 per Institute of Education Sciences restrictions. Analyses were weighted using wtb000 and bootstrap replicate weights. Data are from *2012/2017 Beginning Postecondary Students Longitudinal Study (BPS:12/17)*, by M. Bryan, D. Cooney, and D. Richards, 2019, U.S. Department of Education, National Center for Education Statistics, Institute of Education Sciences (https://nces.ed.gov/pubs2020/2020522.pdf). In the public domain.

Table 3.4

*Differences in Socioacademic Postsecondary Experiences by Disability Self-Disclosure Status (N = 18,990)*

| Student category | Students with disabilities (*N* = 2,120) | Students without disabilities (*N* = 16,870) |
|---|---|---|
| Felt like a part of institution | 0.7 (0.5)** | 0.8 (0.4)** |
| Interactions with faculty | 0.8 (0.4)** | 0.9 (0.3)** |
| Interactions with other students | 0.8 (0.4)* | 0.9 (0.4)* |
| Satisfaction with studies | 0.7 (0.4)** | 0.8 (0.4)** |
| Satisfaction with social experience at institution | 0.7 (0.5)* | 0.8 (0.4)* |

*Note.* Sample size is rounded to the nearest 10 per Institute of Education Sciences restrictions. Data are from *2012/2017 Beginning Postsecondary Students Longitudinal Study (BPS:12/17)*, by M. Bryan, D. Cooney, and D. Richards, 2019, U.S. Department of Education, National Center for Education Statistics, Institute of Education Sciences (https://nces.ed.gov/pubs2020/2020522.pdf). In the public domain.

*Indicates a significant difference between students who disclose and students who did not disclose disability status in survey base year (2012) with $p < .05$.

**Indicates a significant difference between students who disclosed and students who did not disclose disability status in survey base year (2012) with $p < .01$. Analyses were weighted using wtb000 and bootstrap replicate weights.

## Discussion and Implications

In addition to exploring socioacademic experiences contributing to a sense of belonging among students with self-disclosed disabilities, this chapter addresses stakeholders in the campus community who can support the success of those students. Stakeholders include faculty members, disability resource professionals, and other institutional administrators.

As previously noted, statistically significant differences existed in all socioacademic experiences between students with and without self-identified disabilities during their first year in postsecondary education. Students with disabilities had lower percentages of perceived belongingness, including in their interactions with faculty and other students, and their perceived satisfaction with their studies and social experiences at their institution. These findings support previous research that highlights obstacles to socialization, perceived belongingness, and successful transitioning into and throughout the higher education environment for students with disabilities (Brown & Broido, 2019; Collins et al., 2018; Venville et al., 2016). De Sisto et al. (2022) indicated the importance of students participating in activities that incorporate both academic and social elements for their overall sense of belonging in their campus environment.

Overall, socialization and perceived belongingness greatly contribute to student success in the various stages of their postsecondary journey. Student groups with decreased opportunities for success in various socioacademic postsecondary opportunities can be at a greater risk for disengagement and related obstacles in their overall higher education experience (Linley, 2017). It is then essential for the higher education environment to create and maintain a supportive and positive environment for student success, especially for students with disabilities (Sachs & Schreuer, 2011; Yssel et al., 2016). The findings stress the importance and overall need for members of the postsecondary community, including faculty, disability resource professionals, and other institutional leaders, to establish supportive and positive outreach to engage and advocate for students with disabilities.

## Supporting Successful Socialization and Transitioning of Students With Disabilities: Stakeholder Responsibilities

Students experience many transitions in the higher education environment, including the transitions of initial entry into their institution and transitions related to academic years, different institution types, and/or course modalities. It is important to recognize the sensitivity and potential disruption to student success during these transition periods (Naphan & Elliott, 2015; Turnbull et al., 2021). Thoughtful support for students with disabilities can be especially beneficial for their overall success. This support allows students not only to thrive in the transition points but also to further engage in the various academic and social experiences that contribute to positive belongingness in their campus community (Hadley, 2018; Schroeder et al., 2021; Spencer et al., 2018).

Several stakeholders in a student's life can support their success during transition periods. Members of a campus community can influence how a student perceives their experience (Museus et al., 2017; Stebleton et al., 2014; Strayhorn, 2019; Tovar, 2015). Leake and Stodden (2014) stressed that establishing an environment "where disability is not seen as a marker of membership in a 'special' group virtually nobody wants to be a part of but is, rather, accepted and appreciated as an element in a valued range of diversity" (p. 399) can aid in the success of students with disabilities. When postsecondary stakeholders create a supportive and engaging environment for students with disabilities, a disability may no longer be addressed as an impairment but instead as a characteristic of diversity (Aquino, 2016a).

**Faculty**

To further create an environment that fosters a sense of belonging for students with disabilities, faculty need to be aware of the various elements that may hinder this student group's ability to thrive in an inclusive environment. More specifically, concepts related to accessibility and transparency can give students with disabilities the opportunity to succeed in various socioacademic activities throughout their academic career.

One important area for the success of students with disabilities is coursework that is accessible to those with diverse needs (Burgstahler, 2020).

Research notes that there are more students who need potential accommodations and who may self-identify as having a disability than those who actually disclose their disability and receive disability support services from their institution (Aquino & Bittinger, 2019; Lovett et al., 2015). The proactive use of inclusive strategies that can support diverse learning needs, like the incorporation of universal design approaches, can be easily embedded within course design to increase student access to materials, modalities, and supporting resources.

Universal design, the "process of creating products that are accessible to people with a wide range of abilities, disabilities, and other characteristics" (Disabilities, Opportunities, Internetworking, and Technology Center, 2022, para. 1), allows for an individualized experience that accommodates various preferences and needs in an approachable and inclusive structure. When creating more accessible coursework spaces, one must realize the potential variation in self-identifying disability status and the need, or formal request, for accommodations to support the user's experience within a particular setting. When faculty members embed accessible content in their classroom, more individuals have an equal opportunity to learn in the same environment (Burgstahler & Cory, 2010). If learning spaces are not constructed with all students' abilities in mind, the specific learning experience may limit one or more individuals, thus creating a diminished, or inaccessible, learning experience. By integrating key planning features in course development, the instructor can better address the inclusiveness of the intended class session or assignment. By focusing on the positive and supportive interaction of an individual and their environment, a faculty member can accommodate diverse needs and can truly promote learning (McGuire et al., 2006).

Although faculty members can create a learning environment that promotes belongingness through accessible and inclusive course design techniques, they must also recognize and support accommodation policies and procedures for students who require and request additional support services. After the development of an accommodation plan between the student and the institution's disability resource office, it is the faculty member's responsibility to ensure that the accommodation is supported and implemented in the classroom. Failure to support a student's accommodation plan can create liability because this action would indicate noncompliance with associated federal law (Khouri et al., 2022; Neal-Boylan et al., 2021). Before a faculty member may receive an accommodation letter from a student with a self-disclosed disability, it is recommended to have language in the course syllabus about seeking accommodations and contact information for the institution's disability resource office, which can foster a setting that openly supports the sharing of important (and available) information for students who may need services (Cole & Cawthon, 2015; Terras et al., 2015). Including language related to the accommodation process and disability support services in a syllabus does not mean the faculty is or must be an expert on policies on student disability and accommodations; however, it can establish a more supportive learning environment for accommodation use (Mamboleo et al., 2020).

**Student Affairs Administrators**

Through their role in program and policy development and implementation, administrators can support the needs of students with disabilities who enter the higher education environment. Administrators can support initiatives that foster various socioacademic experiences for students with disabilities, which can positively contribute to students' perceived belongingness and overall success (Brinckerhoff et al., 2002; Hadley, 2011). The potential lack of understanding and vigilance in supporting this student group can have a lasting impact on their sense of belonging within specific institutional environments and on their road to degree completion (Barnard-Brak et al., 2010; Hong, 2015). As recommended by Newman et al. (2021), it is important that institutions provide the appropriate and ongoing guidance and professional development opportunities for administrators to "better understand how to respond to the needs of students with disabilities" (p. 353). Professional organizations, including NASPA–Student Affairs Administrators in Higher Education, as well as NASPA's learning communities like the Disability Knowledge Community, are fantastic places to engage with other institutions and administrators on how to best support this student group.

## Disability Resource Professionals

Administrators in an institution's disability resource office are integral to the advocacy and support of disability-related initiatives and policy development. Disability resource professionals are responsible for engaging with students to establish support services that aid in postsecondary access and ensure their institution's compliance with related disability policies and mandates (Banerjee et al., 2020; Kroeger & Kraus, 2017). As noted by Scott and Marchetti (2021), disability resource professionals are frequently employed as full-time institutional staff members, have significant experience in academic and student affairs, and have expertise in disability resource work. Although their work is essential for supporting the needs of students with disabilities, disability resource offices are often understaffed and operate with limited resources and institutional support (Aquino & Scott, 2022). Disability resource professionals are guided by the need to support student disability; however, it is essential that institutions continue to support the needs of the disability resource office to ensure that administrators dedicated to students with disabilities are available to best engage with this work. Disability resource professionals can seek support and guidance in engaging with and advocating for students with disabilities by seeking resources and professional development opportunities through organizations such as the Association on Higher Education and Disability.

## Conclusion

Connected to this book's framework, positive socioacademic experiences throughout the numerous transition points and with various stakeholders in the higher education setting can have a significant impact on the success of students with disabilities (Hope, 2021). Findings from research indicate statistically significant differences in perceived positive experiences in the campus community for students with and without self-disclosed disabilities. Students with disabilities had a lower percentage of perceived belongingness, including in their interactions with faculty and other students, and lower satisfaction with their studies and social experiences at their institutions. This chapter highlights the importance of student stakeholders, including faculty and administrators, in ensuring the support and success of this student group.

## References

Aguirre, A., Carballo, R., & Lopez-Gavira, R. (2021). Improving the academic experience of students with disabilities in higher education: Faculty members of social sciences and law speak out. *Innovation: The European Journal of Social Science Research, 34*(3), 305–320. https://doi.org/10.1080/13511610.2020.1828047

Ahn, M. Y., & Davis, H. H. (2019). Four domains of students' sense of belonging to university. *Studies in Higher Education, 45*(3), 622–634. https://doi.org/10.1080/03075079.2018.1564902

Ahn, M. Y., & Davis, H. H. (2020). Students' sense of belonging and their socio-economic status in higher education: A quantitative approach. *Teaching in Higher Education*, 1–14. http://dx.doi.org/10.1080/13562517.2020.1778664

Akin, D., & Huang, L. M. (2019). Perceptions of college students with disabilities. *Journal of Postsecondary Education and Disability, 32*(1), 21–33. https://www.ahead.org/professional-resources/publications/jped/archived-jped/jped-volume-32/jped-volume-32-issue-1/jped-volume-32-2019-issue-1-table-of-contents

Aquino, K. C. (2016a). A new theoretical approach to postsecondary student disability: Disability-diversity (dis)connect model. *Journal of Postsecondary Education and Disability, 29*(4), 317–330. https://www.ahead.org/professional-resources/publications/jped/archived-jped/jped-volume-29

Aquino, K. C. (2016b). *The disability-diversity disconnect: Redefining the role of student disability within the postsecondary environment* [Doctoral dissertation, Seton Hall University]. Seton Hall University eRepository. https://scholarship.shu.edu/dissertations/2218

Aquino, K. (2020). Exploring postsecondary administrators' inclusion of disability within their definition of student diversity. *International Journal of Disability, Development and Education, 69*(5), 1565–1572. https://doi.org/10.1080/1034912X.2020.1808951

Aquino, K. C., Alhaddab, T. A., & Kim, E. (2017). "Does disability matter?": Students' satisfaction with college experiences. In E. Kim & K. C. Aquino (Eds.), *Disability as diversity in higher education: Policies and practices to enhance student success* (pp. 47–60). Routledge.

Aquino, K. C., & Bittinger, J. D. (2019). The self-(un) identification of disability in higher education. *Journal of Postsecondary Education and Disability, 32*(1), 5–19. https://www.ahead.org/professional-resources/publications/jped/archived-jped/jped-volume-32

Aquino, K. C., & Scott, S. (2022). "They're coming in pretty defeated": Mental health during the COVID-19 pandemic. *Journal of Postsecondary Education and Disability, 35*(2), 175–182. https://www.ahead.org/professional-resources/publications/jped/archived-jped/jped-volume-35

Association on Higher Education and Disability. (n.d.). *AHEAD statement of language.* https://www.ahead.org/professional-resources/accommodations/statement-on-language

Banerjee, M., Lalor, A. R., Madaus, J. W., & Brinckerhoff, L. C. (2020). A survey of postsecondary disability service websites post ADA AA: Recommendations for practitioners. *Journal of Postsecondary Education and Disability, 33*(3), 301–310. https://www.ahead.org/professional-resources/publications/jped/archived-jped/jped-volume-33

Barnard-Brak, L., Lechtenberger, D., & Lan, W. Y. (2010). Accommodation strategies of college students with disabilities. *Qualitative Report, 15*(2), 411–429. https://doi.org/10.46743/2160-3715/2010.1158

Bettencourt, G. M. (2021). "I belong because it wasn't made for me": Understanding working-class students' sense of belonging on campus. *The Journal of Higher Education, 92*(5), 760–783. https://doi.org/10.1080/00221546.2021.1872288

Bialka, C. S., Morro, D., Brown, K., & Hannah, G. (2017). Breaking barriers and building bridges: Understanding how a student organization attends to the social integration of college students with disabilities. *Journal of Postsecondary Education and Disability, 30*(2), 157–172. https://www.ahead.org/professional-resources/publications/jped/archived-jped/jped-volume-30

Booker, K. (2016). Connection and commitment: How sense of belonging and classroom community influence degree persistence for African American undergraduate women. *International Journal of Teaching and Learning in Higher Education, 28*(2), 218–229. https://www.isetl.org/ijtlhe/ijtlhe-issue.php?v=28&n=2&y=2016

Bowman, N. A., Miller, A., Woosley, S., Maxwell, N. P., & Kolze, M. J. (2019a). Understanding the link between noncognitive attributes and college retention. *Research in Higher Education, 60*(2), 135–152. http://dx.doi.org/10.1007/s11162-018-9508-0

Bowman, N. A., Jarratt, L., Polgreen, L. A., Kruckeberg, T., & Segre, A. M. (2019b). Early identification of students' social networks: Predicting college retention and graduation via campus dining. *Journal of College Student Development, 60*(5), 617–622. https://doi.org/10.1353/csd.2019.0052

Brinckerhoff, L. C., McGuire, J. M., & Shaw, S. F. (2002). *Postsecondary education and transition for students with learning disabilities*. PRO-ED.

Brown, K. R., & Broido, E. M. (2019). Engaging students with disabilities. In S. J. Quaye, S. R. Harper, & S. L. Pendakur (Eds.), *Student engagement in higher education: Theoretical perspectives and practical approaches for diverse populations* (pp. 237–255). Routledge.

Bryan, M., Cooney, D., Elliott, B., & Richards, D. (2019). *2012/2017 beginning postecondary students longitudinal study (BPS:12/17)* [Data set]. U.S. Department of Education, National Center for Education Statistics, Institute of Education Sciences. https://nces.ed.gov/pubs2020/2020522.pdf

Burgstahler, S. (2020). *Creating inclusive learning opportunities in higher education: A universal design toolkit*. Harvard Education Press.

Burgstahler, S. E., & Cory, R. C. (Eds.). (2010). *Universal design in higher education: From principles to practice*. Harvard Education Press.

Cole, E. V., & Cawthon, S. W. (2015). Self-disclosure decisions of university students with learning disabilities. *Journal of Postsecondary Education and Disability, 28*(2), 163–179. https://www.ahead.org/professional-resources/publications/jped/archived-jped/jped-volume-28

Collins, A., Azmat, F., & Rentschler, R. (2018). "Bringing everyone on the same journey": Revisiting inclusion in higher education. *Studies in Higher Education, 44*(8), 1475–1487. https://doi.org/10.1080/03075079.2018.1450852

De Sisto, M., Huq, A., & Dickinson, G. (2022). Sense of belonging in second-year undergraduate students: The value of extracurricular activities. *Higher Education Research & Development, 41*(5), 1727–1742. https://doi.org/10.1080/07294360.2021.1902951

Deil-Amen, R. (2011). Socio-academic integrative moments: Rethinking academic and social integration among two-year college students in career-related programs. *The Journal of Higher Education, 82*(1), 54–91. https://doi.org/10.1080/00221546.2011.11779085

Disabilities, Opportunities, Internetworking, and Technology Center. (2022). *What is universal design?* https://www.washington.edu/doit/what-universal-design-0#

Dolmage, J. T. (2017). *Academic ableism: Disability and higher education*. University of Michigan Press.

Dunn, D. S., & Andrews, E. E. (2015). Person-first and identity-first language: Developing psychologists' cultural competence using disability language. *American Psychologist, 70*(3), 255. https://psycnet.apa.org/doi/10.1037/a0038636

Ferrigon, P., & Tucker, K. (2019). Person-first language vs. identity-first language: An examination of the gains and drawbacks of disability language in society. *Journal of Teaching Disability Studies, 1*. https://jtds.commons.gc.cuny.edu/person-first-language-vs-identity-first-language-an-examination-of-the-gains-and-drawbacks-of-disability-language-in-society

Fleming, A. R., Oertle, K. M., Plotner, A. J., & Hakun, J. G. (2017). Influence of social factors on student satisfaction among college students with disabilities. *Journal of College Student Development, 58*(2), 215–228. https://psycnet.apa.org/doi/10.1353/csd.2017.0016

Gillen-O'Neel, C. (2021). Sense of belonging and student engagement: A daily study of first- and continuing-generation college students. *Research in Higher Education, 62*(1), 45–71. http://dx.doi.org/10.1007/s11162-019-09570-y

Hadley, W. M. (2011). College students with disabilities: A student development perspective. In W. S. Harbour & J. W. Madaus (Eds.), *Disability services and campus dynamics* (New Directions for Higher Education, No. 154, 77–81). http://dx.doi.org/10.1002/he.436

Hadley, W. (2018). A sense of belonging: First-year students with learning disabilities' campus engagement. *Journal of College Orientation, Transition, and Retention, 25*(2). https://doi.org/10.24926/jcotr.v25i2.2116

Hoffman, M., Richmond, J., Morrow, J., & Salomone, K. (2002). Investigating "sense of belonging" in first-year college students. *Journal of College Student Retention: Research, Theory & Practice, 4*(3), 227–256. https://doi.org/10.2190/DRYC-CXQ9-JQ8V-HT4V

Hong, B. S. (2015). Qualitative analysis of the barriers college students with disabilities experience in higher education. *Journal of College Student Development, 56*(3), 209–226. https://doi.org/10.1353/csd.2015.0032

Hope, J. (2021). Adopt framework that promotes collaboration for providing disability services. *Disability Compliance for Higher Education, 26*(11), 6–7. https://doi.org/10.1002/dhe.31081

Jiang, L., & Altinyelken, H. K. (2022). Understanding social integration of Chinese students in the Netherlands: The role of friendships. *Journal of Intercultural Communication Research, 51*(2), 191–207. https://doi.org/10.1080/17475759.2021.1877178

Kane, S., Chalcraft, D., & Volpe, G. (2014). Notions of belonging: First year, first semester higher education students enrolled on business or economics degree programmes. *The International Journal of Management Education, 12*(2), 193–201. https://doi.org/10.1016/j.ijme.2014.04.001

Kim, E., & Aquino, K. C. (2017). *Disability as diversity in higher education*. Routledge.

Kimball, E. W., Wells, R. S., Ostiguy, B. J., Manly, C. A., & Lauterbach, A. A. (2016). Students with disabilities in higher education: A review of the literature and an agenda for future research. In M. B. Paulsen (Ed.), *Higher Education: Handbook of Theory and Research* (pp. 91–156). Springer. https://doi.org/10.1007/978-3-319-26829-3_3

Khouri, M., Lipka, O., & Shecter-Lerner, M. (2022). University faculty perceptions about accommodations for students with learning disabilities. *International Journal of Inclusive Education, 26*(4), 365–377. https://doi.org/10.1080/13603116.2019.1658812

Kroeger, S., & Kraus, A. (2017). Thinking and practicing differently: Changing the narrative around disability on college campuses. In E. Kim & K. Aquino (Eds.), *Disability as diversity in higher education: Policies and practices to enhance student success* (pp. 216–229). Routledge.

Kutscher, E. L., & Tuckwiller, E. D. (2019). Persistence in higher education for students with disabilities: A mixed systematic review. *Journal of Diversity in Higher Education, 12*(2), 136. https://doi.org/10.1037/dhe0000088

Leake, D. W., & Stodden, R. A. (2014). Higher education and disability: Past and future of underrepresented populations. *Journal of Postsecondary Education and Disability, 27*(4), 399–408. https://www.ahead.org/professional-resources/publications/jped/archived-jped/jped-volume-27

Linley, J. L. (2017). We are (not) all bulldogs: Minoritized peer socialization agents' meaning-making about collegiate contexts. *Journal of College Student Development, 58*(5), 643–656. https://doi.org/10.1353/csd.2017.0051

Linton, S. (1998). *Claiming disability: Knowledge and identity*. NYU Press.

Lovett, B. J., Nelson, J. M., & Lindstrom, W. (2015). Documenting hidden disabilities in higher education: Analysis of recent guidance from the Association on Higher Education and Disability (AHEAD). *Journal of Disability Policy Studies, 26*(1), 44–53. https://doi.org/10.1177/1044207314533383

Mahar, A. L., Cobigo, V., & Stuart, H. (2012). Conceptualizing belonging. *Disability and Rehabilitation, 35*(12), 1026–1032. https://doi.org/10.3109/09638288.2012.717584

McGuire, J. M., Scott, S. S., & Shaw, S. F. (2006). Universal design and its applications in educational environments. *Remedial and Special Education, 27*(3), 166–175. https://doi.org/10.1177/07419325060270030501

Miller, A. L., Williams, L. M., & Silberstein, S. M. (2018). Found my place: The importance of faculty relationships for seniors' sense of belonging. *Higher Education Research & Development, 38*(3), 594–608. https://doi.org/10.1080/07294360.2018.1551333

Mamboleo, G., Dong, S., & Fais, C. (2020). Factors associated with disability self-disclosure to their professors among college students with disabilities. *Career Development and Transition for Exceptional Individuals, 43*(2), 78–88. https://doi.org/10.1177/2165143419893360

Museus, S. D., Yi, V., & Saelua, N. (2017). The impact of culturally engaging campus environments on sense of belonging. *The Review of Higher Education, 40*(2), 187–215. https://doi.org/10.1353/rhe.2017.0001

Naphan, D. E., & Elliott, M. (2015). Role exit from the military: Student veterans' perceptions of transitioning from the US military to higher education. *The Qualitative Report, 20*(2), 36. https://doi.org/10.46743/2160-3715/2015.2094

National Center for Education Statistics. (n.d.). *Beginning postsecondary students*. https://nces.ed.gov/surveys/bps

Neal-Boylan, L., Miller, M., & Lussier-Duynstee, P. (2021). Failing to fail when disability is a factor. *Nurse Educator, 46*(4), 230–233. https://doi.org/10.1097/nne.0000000000000965

Newman, L. A., Madaus, J. W., Lalor, A. R., & Javitz, H. S. (2021). Effect of accessing supports on higher education persistence of students with disabilities. *Journal of Diversity in Higher Education, 14*(3), 353–363. https://doi.org/10.1037/dhe0000170

Noyens, D., Donche, V., Coertjens, L., Van Daal, T., & Van Petegem, P. (2019). The directional links between students' academic motivation and social integration during the first year of higher education. *European Journal of Psychology of Education, 34*(1), 67–86. https://doi.org/10.1007/s10212-017-0365-6

O'Keeffe, P. (2013). A sense of belonging: Improving student retention. *College Student Journal, 47*(4), 605–613.

Pedler, M. L., Willis, R., & Nieuwoudt, J. E. (2022). A sense of belonging at university: Student retention, motivation and enjoyment. *Journal of Further and Higher Education, 46*(3), 397–408. https://doi.org/10.1080/0309877X.2021.1955844

Pesonen, H. V., Nieminen, J. H., Vincent, J., Waltz, M., Lahdelma, M., Syurina, E. V., & Fabri, M. (2020). A socio-political approach on autistic students' sense of belonging in higher education. *Teaching in Higher Education*, 1–19. https://doi.org/10.1080/13562517.2020.1852205

Rainey, K., Dancy, M., Mickelson, R., Stearns, E., & Moller, S. (2018). Race and gender differences in how sense of belonging influences decisions to major in STEM. *International Journal of STEM education, 5*(1), 1–14. https://doi.org/10.1186/s40594-018-0115-6

Rajkumar, S. (2022, August 8). *How to talk about disability sensitively and avoid ableist tropes*. NPR. https://www.npr.org/2022/08/08/1115682836/how-to-talk-about-disability-sensitively-and-avoid-ableist-tropes

Rivas, J., Hale, K., & Burke, M. G. (2019). Seeking a sense of belonging: Social and cultural integration of international students with American college students. *Journal of International Students, 9*(2), 682–704. https://doi.org/10.32674/jis.v9i2.943

Rubin, M., & Wright, C. L. (2015). Time and money explain social class differences in students' social integration at university. *Studies in Higher Education, 42*(2), 315–330. https://doi.org/10.1080/03075079.2015.1045481

Sachs, D., & Schreuer, N. (2011). Inclusion of students with disabilities in higher education: Performance and participation in student's experiences. *Disability Studies Quarterly, 31*(2). https://dsq-sds.org/index.php/dsq/article/view/1593/1561

Schroeder, E. T., Carter, E. W., & Simplican, S. C. (2021). Inclusive first-year orientation programs involving undergraduates with intellectual disability: Exploring barriers and belonging. *Journal of Postsecondary Education and Disability, 34*(3), 239–252. https://www.ahead.org/professional-resources/publications/jped/archived-jped/jped-volume-34

Scott, S., & Marchetti, C. (2021). A review of the biennial AHEAD surveys: Trends and changes in the demographics and work of disability resource professionals in the U.S. *Journal of Postsecondary Education and Disability, 34*(2), 108–129. https://www.ahead.org/professional-resources/publications/jped/archived-jped/jped-volume-34

Shea, L. C., Hecker, L., & Lalor, A. R. (2019). *From disability to diversity: College success for students with learning disabilities, ADHD, and autism spectrum disorder.* National Resource Center for The First-Year Experience.

Shepler, D. K., & Woosley, S. A. (2012). Understanding the early integration experiences of college students with disabilities. *Journal of Postsecondary Education and Disability, 25*(1), 37–50. https://www.ahead.org/professional-resources/publications/jped/archived-jped/jped-volume-25

Spencer, B., Sherman, L., Nielsen, S., & Thormodson, K. (2018). The effectiveness of occupational therapy interventions for students with mental illness transitioning to higher education: A systematic review. *Occupational Therapy in Mental Health, 34*(2), 151–164. https://commons.und.edu/ot-grad/347

Stebleton, M. J., Soria, K. M., & Huesman, R. L., Jr. (2014). First-generation students' sense of belonging, mental health, and use of counseling services at public research universities. *Journal of College Counseling, 17*(1), 6–20. https://doi.org/10.1002/j.2161-1882.2014.00044.x

Strayhorn, T. L. (2012). *College students' sense of belonging: A key to educational success for all.* Routledge.

Strayhorn, T. L. (2019). *College students' sense of belonging: A key to educational success for all students* (2nd ed.). Routledge.

Sun, J., & Hagedorn, L. S. (2016). Homesickness at college: Its impact on academic performance and retention. *Journal of College Student Development, 57*(8), 943–957. https://doi.org/10.1353/csd.2016.0092

Terras, K., Leggio, J., & Phillips, A. (2015). Disability accommodations in online courses: The graduate student experience. *Journal of Postsecondary Education and Disability, 28*(3), 329–340. https://www.ahead.org/professional-resources/publications/jped/archived-jped/jped-volume-28

Tinto, V. (1997). Classrooms as communities: Exploring the educational character of student persistence. *The Journal of Higher Education, 68*(6), 599–623. https://doi.org/10.2307/2959965

Tinto, V. (2015). Through the eyes of students. *Journal of College Student Retention: Research, Theory & Practice, 19*(3), 254-269. https://doi.org/10.1177/1521025115621917

Tovar, E. (2015). The role of faculty, counselors, and support programs on Latino/a community college students' success and intent to persist. *Community College Review, 43*(1), 46–71. https://doi.org/10.1177/0091552114553788

Turnbull, D., Chugh, R., & Luck, J. (2021). Transitioning to e-learning during the COVID-19 pandemic: How have higher education institutions responded to the challenge? *Education and Information Technologies, 26*(5), 6401–6419. https://doi.org/10.1007/s10639-021-10633-w

Vaccaro, A., Daly-Cano, M., & Newman, B. M. (2015). A sense of belonging among college students with disabilities: An emergent theoretical model. *Journal of College Student Development, 56*(7), 670–686. https://doi.org/10.1353/csd.2015.0072

Vaccaro, A., & Newman, B. M. (2016). Development of a sense of belonging for privileged and minoritized students: An emergent model. *Journal of College Student Development, 57*(8), 925–942. https://doi.org/10.1353/csd.2016.0091

Venville, A., Mealings, M., Ennals, P., Oates, J., Fossey, E., Douglas, J., & Bigby, C. (2016). Supporting students with invisible disabilities: A scoping review of postsecondary education for students with mental illness or an acquired brain injury. *International Journal of Disability, Development and Education, 63*(6), 571–592. https://psycnet.apa.org/doi/10.1080/1034912X.2016.1153050

Verdinelli, S., & Kutner, D. (2016). Persistence factors among online graduate students with disabilities. *Journal of Diversity in Higher Education, 9*(4), 353–368. https://doi.org/10.1037/a0039791

Vogel, F. R., & Human-Vogel, S. (2018). The relevance of identity style and professional identity to academic commitment and academic achievement in a higher education setting. *Higher Education Research & Development, 37*(3), 620–634. https://doi.org/10.1080/07294360.2018.1436526

Wegemer, C. M., & Sarsour, N. (2021). College services, sense of belonging, and friendships: The enduring importance of the high school context. *Journal of Latinos and Education, 22*(3), 1046–1064. https://doi.org/10.1080/15348431.2021.1899926

Wong, A. (Ed.). (2020). *Disability visibility: First-person stories from the twenty-first century*. Vintage.

Yssel, N., Pak, N., & Beilke, J. (2016). A door must be opened: Perceptions of students with disabilities in higher education. *International Journal of Disability, Development and Education, 63*(3), 384–394. https://psycnet.apa.org/doi/10.1080/1034912X.2015.1123232

# PART III

# Individual Differences, Life Transitions, and Attitudes

CHAPTER 4

# My Search for Access and Accommodations in Higher Education

Valerie Piro

After I became a wheelchair user at age 16, my life became a bit more complicated. There were physical changes that came with a spinal cord injury, which included a loss of movement and feeling in my torso and legs, an inability to write by hand for long periods, and fluctuations in blood pressure and temperature regulation. There were hours of physical therapy to maintain the capabilities I had and to prevent things from getting worse, but I never lost sight that I was still a high school student applying to college.

Years later, I am now in the final years of a history PhD program. I have completed my BA, MPhil, EdM, and (incidental) MA degrees; navigated the disability accommodation process with four access and disability services (ADS) offices; and found access in three different universities. In that time, I have seen—from the perspective of a student and that of an ADS intern—how students with both visible and hidden disabilities have sought accommodations and gained access. What follows are accounts of how I sought accommodations and achieved access in higher education with each degree program; these accounts are expressed through the lenses of individual differences and attitudes. As I eventually learned as an intern and coach in the ADS office at my graduate school, students with disabilities have a wide range of interactions with disability services and academic staff. Although faculty and staff can assist students with disabilities in accessing content and facilitating inclusion, granting accommodations is the legal responsibility of the ADS office.

## An Introduction to Disability Services in Colleges

I returned as a wheelchair user to my New York City high school for my senior year. My accommodations included what I called a bare-bones course load (just the requirements for graduation), a space for me to take SAT II exams (and any other exams if I needed extra time), and an exemption from gym class (I used adaptive exercise equipment at home). There had not been any discussions with my guidance or college counselors about how to choose an appropriate college campus. No one suggested that I had to do anything differently from my nondisabled peers when applying to college.

And so I began my college search as if each school were fully wheelchair accessible. After one visit to a particularly old campus, I learned that this was an unwise strategy and changed tactics to base my search on which college websites included information on their ADS office or which had photos of students in wheelchairs (Piro, 2017). Most nondisabled students chose schools based on academics, cost, and location, but I had the extra factor of physical accessibility to consider: Could I live on campus and easily wheel to the library? Would a residence hall room be large enough to fit my physical therapy equipment? Were shuttles accessible, and how frequently did they run?

After I had been accepted to seven schools, it was time to visit their campuses. My mother accompanied me to one school in the

Midwest, where I had the opportunity to speak with staff in the ADS office and see a wheelchair-accessible residence hall. To my dismay, although the disability services administrator seemed helpful and attentive, the university did not offer what I needed: The room was too small for my physical therapy equipment, and the residence hall itself was located at the bottom of a hill. The library was at the top of the hill, along with much of the campus. My mother asked the disability services administrator questions, many of which I had not even considered. In general, my parents did much of my advocating while I adjusted to life with paralysis. For those individuals who acquire a disability suddenly, the transition to a new normal can take some time, and parental support can be very helpful.

The college I eventually attended did just about everything it could have to convince me and my parents that this was the best option for me, even though the campus was one of the oldest in the country and still had some physical accessibility issues (Nam & Wang, 2021; Yao et al., 2019). After I was accepted, I contacted the ADS office, which set up meetings for me and my parents that included members of campus security and the head of operations (who maintain the freshman residence halls, freshman dining hall, and academic buildings). Disability services also informed me about transportation services and the types of classroom accommodations they had provided for students with my disability in the past. For someone unsure about what accommodations could be requested, or what was typically granted, this outreach was immensely helpful.

While visiting, my parents and I were also shown the very room where I would live during freshman year. It was a double, with large windows, that would easily fit my physical therapy equipment. The main research library and dining hall were close by, and I never had to wheel farther than 10 minutes to get to class. I felt like I was meant to be part of the campus—and that the disability accommodations granted had been tailored for my individual differences.

**Main Takeaways**

- Students with disabilities often must do their own research to determine which colleges might be the best fit—while also considering other basic factors (e.g., financial aid, location).
- High school guidance and college counselors may not be familiar with what disability services offer at potential colleges and should request materials from colleges' disability services to distribute to prospective students.
- College representatives who visit high schools may not be familiar with what disability services offer at their own colleges and should be given access-related materials to distribute to prospective students.
- Parents may need to take a larger role in advocating for their students at the beginning of the college application process. This likely will be the first time students are in a position to self-advocate, and they might not know what to ask for.
- Before meeting with admitted students (and their parents), ADS offices should coordinate with other offices (e.g., security, housing, dining, paratransit, facilities) and let students know the full range of accommodations that have been granted to students with similar disabilities in the past.

## Undergraduate Years

From my sophomore year onward, my parents took on less of a role. They trusted me to interact with disability services to advocate for what I needed. My accommodation needs had not changed much from the previous year, except concerning transportation. I was now in upperclassman housing and needed the university's paratransit van service to get around. Disability services gave me the email address of the dispatcher, who coordinated my transportation to and from class each semester.

I received help from many quarters. The house master, or resident assistant (RA), of my upperclassman residence hall saw to it that I had accessible housing and alerted the dining hall staff that I might need assistance with reaching things at mealtimes. The RA also coordinated with facilities personnel to ensure the ramps were cleared and salted when it snowed.

After I chose my major, I also received help from the history department faculty and staff, since some offices were inaccessible to me in the building. I felt comfortable asking the history department staff what could be done, and they gave my advisor a wheelchair-accessible office.

When I first started as an undergraduate, I was under the impression that any time I needed an accommodation or assistance, I should first contact disability services. After a few years, I realized that I could easily have many of my needs met by asking academic staff or the RA, and I became more at ease with asking staff and fellow students to help me with immediate or everyday needs, such as reaching for and using food trays in the dining hall. I knew that I could always contact disability services if the issue was more complicated and required an Americans with Disabilities Act accommodation.

**Main Takeaways**

- After the first year of college, parental advocacy makes way for greater student self-advocacy.
- ADS connects students with other departments and offices (e.g., transportation) and acts as an advocate if the student encounters issues.

## Graduate School 1: Disability Accommodations and Access in the United Kingdom

Upon completing my BA, I began an MPhil program in medieval history at a university in England. Seeking accommodations there was an entirely different experience from when I was a college student in the United States.

Although this university was vastly different from a U.S. university, I had not given much thought to how the university's disability services fit into this overall structure; I initially believed that disability services could not have been too different from its U.S. counterpart. But then I ran into a major problem: I had been accepted to my department, but my soon-to-be college's only accessible residence hall for graduate students was going to be under renovation for the sole year of my MPhil program. The college informed me that because I would not have a place to live while the accessible housing was being renovated, I would have to resubmit an application the following year (i.e., reapply to the program that already had accepted me).

I tried to work with a disability resource center (DRC) administrator to help me find another college where I could live, but I had to work with each individual college. I investigated which colleges had wheelchair-accessible housing but was told that they were not accepting students at that time. Only one college had space for me, because my DRC contact specifically knew someone who worked at that particular college.

Once I began my program at this university, I relied on the DRC for such accommodations as extra funding to pay for taxi rides to and from my department as well as a laundry service. For access needs I contacted my college's administrator and the history department staff. At my undergraduate institution, I was given accommodations and access that I had not even thought to ask for, but at my graduate program in England, I found that active advocacy was required to achieve access to the full student experience.

**Main Takeaways**

- Universities abroad may have an overall different setup than that of U.S. universities; a central ADS office may provide only limited accommodations.
- Students who study abroad must be prepared to advocate with providers who are not specifically in disability services, such as department or college staff.

## Graduate School 2: Both Student and Disability Services Intern

Following my MPhil in history, I enrolled in a higher education (EdM) program, returning to my undergraduate university in its Graduate School of Education. I focused on access for students with disabilities in higher education, specifically as they transitioned from high school to college. By this point, I knew which accommodations I needed both in the classroom and in graduate housing. I was already familiar with my university's paratransit service, and the disability services office served as a liaison between me and the housing office. The ADS administrator reviewed my documentation, interviewed me, and began an interactive accommodations process that was uniquely different from that of my undergraduate experience.

There was one setback: Although I was provided letters to give to faculty at the beginning of each semester to alert them to my accommodation needs, I did not distribute those letters. Giving letters with approved accommodations to faculty is standard practice for students with disabilities; however, I had never previously been given these letters to distribute before. When I was an undergraduate, disability services ensured that my classrooms were held in accessible locations, which was the only academic accommodation I had requested; perhaps this accommodation would not have required direct communication with faculty. My accommodation needs had shifted since then. Faced with this method of conveying a need for accommodations, I felt unexpectedly awkward and opted to speak to each professor if a situation emerged in which I would require an accommodation. This typically involved requesting a longer midclass break so that I had enough time to catheterize myself. I felt comfortable enough self-advocating that the letters seemed unnecessary, although looking back, I realize they were how I legally was meant to tell my instructors that I required accommodations. It was not good practice to circumvent the letter distribution process, however awkward it may have felt at the time.

Despite my hesitance to hand these letters to faculty, the transition to this graduate program was a seamless process, in part because disability services worked so effectively with other departments on campus. I regularly spoke with the head of disability services, who checked in on how I was progressing during each semester. I also became one of her interns for the duration of my one-year program; this role allowed me another perspective on disability accommodations.

Previously, I had understood disability services only from the student's perspective—specifically, the perspective of a student with a mobility impairment. However, working in the graduate school's ADS office as an intern broadened my understanding of disability and what kinds of accommodations disability services could provide for a range of individual differences among students with disabilities. The director of disability services mentored me so that I could provide alternative reading formats for students, transcribe audio files into text, and serve as a writing coach.

I learned that although students with mobility impairments constitute about 3% of students with disabilities on any given college campus, improvements in physical accessibility (i.e., construction of ramps and building renovations) usually receive the most publicity when institutions of higher education make a point of discussing their commitment to students with disabilities (Biemiller, 2016). Meanwhile, the majority of student disabilities are hidden, and these students may pass as nondisabled. Therefore, those with visible disabilities might be thought of as the only students on campus with disabilities.

In fact, that had been my own perception. When I was in my higher education program, I assumed that I was one of only a handful of students with disabilities because I did not see anyone who looked like me. I was far too engrossed in my academic ambitions and maintaining a sustainable health management routine to reflect on the presence of students with sensory, neurological, and medical conditions that required modifications and accommodations in housing and classes just as I did. I came to realize that many students had nonvisible disabilities. An op-ed in *The Chronicle of Higher Education* questioned whether students who sought extra time on exams were cheating (Trachtenberg, 2016). The author, a professor, had no access to students' medical histories. I look back on my hesitance to give professors accommodation letters. I now realize that a professor would be likely to grant me an academic accommodation that related directly to my wheelchair despite never having received a letter. A visible disability can create its own implicit bias and attitudes about abilities.

One of my roles as an intern in the ADS office was to schedule the delivery of accommodations. I asked my ADS director about the range of disabilities in the school. She was very careful to speak broadly and never violated the private documentation of any student. Because I was unfamiliar with nearly every disability that was not my own, I listened carefully to students I spoke with to understand their needs, and I was considerate of their individual differences. Significantly, my other role, as a writing coach, broadened my understanding of students' individual needs. Some students required more structure, or someone to hold them accountable to their scheduled deadlines, or a person to provide motivation. In one case, a student had their final paper all mapped out in their head but seemed uneasy about starting. I asked them to dictate how they would write the paper, and as they spoke, I typed, and the paper started to come together. I was an intern, but the inclusive culture in this ADS office underscored that these students belonged here—and that they were more than capable of doing the work. I learned that while some strategies might work for some students, not every strategy is ideal for every student.

**Main Takeaways**

- Although I was confident in my ability to self-advocate, handing a letter with stated disability accommodations to a professor at the beginning of the semester felt uncomfortable. Having a visible disability gave me an implicit advantage when I asked a professor outright for an accommodation related to my mobility impairment.
- It is important for students to share accommodation letters from the ADS office with their professors.
- While interning at this program's ADS office, I learned more about individual differences among students and how best to tailor an accommodation to help level the playing field for any particular student.

## Choosing a PhD Program

Doctoral programs are specialized, and often students apply to certain programs to work with specific faculty. As a result, I applied to the programs that most appealed to me as an aspiring academic and then worried about accessibility only after I had been admitted. Before visiting campuses, however, I told each potential advisor that I could not attend the school unless I could first meet with disability services and secure housing.

The decision came down to two schools. My potential advisor at the first school emailed me to let me know that I had been accepted and asked if I wanted to meet with anyone specifically during admitted students' weekend; they also set up meetings between me and disability services, met with me when I visited campus, and coordinated with housing to show me a wheelchair-accessible graduate apartment. While I was able to meet with disability services at the second school and attended a presentation from the housing department with all admitted students, I could not view a wheelchair-accessible graduate apartment because it was occupied at the time. Disability services at both universities assured me that if I were to attend, my accommodation needs would be met. This assurance allowed me to judge between the two programs based on their academics and funding, which was how I knew the nondisabled admitted students were making their decisions.

Campus visits revealed both schools were wheelchair friendly. One school had outdoor elevators, which were broken or being repaired three out of the four times I needed to use them. The other school's history department building lacked an elevator, and the department's director of graduate studies informed me that not only would I be the department's first "wheeled graduate student," but I would also need to let the department know of my acceptance as soon as possible so they could commence work on the stairlift that would have to be installed for my use. Perhaps such accessibility issues should have been a deterrent, but these places were two of my dream programs. If it meant setting aside extra time for a slow stairlift or waiting for a minor elevator repair, then I would make it work. The important thing was that the faculty at both institutions wanted me to succeed.

## Main Takeaways

- Graduate schools have more specialized programs, which means that students will apply based on the program and faculty.

- Faculty (i.e., potential advisors) are often the first point of contact for admitted students and can arrange meetings between admitted students and disability services when students visit.
- The attitudes of disability services administrators can be the deciding factor for students with disabilities selecting among graduate programs.

## Graduate School 3: Navigating a PhD Program

My university's history department played a major role in providing access and inclusion. The department chair reached out to me when it was time for departmental language exams. Generally, students pick up the language exams from the department and have one hour to take each test. Most students go to their carrels in the nearby library to take the exams, but this effort would have been an issue for me because of how slowly the history department stairlift moved. The department chair asked if I would like to reserve a small room in the department in which I could take the exam so that I would not lose time. I had not even considered that possibility and was grateful for the offer.

Unfortunately, I had not been allowed to view a wheelchair-accessible graduate apartment prior to matriculating. The apartment was technically wheelchair accessible (it was renovated right before I moved in); however, the shower just barely fit my shower wheelchair, and I did not feel safe using the oven, which was located directly below the stove range. This is a typical oven configuration for nondisabled individuals, but I have found that a wall oven is much safer for my own use. When I discussed the oven issue with disability services, I opted for a countertop oven.

I had asked disability services whether the kitchen could be renovated in the style of wheelchair-accessible kitchens I had used in my housing at my previous graduate schools. Disability services spoke with the housing office, which stated that the town would have to approve the renovation. The modifications were never done.

There were additional accessibility problems. Graduate housing was located at the bottom of a hill, so I relied on a shuttle to get to campus. Disability services put me in touch with the dispatcher at transportation services. I would call the dispatcher to let the incoming shuttle driver know that I planned to get on the shuttle, and they would drive down to my building.

Getting back to my apartment was more difficult. In the evening, when I typically left campus, shuttles came less frequently, and if I missed the shuttle, I would have to wait for the next one. This became an issue in the late fall and winter, when I would sit in freezing or near-freezing weather for more than 20 minutes. My spinal cord injury prevents me from regulating my body temperature, which makes me prone to hypothermia. It was then that I realized how much I depended on the frequent shuttles, paratransit, and taxi cabs at my previous universities. I would return to my apartment and spend an hour drinking hot tea while bundled in hoodies and a blanket as I warmed up, all the while unable to focus on my coursework.

Although the ADS office sought to deliver meaningful accommodations, and academic staff sought to provide me access, the housing office could not furnish what I needed. So, two years into the program, I moved off campus even though I knew this decision would limit my teaching options, as remote or online teaching did not yet exist. Within a few months, I had my ideal apartment about an hour and a half away from campus. Although I wished I could participate more fully in my PhD program, I did not regret the move.

**Main Takeaways**

- Disability services can have a major impact on the experience of students with disabilities, but there are limits to

- what it can provide because it works with other offices in the institution.
- Sometimes students with disabilities must accept an accommodation that can restrict them from the full experiences that other students enjoy.

## Conclusion

When I began applying to colleges, I knew next to nothing about disability accommodations and went about my college search as if each institution were fully wheelchair accessible. Now, 10 years and four institutions of higher learning later, I have learned that each university has its own administrative culture when it comes to disability accommodations. Not only does each student have individual differences regarding their disability, but stakeholders in the institution have their own distinct attitudes when providing accommodations or access. Ultimately, each student's experience is different, and I can speak only to my own time as a student and disability services intern.

My undergraduate college experience showed me that parents can play an important role in advocating for their children, who are often registering for disability services for the first time. It may be helpful for parents to sit in on initial meetings with disability services administrators, especially after students have been given offers of admission. After these introductory meetings, parents should trust their children to self-advocate after they fully transition to college. Once in college, students should be comfortable with discussing accommodations not only with disability services administrators but also with faculty and staff.

In my graduate school experience, I came across three different administrative cultures and attitudes. In the United Kingdom, I learned that disability services might be a centralized office, but the overall structure of a British university might grant authority to an individual college that cannot be overruled by disability services. Much of a student's interactions will take place within their own college or department, while disability services may serve more as a liaison or as a bursar. After returning to the United States, I was able to focus on my coursework and internship at a graduate school of education because the ADS office could collaborate with other departments to provide the accommodations to which I was entitled.

As an intern in an ADS office, I learned about individual differences among students with hidden disabilities when I served as a writing coach and supplied alternative course materials. Academic coaching helps to level the playing field when students who are fully capable of doing the work are given the tools to do so. Most importantly, the disability services administrator is the one who determines the accommodations to which a student is legally entitled. It is not the place of faculty to judge whether a student is truly in need of an accommodation; rather, it is the ADS office's role to grant accommodations.

By the time I reached my doctoral program, I became more confident in asking department faculty and staff for access. Coordination and collaboration between the ADS office and other administrative functions, such as housing and facilities, are essential for ensuring that a student is fully included in any university setting.

## References

Biemiller, L. (2016, September 18). College facilities evolve from accommodation to inclusivity. *The Chronicle of Higher Education.* https://www.chronicle.com/article/college-facilities-evolve-from-accommodation-to-inclusivity

Nam, J. S., & Wang, A. Z. (2021, October 21). "It wasn't enough": Disabled students join forces for accessibility. *The Harvard Crimson.* https://www.thecrimson.com/article/2021/10/21/accessibility-on-campus

Piro, V. (2017, April 6). Applying to college as a wheelchair user. *Inside Higher Ed.* https://www.insidehighered.com/views/2017/04/06/challenges-wheelchair-users-face-when-visiting-colleges-essay

Trachtenberg, A. (2016, September 18). Extra time on an exam: Suitable accommodation or legal cheating? *The Chronicle of Higher Education.* https://www.chronicle.com/article/extra-time-on-an-exam-suitable-accommodation-or-legal-cheating

Yao, W. Y., Isselbacher, J. E., & Su, A. Y. (2019, May 28). Barriers to entry. *The Harvard Crimson.* https://www.thecrimson.com/article/2019/5/28/barriers-to-entry

# CHAPTER 5

# Disability Rights Are Civil Rights

Mary Lee Vance

By now, almost every industry recognizes how important it is for different genders and races to be represented in the workplace, but the same level of recognition has not yet been achieved for the need to have a diversity of disabled employees—and institutions of higher education are even further from having this kind of attention to disabled representation in the senior-level administrative ranks.

I have worked at campuses that range from small to large: Michigan State University; Iowa State University; George Mason University; University of Wisconsin–Superior; University of Montana; Purdue University–Calumet; University of California, Berkeley; Orange Coast College; and now California State University, Sacramento.

I represent an intersection of identities. I was born in South Korea to a single woman, who was possibly a waitress in a tea shop in Seoul. During my first years of life, I was infected by the polio virus, which left my legs paralyzed. Years later, doctors would say I am a walking miracle because I have virtually no muscles in my legs and rely on my abdominal muscles to propel my legs forward.

At some stage, I was taken to an orphanage; the staff there placed me in a hospital for medical attention. The nurses at the hospital took excellent care of me but were afraid that if I were sent away from Korea, I would be exhibited like a freak and mistreated. Despite their concerns, the orphanage proceeded to process my adoption.

I was adopted by a U.S. couple with Swiss, German, and English ancestry and raised in a community where I and my adopted sister were the only non-Whites. In elementary school, I started to lose my vision and had to wear very thick glasses to see what was on the chalkboard.

My kindergarten through undergraduate college years were not academically stellar. I struggled with math—whatever stereotypical gene that "makes Asians brilliant in the sciences" totally missed me. After completing my graduate degree, I learned from a friend about a job opportunity at Michigan State University. They were looking for an Asian American liaison and computer specialist. Reading the post, I felt totally unqualified. What did I know about being Asian American? And of course, I was a near failure with computers. By some miracle I did get the position and, in the process, met the director of disability services, who took me under her wing.

Until I moved to California, I had never met another Korean adoptee with a disability employed in higher education. To date, I have yet to meet a person of color who also has a disability employed in higher education at a senior-level administrative rank. Known senior administrators with visible disabilities were invariably in their positions before becoming disabled. There have been no known openly disabled (although there may have been ones with nonvisible disabilities) senior-level administrators except for those at Gallaudet. It is one thing to become disabled after having achieved a certain rank or career level; it is another to have a visible disability and seek those higher-level positions.

## The Fight for Disability Rights as Civil Rights

It is well known that as we age, we lose some if not all of our bodily functions. In other words, we will, if we are fortunate to live long enough, eventually experience at least one functional limitation. While some of us may have experienced functional limitations since birth, others will face reduced functions later in life as the result of accidents, health-related complications, or simple aging. It is not something we can avoid, and regardless of age, economic class, race, sexual orientation, religion, or any other identification, disability and functional limitation status is equal opportunity.

It was not until 1973, when Section 504 of the Rehabilitation Act was passed into law, that discrimination based on disability was prohibited. As of 1977 students were guaranteed equal educational access through Section 504, and in 1990 the Americans with Disabilities Act (ADA) provided disability rights. The only schools exempt from complying with Section 504 or the ADA were private ones that did not accept any federal aid.

Recognizing that disability rights are, in fact, civil rights, it follows that racism and ableism are similar. Racism, the belief that different races possess distinct characteristics, leads to the idea that one race is superior to another, which breeds prejudice, discrimination, and even laws to marginalize specific groups. With ableism, there is a similar belief that individuals with physical, intellectual, and/or psychological disabilities are less valuable than people without disabilities; this leads to the same form of discrimination—in this case, favoring the nondisabled.

The world of education is full of ableism. Ableist educators, committed to educating students, fail to understand that their curricula automatically discriminate and exclude students who have disabilities. Although disabled activists were able to get regulations for Section 504 and the ADA passed into law, the world of education is still filled with barriers that prevent students who learn and perform differently, because of disability, from being able to achieve their potential.

Both Section 504 and the ADA are very clear about the requirement to provide equal access. Less clear is how to do it. As a result, very little consistency exists for how accommodations are approved and afforded in elementary schools, through middle schools, through high schools, and ultimately in colleges and universities. The good news is that each institution can establish processes and accommodations according to their available resources; however, this can also be bad news because, for parents and students, the inconsistencies are confusing. Often, the differences can be traced back to how accommodations and resources are funded or are considered essential. For example, if a college has a doctoral program in clinical psychology, the possibility of doctoral candidates administering psychological assessments and providing specialized counseling and programs would be quite possible, whereas a smaller college without such a program or doctoral-level students would not be able to provide such services. Some colleges and universities have sophisticated and privately funded technology centers, able to offer innovative technology and resources that institutions without similar funding sources cannot. Not all colleges and universities have learning specialists on staff; for those that do, the fee process will differ from campus to campus, depending on how the service is coordinated and funded.

## Transition to College

As a disabled student who graduated from college before Section 504 regulations, I did not have the benefit of the law on my side when it came to my education. My parents did not push the school for me to have any special favors, although I did spend quite a bit of time in "detention," a place where misbehaving students were placed for a time-out—in my case, it was a place for me to wait while my classmates were in a gym class. Although it was always a given that I would go to college, it was not necessarily a given that I would graduate.

Going to college was a wonderful opportunity to learn independence. My parents sheltered and protected me too much when I was young, I thought. When I was in elementary school they feared that I would get hurt. Without my parents at college, I had to take responsibility for getting to classes on my own and for managing my disability. Without fully understanding the concept of self-advocacy, I had to develop a sense of responsibility for obtaining any needed accommodations early on.

Transitioning from high school to college is a major change for all students and parents, regardless of whether a disability is part of the equation. FERPA (Family Educational Rights and Privacy Act) rights transfer from the parent to the child upon the child's graduation from high school. As difficult as it may seem for parents to comprehend, their child is now considered an adult and has the right (and responsibility) to determine how their educational records are shared. Parents who have had to fight a school system to get what they believed their child needed to be successful will have a rude awakening when they accompany their child (now considered an adult) to a college's disability services intake. Unless they are prepared to recognize that the child must assume responsibilities they previously held, the parents may have a hard time stepping back so their child can start assuming responsibility for their disability management.

At the college level, because FERPA rights have transferred to the student, parents no longer can call on behalf of their child and expect a college official to respond to their inquiries about how their child is doing. The disability services office (DSO) may not even acknowledge that the student is registered with them, much less agree to be a messenger or mediator between student and parents.

To add to the confusion, even though a college may request medical documentation to verify a student's disability, the DSO is merely the recipient of medical information for the purpose of determining appropriate academic-related disability accommodations. Therefore, the DSO is not governed by HIPAA (Health Insurance Portability and Accountability Act), with its strict confidentiality requirements for health information. DSO staff do not treat, deliver therapy, or make any health-related diagnoses. This means that, under FERPA, college officials may share information about the student with other campus departments as needed, since all college employees, unless working in counseling or a unit under HIPAA, are mandated reporters. For example, although a diagnosis may be kept confidential by the DSO, a student's accommodation status may be shared with police or other offices if the student is in danger of harming themself or others.

And then there is Free and Appropriate Public Education (FAPE), which guarantees students a free and appropriate education through high school. FAPE ensures that all students are afforded every opportunity possible to either graduate with a diploma or, at the very least, leave with a certificate of attendance. These entitlements can then lead to unrealistic expectations among students and parents of what a postsecondary school must provide for the student to succeed in college. The ADA is not an *entitlement* law; it is an *antidiscrimination* law that does not guarantee student success.

Some parents, unfortunately, do not do their students any favors by advocating that they be excused from the rigors of academia. Accommodations that parents may have lobbied for—such as extreme curriculum changes, alternative assignments and assignment deadline extensions, unlimited time and open-book exams, tutoring, coaching, course waivers, no penalty for absences, and even exam questions given a week in advance of exams with the option to bring in a filled-out answer book—may have gotten a student through high school, but these accommodations may not prepare them for college.

Under the Individuals with Disabilities Education Act (IDEA) and Section 504 of the Rehabilitation Act, students legally entitled to disability accommodations during kindergarten through 12th grade receive accommodations that are not necessarily reasonable and appropriate in higher education under the ADA. Although Section 504 provides much of the guidance on Individualized Education Programs (IEPs), IEP discussions for the most part are held without the student present—and often with no medical documentation required. As a result, many students enter college without having had any medical diagnosis conducted, yet with a history of accommodations—and not even understanding they have disabilities.

At the college level, under ADA requirements, students engage in an interactive process with the campus DSO. Unless the disability and accommodation are clearly obvious—such as a scooter or chair user needing an accessible table and chair in classrooms, a cane user needing braille or specific alternative media, or someone using sign language and requiring an interpreter—the student must be present in a meeting in which medical documentation is reviewed along with accommodation requests. This meeting clarifies, first, whether the student even meets the disability definition and, second, whether the accommodation request has a direct nexus to the identified disability. Most students participate on their own in these meetings, but some elect to bring in their parents or guardians. In some cases, the parents or guardians may be the ones dragging their student to the intake meeting to make sure the student is provided the accommodations they believe are needed. However, under the ADA, a college cannot force a student to register with a DSO, much less require the student to use any approved accommodations.

Parents accustomed to speaking on behalf of their student are often shocked at being informed they need to let the student speak at a college intake, as the student is now considered an adult, due to FERPA, and must demonstrate the ability to be considered "otherwise qualified" to be in college, under the ADA. If a student cannot articulate their educational barriers or cannot succeed academically, with or without accommodations, then the question of whether the student is otherwise qualified to be in college may be raised.

## The Accommodation Process

My first professional job at Michigan State University was in TRIO, a federally funded opportunity program for first-generation (neither parent graduated from college), low-income, and underrepresented students. Although not officially recognized as first generation, all disabled college students, I firmly believe, are also "first generation" unless they are living in a home with a college-educated parent who shares their disability.

I didn't have my parents communicating with my college about any of my needs. I took the initiative and called facilities early in the morning after a heavy snowfall to request they clear sidewalks from my residence hall to the building where my first class was being held because I couldn't pick up my feet over the snow. I requested permission to record lectures so I could listen to them afterward and thus catch bits my hearing had missed. I always went to class early to make sure I could be in the front of the room, and I sat near a wall so my good ear was pointed in the direction of the instructor.

As a junior, I started the Handicapped Student Organization at the prompting and encouragement of my academic advisor Cal Helming. (Little did I know what was brewing at Berkeley at the time regarding Section 504: the 1977 occupation of the San Francisco Federal Building at United Nations Plaza by 150 medically fragile protestors fighting for Section 504 regulations; see Cone [n.d.] for more information on the sit-in.) The media immediately wanted to interview me. Reporters asked why I was so interested in having an elevator installed in the administration building when there were only two students in wheelchairs at the time. I responded, "Why only two? Maybe with more elevators, there would be more students."

The housing director decided that the all-female residence hall I was in needed to become coed and that females would occupy the second and fourth floors. I protested—I was on the ground floor and the building had no elevators. He was firm that males had to be on the ground floor for "protection."

To what extent is a college responsible for providing what a student (and/or parents) wants versus what a student is required to have under ADA? First, as hard as it may be to understand, the DSO serves the student, and parents need to be informed that their child must now begin to self-advocate and articulate what they need.

Students in college are not guaranteed a free (taxpayer-paid) education. Students must pay for their college education and earn their grades to remain enrolled. The ADA guarantees equal *access* but does not guarantee *success*. And, unfortunately, students are not always willing to accept that what they request is not always reasonable and will not always be approved.

Depending on the state or school system, community colleges may have policies that allow easy transfer of high school IEPs; however, under the ADA, some accommodations may not be approved if it is determined that the request would pose a fundamental alteration or an undue burden. Colleges have a responsibility to provide anything that would foster equal participation or that would best ensure valid results, unless it is

- a fundamental alteration or lowering of academic standards
- an undue burden
- a personal service
- a direct threat to the health and safety of *others*

Today, students shouldn't need to ask faculty directly to provide accommodations, because once academic modifications or adjustments have been approved by the DSO, students must notify faculty, who are then responsible for implementing any necessary academic accommodations. Students planning to live on campus are not always aware that they must also contract for a meal plan; as a result, requests to break the meal contracts are quite common. By choosing to live on campus, students may think their disability entitles them to a private room with a private bathroom and a kitchen suite with no meal plan; in fact, the point of living on campus and being on the meal plan is to build relationships with other people and learn about new food options. Thus, a student claiming they can't have roommates, that they must have a private bathroom, and that they need a private kitchen to cook their own food should undergo a rigorous review process.

Although it can be easier and less stressful to approve anything a student wants, it is not always possible. And it is when a DSO must decline or deny an accommodation that things can become legally messy very fast. A team should review requests for obtaining single rooms, canceling meal plans, and getting an emotional support animal, as these cases are the ones most likely to escalate, and a team decision makes the process less arbitrary and stronger to defend.

## Collaborations

Having grown up as intersectional as I am, I have always been interested in meeting diverse people from different cultures. Early on, I learned the value of collaboration. I don't drive, so I can't always go where I want, when I want. Compromise has been a huge skill to acquire, and I have learned the importance of providing compensation or fair trade to achieve desired results.

At each campus, I have made it a point to have faculty allies and a student advisory group. They have paid for themselves many times over by bringing issues to the faculty senate agenda and getting students involved.

The DSO cannot perform its mandated functions without collaboration with other campus stakeholders. Faculty members need guidance when a student self-identifies a disability to get some form of preferential treatment—with or without an accommodation letter from the DSO. Senior administrators may not know what their DSO provides and may not understand the legal ramifications associated with being noncompliant with ADA mandates.

Collaboration between DSO and campus partners, such as counseling, academic advising, parking, police/security, Title IX, and the ADA coordinator, is obviously important. The local community is also an essential collaborator. It is surprising the number of students who come to college unaware of the state rehabilitation office and what the department of rehabilitation (or similar agency, depending on the state) has to offer. Taxpayer funds cover the cost of the services, which include tuition support, technology, coaching, training, and other resources for eligible clients.

And, of course, there is collaboration with the faculty. At most colleges, faculty and students have shared governance. Having strong faculty connections in the senate and student organizations is crucial for getting new initiatives off the ground. When students speak, administrators listen. When faculty speak, administrators listen. An important recommendation is to form a campuswide faculty and student advisory board to advise the provost, vice president of inclusive excellence, or vice president of student affairs on campus disability priorities.

## Grievances

Before the Section 504 regulations in 1977, there were no consequences for a school that opted not to do anything for a "handicapped" child. Today, it seems that more and more parents want to blame everyone and everything except their child for failing to succeed. The emphasis on success is very strong today because there is a major legal shift from high school to college, when success is no longer an educational institution's responsibility. In college, there is no right to succeed.

In nearly every case of a student or parent acting entitled, it was because they did not understand the FERPA rights-transfer process or the difference between FAPE and the ADA. There was always a misbelief that it was the college's duty to ensure the student would be successful and graduate on time, regardless of the student's fit for the major or the rigor of the academic program or the disability conditions that might prevent the student from completing a full credit load.

Students have every right to protest and complain about the quality of their accommodations; however, disability services professionals have a responsibility to resolve the issues, as much as possible, at the lowest possible administrative level. This means recognizing when a student situation could escalate—and informing superiors in a timely manner as well as seeking their assistance if needed.

When complaints escalate beyond the internal resolution process within a DSO, the complaint process needs to be easily available. If a complaint is escalating, the most important process for a DSO to remember is not to shut the door to communication with the student. A review of Office for Civil Rights complaints and settlements shows that one of the areas where DSOs got into trouble was when they stopped communicating with the student. Granted, some students, especially when they are complaining and have an attorney on retainer, can be very difficult to work with, but the DSO has a duty to keep the interactive process open.

With rights come responsibilities. Students must take responsibility for their own learning. Colleges and universities do not have a legal responsibility for ensuring students are successful; they are responsible for ensuring equal access. Information must be easily accessible and updated as needed.

## Working With Senior-Level Administration

Senior-level administrators use a variety of models to control internal budgets. However, in trying to control a departmental budget, such as that of a DSO, administrators must recognize that if a student requires sign-language interpretation services, braille, or other very expensive accommodation, the institution has a responsibility to provide not only the preferred but also the most effective accommodation. The DSO should never bear sole budget responsibility. The DSO, the budget office, and senior administration must decide from where the necessary additional institutional funds will be drawn in the event the department has to cover a student wanting to complete an internship, attend a campus-sponsored event, or engage in another activity that the college would have a duty to accommodate.

It is good practice for the disability services director to meet in person with their superior at least once a month. At these meetings the senior administrator must be informed of any student cases that may be escalating. Administrators do not like surprises. During these regular meetings, issues related to personnel, budget, space, new projects, collaborations, and presentations should be shared. An agenda outlining topics and highlights, developed by the disability services director, not only keeps the meeting focused but also serves as documentation when it is time to develop a summary for the annual performance evaluation.

## Human Resources

In the past, whenever I was interviewing, I would try not to identify my disabilities until there was a need to know. On paper, my disabilities as well as my race were no one's business. My credentials were all that a future employer needed to know at that stage. However, once a phone or Zoom interview was required, I would have to disclose my hearing loss—to make sure the committee members wouldn't think I was rude or stupid if I misunderstood or misheard a question. Finally, if invited to an in-person interview, I would need to disclose my physical disability. I can only imagine the opportunities that might have been if I could have done all my interviews via Zoom and never provided any clues to the interviewers that I was physically disabled.

During the COVID-19 pandemic, professionals with disabilities found employability in a variety of careers; whereas before, their disabilities may have been considered too overwhelming for employers to handle. I filled five positions in my department via only Zoom interviews. The candidates and I did not meet in person until months after they had been on board and had been working remotely for nearly a year. By that time, my department, and the campus as a whole, had demonstrated the ability to teach courses and keep the university running remotely.

How can the higher education landscape change to reflect the diversity of the workforce, including hiring more employees with disabilities? With any vacancy, a position description identifying the requirements versus the wants will influence the applicant pool. Job duties that are often "required" in a position description include ability to stand, twist, kneel, lift 10 or more pounds, walk, type, and perform other functions that don't acknowledge how technology, reasonable accommodations per Title I of the ADA, and creativity can revamp essential duties. Hiring officials need to eliminate, if not radically modify, such antiquated and ableist screening criteria in favor of requirements that specifically address needed skills and experiences.

## Final Thoughts

Although I am a unicorn still, since I have yet to meet another person of color with a visible disability in a senior-level administrative position, I will continue to outproduce my peers. I have just finished editing my fourth book—and at the time of this volume's printing will have completed editing my fifth. I serve as a reviewer for two blind-refereed scholarly journals, have written multimillion-dollar federal grant applications that were approved, initiated radical technological innovations in departments that were still paper-file dependent, and achieved other triumphs all while directing comprehensive services for a very complex student population.

When I have left positions, I have often been replaced by two or more employees. Even though I never actively sought a position in disability services until about 20 years ago, I was constantly getting it added to my duties, often with no additional personnel. As one colleague observed, several institutions clearly believed in giving the "disability services responsibility to the person with the disability." In one situation, I was given disability services because the previous director could not handle the personnel responsibility.

In the early days of being responsible for disability services, I was rather clueless because I had no training or experience other than *having* disabilities. Since then, I have learned a great deal about what it takes to stay in the profession. What keeps me going and remaining in the field? The students. I believe in what I do and what DSOs provide. Mostly, though, I am particularly committed to the value of universal design and universal access so that more students with disabilities succeed in becoming independent.

Teaching faculty and administrators about universal access and inclusivity is my mission, and it's what keeps me working. The inclusive light bulb going off in people's heads not only empowers them but also gives me a shot of adrenaline. It is only after institutions of higher education recognize that without disability there is no diversity, and that disability rights are civil rights, that individuals with disabilities will finally see ourselves reflected in a full-length mirror.

## Resources for Additional Information

Connelly, E. A. J. (2020, July 20). Overlooked no more: Brad Lomax, a bridge between civil rights movements. *The New York Times*. https://www.nytimes.com/2020/07/08/obituaries/brad-lomax-overlooked.html

Newnham, N., & LeBrecht, J. (Directors). (2020). *Crip camp: A disability revolution* [Film]. Netflix; Higher Ground; Rusted Spoke Productions. https://www.youtube.com/watch?v=OFS8SpwioZ4

Vance, M. L., & Thompson, T. (Eds.). (2023). *Laws, policies and procedures: Tools for postsecondary student accommodations*. Association on Higher Education and Disability.

## References

Americans with Disabilities Act of 1990, 42 U.S.C. § 12101 *et seq.* (1990). https://www.ada.gov/pubs/adastatute08.htm

Cone, K. (n.d.). *Short history of the 504 sit-in*. Disability Rights Education & Defense Fund. https://dredf.org/504-sit-in-20th-anniversary/short-history-of-the-504-sit-in

Individuals with Disabilities Education Act, 20 U.S.C. § 1400 *et seq.* (2004).

Rehabilitation Act of 1973 § 504, 29 U.S.C. § 794 *et seq.* (2012).

# CHAPTER 6

# Neurodiversity

Neal E. Lipsitz

How we *think* about disability has evolved over time. And, it continues to change. One example includes the various models of disability that have been articulated since the 1980s. According to Ashmore and Kasnitz (2014), a major distinction has been made between the medical model of disability and the social, sociocultural, or cultural models, each of which "reframe[s] the focus from individuals and their perceived impairments to beliefs, experiences, and societal practices that create and manipulate disability. . . . A cultural model of disability recognizes disabling barriers as not only physical but also attitudinal, procedural, legal, religious, historical, and linguistic" (p. 27). A central concern has been that the medical model alone (e.g., perceiving disability as a medical problem) does not account for the barriers that exist within the totality of the environment for many individuals with disabilities, and this omission can lead to discrimination (Andrews, 2020).

A related change in how we think about disability comes from the neurodiversity movement, which, over the past 25 years, has aimed to shift thinking about autism and other neurological differences from something pathological to a natural and valuable variation in neurology. The neurodiversity movement dovetails with the social, sociocultural, or cultural models of disability in that the environment is seen as the cause for manifestation of an impairment, not some defect within the individual. There is no perceived need to "fix" the person who is neurodiverse; rather, the aim is to remove for these individuals the barriers created by an unaccommodating environment.

Two essays by recent college graduates follow. These essays highlight their authors' personal experiences during college and, to some extent, within their everyday lives. Both contributors had been diagnosed with autism earlier in their lives.

## How to Think About Neurodiversity

### Clara Gibson

Though the term *neurodiversity* has begun to enter the common parlance, much discussion of the concept has been siloed within the disabled community. Neurodiversity refers to the belief that neurological and developmental disabilities are not disabling in and of themselves; rather, they are natural variations within the human condition, much like hair color, height, or eye color. Neurodiversity, however, should not obfuscate the fact that neurodivergent individuals—including neurodivergent college students—face significant challenges in participating in a society designed for neurotypical (nondisabled) individuals. To approach higher education policy through the lens of neurodiversity is to adopt what is also referred to as the *social model of disability*, which acknowledges that individuals with certain neurologies are handicapped not by any intrinsic inferiority but by the fact that social institutions are not designed for them. Although neurodiversity is a concept developed primarily within the autism and ADHD (attention-deficit/hyperactivity disorder) communities, and every person with a disability has a unique and shifting understanding of their own abilities, the notion of disability as constituted by a mismatch between accessibility needs and existing social structures can be used to address inequalities for all individuals with disabilities.

To meaningfully improve the lives of students with disabilities is to attempt to carve a path through centuries of silence and inertia. From a historical perspective, we, as a society, have only just begun to treat people with disabilities as human beings. In 1970, within the lifetime of my parents' generation, children with developmental and intellectual disabilities were warehoused in institutions and used as lab rats in medical experiments. More recently, even movies have become a battleground. In 2021, pop star Sia's directorial debut *Music* drew harsh criticism for its portrayal of autism. Autistic viewers criticized Sia's decision to cast a non-autistic actress to play the role, while the film was praised by the anti-neurodiversity National Council on Severe Autism (NCSA; Luterman, 2021). On the NCSA blog, Jill Escher (2021), council president, wrote of the controversy:

> Okaaaaaayyyy . . . say what? Let me tell you what would have happened if Sia had cast Sophie as Music. She would have wandered off the set, flung off her costume and headphones, flipped out at the lights and noise, fell asleep at the late hours, and failed at following a single directorial direction. In other words, disaster. (para. 13)

Neurodiversity advocates, who are typically young people with developmental or learning disabilities, often struggle to find their voices in a field that is dominated by neurotypical parents or grandparents of children with disabilities. The instance that most shaped my own self-conception, however, was the 2013 attempted murder of Issy Stapleton. I was diagnosed with autism spectrum disorder in the summer of 2013. My parents had never considered that there might be anything wrong with me, a fact for which I will always love them, but a family member had urged them to get me evaluated. After I was diagnosed, my mother took me to my favorite restaurant and held my hand.

"Do you feel different?" I asked. She furrowed her brow, confused. "You know. About me?"

She laughed. "No. No. You're the same person, Clara. And I love you."

In September 2013, only a week or so after my diagnosis, Kelli Stapleton was arrested for attempting to murder her daughter Issy in what Kelli claimed was a failed murder–suicide (Rosin, 2014). In her own defense, Kelli cited only her daughter's autism, her violence, and her desire to take them both to heaven, where they could be free of this burden. I watched as Kelli appeared on *Dr. Phil*, in a now near-impossible-to-find two-episode special, to tell him that the Huron Valley Prison for Women had been much kinder to her than the jail of autism. I watched Dr. Phil McGraw himself wax poetic about the impact of Kelli's incarceration on her two neurotypical children, with barely a mention of the violence and trauma visited upon Issy. I had no idea how to explain it—in fact, I would've sooner gotten a tooth drilled—but I knew that this incident had forever shaped my self-perception. Because of my neurology, my life was worthless—maybe even nothing at all.

As a child, I never fit in with my peers. The older I got, the more it bothered me. I began to withdraw from them, choosing instead to interact with teachers and friends of my parents. My parents told me that I would make friends in college, when my peers were more mature, more forgiving, but by the time I graduated, my Rhodesian ridgeback Ollie was still my only friend. I met many lovely people at college, people who could've been my friends, but it seemed that I was congenitally unable to bridge this gap. This isolation is shared by almost all students with disabilities, and its effects can be devastating. While my experience with autism may differ greatly from that of someone with, for example, cerebral palsy or cancer or spina bifida, all people with disabilities are connected by the social pressure to achieve neurotypicality, or able-bodiedness, as well as by the isolation and burnout that come from constantly having to work twice as hard to accomplish what is expected of them—in school or in the workplace as well as in social interactions, friendships, and even familial relationships.

It was almost impossible to tell my parents the extent of my social isolation, but there came a time when I finally broke down. I was depressed, overworked, and mourning the loss of my only friend. I told them, in tears, this:

> I have been trying to fit in, to be normal, for 20 years. I have to paste a smile on my face, and pretend, and the end result is always the same. I talk to people, I try, but eventually, I make a mistake. And I can see it—something changes in their face, a door slams shut, when they realize that I'm not normal. I never know what they're reacting to, and I don't even know if they know what they're reacting to, but I know what they're thinking: I'm just too weird. I'm just too different. Even when they're shown a still photo of someone autistic, neurotypicals still have a negative reaction. I don't even have to say anything, I'm already just *wrong*.

From a psychiatric perspective, the sequelae of isolation and stigma can manifest as anxiety, depression, and psychosis. Academically, students may fail classes or drop out altogether. To create an environment in which students with disabilities are unable to succeed not only is devastating to individual students but also robs institutions of those students' perspectives and potential contributions. Because we have already established the extent to which ableism is ingrained in both our society and our institutions, it should go without saying that higher education is not immune. In attempting to alleviate the burden ableism places on students with disabilities, institutions must thread the needle between two flawed approaches.

First, there is the tendency to view disability as a private medical problem. The medical model, characterized by a culture of silence around issues of disability and ableism, creates an onerous path toward claiming accommodations. It does not inspire student advocacy and support groups for students with disabilities. The results of the medical model communicate clearly to students with disabilities that they are expected to address their disabilities before they arrive on campus. By putting the onus on students to assimilate perfectly with their nondisabled peers, colleges and universities create a culture of shame and silence that adds to the isolation I described previously. Because large bureaucracies change slowly, and this approach to disability has been the default for decades, elements of this approach are present in the culture of most institutions.

The second imperfect approach is to enforce an atmosphere of toxic positivity surrounding issues of disability. While fostering pride and appreciation for the unique strengths students with disabilities have and the enrichment their perspectives bring to the colleges and universities they attend, administrators and support staff must remember that students with disabilities face serious inequities and challenges every day of their lives. Pushing social acceptance and celebration of students with disabilities is meaningless without serious, practical attempts to create more equitable and accessible conditions. Although most disability-rights organizations support a shift from the medical model of disability to the social model, which acknowledges that, while neurological differences like autism, ADHD, and dyslexia are normal and healthy variations, society is set up to disadvantage people with certain neurological configurations. This disadvantage can be ameliorated only with real structural change.

How, then, can disability services offices begin to attack the barriers facing students with disabilities? The first objective may seem somewhat tautological—disability services offices must find a way to create an atmosphere in which students with disabilities feel comfortable disclosing and registering for accommodations. In a study of the impact of disability services offices on academic outcomes for students with disabilities, Chiu et al. (2019) found that trajectories of students' GPAs improved after they registered with the disability services office. Moreover, there was a significant association between registering with the office early in their matriculation and higher semester GPAs than registering later.... In fact, [students with disabilities] who interacted with student disability services personnel were more likely to meet with their faculty and to report higher levels of satisfaction with other university services. (p. 234)

The main barrier preventing students from registering is ableism, both internalized and external. Abes and Darkow (2020) proposed crip theory as one approach to encouraging student disclosures. Crip theory is a disability studies concept that aims to "expose compulsory able-bodiedness and able-mindedness in all contexts" and "critiques . . . these messages and the disabled/nondisabled binary that deems disability abnormal" (p. 224). Abes and Darkow (2020) acknowledged the aspects of disclosure that lead many students to hide their disabilities:

[A]s Knight (2017) stated: "When we disclose our disabilities, when we publicly acknowledge the particularities of our bodies, we make ourselves vulnerable to backlash." Mingus (2017) described the "forced intimacy" of disclosure: "People are allowed to ask me intrusive questions about my body, make me 'prove' my disability or expect me to share with them every aspect of my accessibility needs." (p. 225)

Another important point Abes and Darkow (2020) made is that of the changeable nature of disability. The fluid nature of disability resists a one-size-fits-all approach, necessitating ongoing dialogue between students, faculty members, and administrators.

When the disability impact on a student is constantly changing, indefinite accommodation plans are necessary. When a student discloses their disability, they may not come to disability services knowing their access needs and may be seeking to engage in a dialogue where professionals validate their experience and work collaboratively in access planning. (Abes & Darkow, 2020, p. 225)

The best approach, then, is not for disability services personnel to be the gatekeepers for a predetermined menu of accommodations, but one of mutual problem-solving and ongoing dialogue regarding access needs. For example, when experiencing difficulties in the classroom, a student or a faculty member should feel that the disability services office is a resource to allow both parties to find a solution. Because most faculty members' training in accessibility is limited to the legal requirements, frustration may ensue when faculty find students with competing accessibility needs in their classes. Disability services offices can be resources to faculty members so they can ensure positive classroom experiences for students with accessibility needs—as well as prevent needless frustration. Moreover,

> [w]hen disability services professionals embrace disability as fluid, disabled students will feel less shame, stigma, and uncertainty around disclosure. Also, when professionals perceive students' physical and emotional labor associated with meeting legal requirements as part of the meaning of their disability, students will feel respected and understood, which also contributes to disclosure. (Abes & Darkow, 2020, p. 226)

In practical terms, Abes and Darkow (2020) suggested

> providing ways for students to engage remotely with disability services offices [to] reduce the number of in-person visits the students must make. . . . [and] lessen[ing] the ableist burden of students' having to disclose their disability multiple times. . . . Processes that require multiple instances of disclosure, whether to multiple faculty members or in other university areas . . . are strenuous on disabled students. When disabilities are not

readily apparent...disclosure to multiple faculty members can be challenging due to the uncertainty of the faculty reaction and power differences. (pp. 226–227)

Familiarizing faculty members with the process by which accessibility services verifies and assigns accommodations, as well as the arduous process students must go through to register in the first place (including phone calls, obtaining medical records, struggles with insurance companies, and costly evaluations), would likely contribute to a deeper understanding of the challenges students with disabilities face as well as increase confidence in the important role accommodations play in ensuring an equitable learning environment for all.

Every interaction in which a student must disclose their disability is another chance that they may face rejection, ableism, or judgment. During my college years, my warmest, most rewarding relationships with faculty members were those in which I was open about my disability. My academic advisor noticed my focused intensity in the classroom and my academic seriousness. I always felt like a valued member of his classroom, rather than being embarrassed by my enthusiasm. A member of the English department responded to my disclosure with genuine interest and empathy, encouraging me to blend my interest in disability theory with literary studies. "Neurodivergent criticism could be the next big thing," she told me. "You can be right at the forefront." As a response to my disclosures, both she and a third, more junior, faculty member took a special interest in my integrating disability studies with literary critique. To hear faculty members see my diagnosis—this embarrassing secret—as an asset was a truly special experience. These collaborations can be life-changing for students who have spent their whole lives ashamed of an essential part of their identity and can provide new perspectives for faculty members as well.

# My Experience as a Neurodiverse College Student

*Terrence Smith*

Human beings have five senses: vision, hearing, smell, taste, and touch. These senses are used to perceive surroundings and make sense of the way the world works. Sometimes, though, what some people see is not necessarily what others see. Everyone has different experiences and perceptions of the world that influence their perspective of things, and these differences can be deeper and more complex than one might realize.

That is something that holds true for me as an individual with autism. A disconnection exists between what my peers and supervisors perceive my actions to be and what was going through my mind about those actions. What can be perceived as rudeness can simply be plain ignorance. I do tend to be a little awkward in social situations. I don't always know the proper way to comport myself around other people, and even when I do think I am behaving appropriately, I am doing something that is not neurotypical without realizing it.

For instance, I attended an on-campus function where one of my friends and his parents would be. I wanted help from my friend identifying whether one of the men attending was his father, so I pointed in his direction and then went over and said hello. Afterward, my friend indicated to me that someone complained that I was being rude by pointing and that I may have been interrupting his father's conversation or standing too close. It did not occur to me that I was performing a gesture that may be perceived in that way.

Perceptions of personal space are something I struggle with. I spent a lot of time in the art studio during my years in college. As a result, I created art among fellow art students, and I enjoyed seeing what they created. Unfortunately, this feeling wasn't reciprocated. I observed one woman drawing an image in the art studio. I stood there for what I felt was only 10 seconds at the most, and I thought I kept an appropriate distance from her. The only thought in my head at the time was *Gee, that drawing is neat.* A few weeks later, another friend told me that I was making the woman uncomfortable and that she thought I had an interest in her. It was one of those "Wait, what?" moments. I thought I was just watching her do art, and I wasn't aware that my brief observation would communicate any kind of intentions. Had I known that action would have been interpreted that way, I would not have done it. Fortunately, I was able to clear things up with her, and while we did not end up as friends, at the very least the misunderstanding was resolved.

Unfortunately, that would not be the only misconception I would have to deal with. I have always failed to see the forest for the trees. I could have such narrow focus on one thing, and be so obsessive with details, that I would lose sight of the big picture. Two sides are constantly battling in my brain: the OCD (obsessive-compulsive disorder), with which I was officially diagnosed, and the ADHD (attention-deficit/hyperactivity disorder), with which I have not been diagnosed but that I strongly suspect I have. This would lead to some sticky situations.

Some of the faculty had concerns about my behavior and performance. One of them thought I was negligent or lazy, partly because I struggled with getting the reading done on time. I tend to be obsessive-compulsive about my work. Scanning reading was never my forte. At the same time I was taking that class, I was taking an art course in which my professor had high expectations for me and my fellow students. Also, I was always trying to put first things first when it came to deadlines. Unfortunately, there are no numerical values indicating when a work of art is finished. The thing about it is that it is done when the artist decides it is done. Conversely, it is always possible to do more, so more is always what I had to do, especially when assignments for other classes had to be put on hold. It was a struggle to balance my time with everyone's expectations. It is not that my professors were not willing to work with me; I was simply expected to live up to their expectations with the accommodations that were given to me, and I did what I could with the expectations that were on me. I was allotted time extensions to complete assignments, although some instructors seemed to be concerned that I kept needing extensions. One professor denied my request for an extension, which the Office of Student Accessibility Services supported denying, since I had not gotten to the work until shortly before it was due. Needless to say, time management was a challenge.

Organization was never my strong point, either. In my first year of college, I had one professor who called himself a "benevolent dictator." He lived up to that name. He loved teaching and cared deeply about his students, but he also was firm with his expectations. There was one moment in class when he called me out for struggling to find a paper in my binder, which was a mess. I was more concerned about getting work done than getting my documents in order, even though having things put together was necessary for success. By senior year, I had my documents tabbed according to subject, and faculty and staff at a meeting I attended were impressed with how organized I was. So, I got there eventually.

College is a place where different voices from different perspectives can be heard. The voices of autistic people and the differently abled need to be heard as well; it would help others better understand their challenges. During one of my early years at college, I checked out a presentation from a professor on campus who discussed his experiences with ADHD. He opened the presentation by pretending he saw a bird and losing focus. It was great that he had a sense of humor about himself. It showed that he did not take himself too seriously and that he was able to laugh at the challenges he faced, which I think is a good coping mechanism. When I spoke to him afterward, he said that his son was also autistic. I was surprised that was something to which we could relate. I did not think of it in this terminology at the time, but looking back, the way that I felt was "seen"—that he understood what I was experiencing and could relate to it.

Speaking of which, the campus's Office of Student Accessibility Services was there to help me out along the journey. Its staff members knew that students were more than what they appeared to be on the surface, that they were capable of succeeding like any other student who did not have disabilities. The office's role was to ensure proper equity for me, act as a facilitator between students and faculty, ensure that everyone's expectations were met, and put in place any tools and support I needed.

The Office of Student Accessibility Services was also there to help with whatever concerns my family had. My parents were worried about how I might handle the transition from home life to college life. They were concerned with how I would manage my time and with whom I would interact. Any parent would worry about their kid going off to college, but I think the fact that I am autistic may have compounded this concern. According to my dad, I tend to be very trusting. He has been around the bend several times before, and he has had his share of experience with people who have been less than honest with him. He doesn't want the same to happen to me. My brother also had his concerns. Having shared a room with me for much of my life, he was uneasy about how my interactions with any future roommates would turn out. He knows a lot about living with someone who is autistic.

I think my parents worried too much when I was away. I did an OK job of taking care of myself, although I forgot there were plenty of clean clothes in my closet, which went unnoticed for months. I was always welcomed home on the weekends, since I was just an hour away, so I didn't have to deal with homesickness. And my dad was on hand to offer advice on issues that I was dealing with. Largely, though, my parents did not get involved in my college life. If I had been right next door, they might have been involved in every aspect of my life.

Fortunately, they felt I was in safe hands. I was at a smaller college, where professors had more opportunity to provide individualized attention. They were concerned that had I attended a larger college or university, I would get lost in the crowds and be in a classroom with at least a hundred other students. All the buildings on my campus were also close together, so I would not get lost (more than I would have anywhere else, at least).

For the most part, I got along well with the faculty and staff on campus. There was one woman at the dining hall who swiped everyone's card upon entry. She always called us by name and always acted like she was glad to see us. She made every student on campus feel welcome. I have heard that dining hall staff are working to emulate her behavior.

As I said, along with the autism comes OCD; my obsession with detail and perfection had people questioning my intellectual abilities. Such an instance was when I had to sign a document about my student loans at the registrar's office. My father told me not to sign something until I read it all the way through, which I did. I even asked for a dictionary so that I made sure I understood every word. Going through the contract with a fine-toothed comb was a great deal of frustration for me. The registrar staff mistook this frustration for incompetence, wondering if I was even intellectually capable of understanding the document, so my father and I, along with the Office of Student Accessibility Services, had to prove that I was in fact competent.

One thing that would have improved my college experience would have been connections with other students with autism. I did not have much experience interacting with others who lived the same experiences as I did. I think that would have been a way for me to feel more comfortable, to not feel so isolated. Ironically, I think that because of my special interests in video games and science fiction, I was able to bond with other people on campus. It was like sharing a common language—except that the language was "nerd" stuff. I also made some friends during a pre-first year summer boot camp who became part of my social group. It was a good way to get accustomed to college life before college actually started.

## Neurodiversity Summary

Clara and Terrence demonstrate the famous quote by Dr. Stephen Shore, an autistic professor in the School of Education at Adelphi University: "When you meet one person with autism, you've met one person with autism" (Healis Autism Centre, 2020, para. 1). Although some characteristics are similar among autistic people, Shore points out that each individual is different. The autistic students you meet on campus have their own strengths and challenges, making each one of them unique. Hence, individual differences are quite pronounced within the realm of neurodiversity—not just diverse from those who are neurotypical but different from one another as well. And this is where the framework (see Chapter 1) comes into play: Each individual can be "mapped" onto the framework, including all of the stakeholders involved, and a real appreciation for who they are and where they're coming from can emerge. This mapping, along with the roles, responsibilities, and attitudes of the relevant stakeholders, can help the team (no matter how it's configured) to organize the available information and collaborate to meet each student's needs in an appropriate way.

Of course, similarities also exist among neurodiverse individuals. The medical model would suggest that behavioral assessments and diagnostic criteria must have certain characteristics that are consistent across the board. Although experienced differently by each person, these characteristics may be put into broad categories and "include having difficulty in communication, social interactions, and having a restricted set of routines, as well as repeated behaviors" (Healis Autism Centre, 2020, para. 1). Clara and Terrence provide plenty of examples of how these characteristics manifested for them in college. However, from the perspective of a social model, these experiences are due to stigma and the assumptions made by others. Again, the framework can help sort out where the stakeholders are coming from and, through understanding and collaboration, help the group move forward.

Finally, Clara and Terrence put forth a variety of suggestions to enhance our work, as student affairs professionals, with neurodivergent students. Paying attention to individual differences is key and fits perfectly with our mandate to engage with students on an individual basis. To improve the lives of neurodiverse students—to help them feel included, have access, and see individualities as assets—we must address harmful attitudes such as ableism, biases, and negative stereotyping, along with inequities, barriers, and stigma. Our students are depending on it.

## References

Abes, E., & Darkow, D. (2020). Using crip theory to create campus cultures that foster students' disability disclosure. *Journal of Postsecondary Education and Disability, 33*(3), 223–231. https://www.ahead.org/professional-resources/publications/jped/archived-jped/jped-volume-33

Andrews, E. E. (2020). *Disability as diversity: Developing cultural competence.* Oxford.

Ashmore, J., & Kasnitz, D. (2014). Models of disability in higher education. In M. L. Vance, N. E. Lipsitz, & K. Parks (Eds.), *Beyond the Americans with Disabilities Act: Inclusive policy and practice for higher education* (pp. 21–34). NASPA–Student Affairs Administrators in Higher Education.

Chiu, Y.-C. J., Chang, H.-Y. V., Johnston, A., Nascimento, M., Herbert, J. T., Niu, X. M. (2019). Impact of disability services on academic achievement among college students with disabilities. *Journal of Postsecondary Education and Disability, 32*(3), 227–245. https://www.ahead.org/professional-resources/publications/jped/archived-jped/jped-volume-32

Escher, J. (2021, February). The Sia shaming spectacle is a tragedy for the arts and the autism community. *National Council on Severe Autism Blog.* https://www.ncsautism.org/blog//sia-shaming

Healis Autism Centre. (2020, July 14). When you meet one person with autism, you've met one person with autism. https://www.healisautism.com/post/when-you-meet-one-person-with-autism

Knight, A. (2017). Feminism, disability, and the democratic classroom. In S. L. Kerschbaum, L. T. Eisenmann, & J. M. Jones (Eds.), *Negotiating disability: Disclosure and higher education* (pp. 57–74). University of Michigan Press.

Luterman, S. (2021, February 12). Sia asked critics to watch her controversial new movie before judging it, so I did. *Slate.* https://slate.com/culture/2021/02/sia-movie-music-autism-golden-globes-review.html

Mingus, M. (2017, August 6). Forced intimacy: An ableist norm. *Leaving Evidence.* https://leavingevidence.wordpress.com/2017/08/06/forced-intimacy-an-ableist-norm

Rosin, H. (2014, October). Kelli Stapleton can't forgive herself for trying to kill her violent, autistic daughter. Can you? *New York Magazine.* https://nymag.com/intelligencer/2014/10/kelli-stapleton-issy-stapleton.html

# PART IV

# Academic Rigor, New Pedagogies, Disability Law, and Technology

# CHAPTER 7

# New Pedagogy With Academic Rigor
## *Universal Design for Learning*

Lyman L. Dukes III and Joseph W. Madaus

During the 2015–2016 academic year, 19.4% of all undergraduate students in the United States reported one or more disabilities (National Center for Education Statistics [NCES], 2018). However, the actual number of students with disabilities on campuses and in online programs is likely higher. For example, in 2022, the NCES (part of the United States Department of Education) reported that 65% of students who were identified with a disability at some point in their lives did not disclose their disability to their college. Students from less traditional groups, such as veterans, students age 30 or older, and students who were independent from their parents, reported disability at higher levels (NCES, 2018). Each of these data points highlights the diversity of learners on campuses and in online programs.

Simultaneously, there has been a greater emphasis on viewing disability through a social justice lens. As described by Evans et al. (2017), this effort begins with the assumption that the abilities and rights of people to contribute to and benefit from higher education do not depend on their bodies or psyches conforming to dominant norms. It means that the barriers to success in higher education lie in the structural, organizational, physical, and attitudinal aspects of institutions.

Disability is also increasingly being included in diversity, equity, and inclusion initiatives at colleges and universities (Shaewitz & Crandall, 2020). These efforts include taking a more flexible approach to the documentation required for students to access necessary services (Tarconish et al., 2021). The intent of these efforts is to recognize the talents these students bring to college campuses and minimize barriers to access based on negative attitudes toward students with disabilities. Moreover, it recognizes that educating and supporting students with disabilities is a campuswide responsibility.

Both of us are professors at large, public 4-year universities, and we teach students with diverse learning needs, including students with disabilities. Lipsitz et al. (as cited in Hope, 2021) identified faculty members as key stakeholders in meeting the needs of students with disabilities. Particularly, Lipsitz et al. pointed to the importance of faculty members simultaneously recognizing individual differences and maintaining academic rigor in their courses. They highlighted the role of faculty in creating access for students with disabilities via inclusive teaching methodologies as well as working with them to clarify course expectations and effective educational behavior—all while maintaining academic integrity (Hope, 2021). We concur with Lipsitz et al.'s assessment and believe universal design for learning (UDL) is a powerful pedagogical mechanism to support student academic and behavioral goals and expectations. UDL is a methodology that allows instructors to proactively anticipate and plan for the needs of a range of diverse learners, including students with disabilities, while maintaining high academic standards. This chapter offers an overview of the concept of UDL and presents examples that can be considered in the design, delivery, and assessment of a variety of courses—whether they are in person, fully online, or hybrid.

## What Is Universal Design for Learning?

The genesis for UDL is universal design, a concept rooted in architecture and the planning of the physical environment. Ron Mace is credited with coining the term *universal design* (UD) to capture "the design of products and environments to be usable by all people, to the greatest extent possible, without the need for adaptation or specialized design" (Center for Universal Design, 2018, para. 2). One of the first published accounts of applying UD to instructional design in higher education was the work of Silver et al. (1998). Using the terminology *universal instructional design* (UID), the authors noted that with UID, students may find that many of the instructional accommodations they would request are already part of the faculty members' overall instructional design. Furthermore, these approaches may benefit all students in the class. For example, "most of the requests by students with learning disabilities at our institution . . . are typically helpful for all students, and in fact may be representative of effective instructional practices" (Silver et al., 1998, pp. 47–48).

In the late 1990s and early 2000s the United States Department of Education provided a series of grants related to the promotion of UD in higher education instruction (Izzo et al., 2008). Several approaches to UD emerged, including UDL (Burgstahler, 2015; Izzo et al., 2008). Although the exact label (i.e., UD, UDI [universal design of instruction], UID, UDL) and some of the language varied, these approaches shared some common ideas—that student diversity is the norm and instructors should anticipate this variance as part of their instructional planning (Dukes et al., 2009; McGuire et al., 2006). Additionally, each approach promotes incorporating accessible instructional strategies to create a more inclusive option to the traditional accommodation process, minimizing the self-disclosure stigma for students and reducing time requirements for faculty to retrofit their instruction for accommodations (Izzo et al., 2008). Importantly, a course designed and delivered using UDL practices does not negatively affect course rigor or high student expectations (Moore, 2017; Scott et al., 2003).

UDL was initially applied in the K–12 environment. Developed by the Center for Applied Special Technology (CAST, 2018), UDL is based in three principles—that instruction should

1. provide multiple means of engagement (referred to as the "why" of learning).
2. provide multiple means of representation (referred to as the "what" of learning).
3. provide multiple means of action and expression (referred to as the "how" of learning).

CAST (2018) developed a set of guidelines that operationalize each of the three principles. Although this model was first used in K–12 settings, it has since been applied in the postsecondary environment. In fact, UDL is specifically noted in the language of the Higher Education Opportunity Act of 2008. According to the legislation, UDL

> means a scientifically valid framework for guiding educational practice that—"(A) provides flexibility in the ways information is presented, in the ways students respond or demonstrate knowledge and skills, and in the ways students are engaged;" and "(B) reduces barriers in instruction, provides appropriate accommodations, supports, and challenges, and maintains high achievement expectations for all students, including students with disabilities and students who are limited English proficient." [§103(a)(24)(A)(B)]

In summary, several UD models have been developed and applied to varying extent in higher education instruction.

# Implementing UDL

When preparing a postsecondary-level course for students, instructors often consider three broad areas: course design and planning, course delivery and instruction, and course assessment and learner evaluation. The following sections organize the process for applying the UDL guidelines using these areas. That is, as courses are initially planned and subsequently updated, instructors are encouraged to concurrently consider how UDL can be continually and consistently embedded into a course. Instructors can start with one piece of the course and iteratively expand the application of UDL over time.

## The UDL Circle

Each UDL guideline does not need to be comprehensively implemented across every part of a course. In fact, as CAST (2018) noted, guidelines sometimes may not be germane to one's learning goals. Likewise, Rao (2013) advised that instructors add UD strategies incrementally and assess what worked for their students; the learning environment can be "built upon and refined as needed" (para. 12). To operationalize these recommendations, instructors can use what Behling and Posey (in press) call the UDL circle (Figure 7.1):

1. Reflect on the intended goals or construct.
2. Identify challenges to achieving those goals.
3. Try a UDL guideline to provide flexible pathways to achieve those goals and overcome the challenges.
4. Gather feedback on the effectiveness.

Figure 7.1
*The UDL Circle*

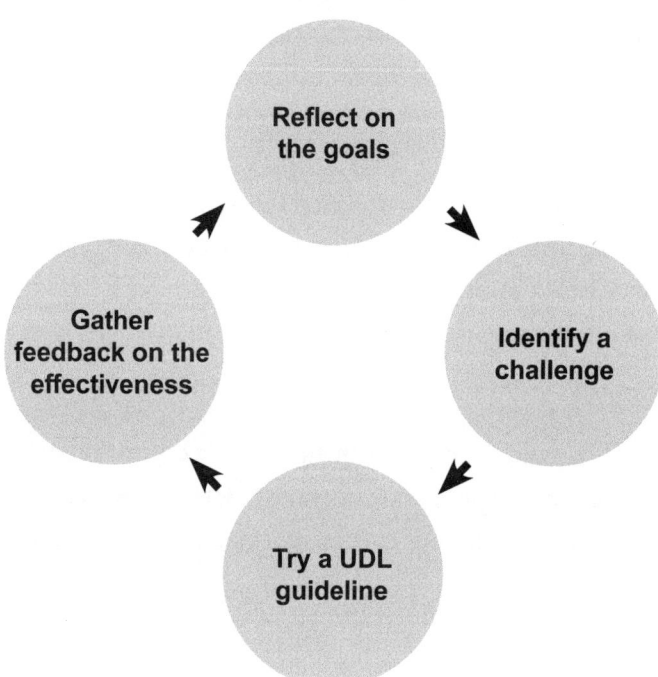

Begin by reflecting on the current course design, delivery, and assessment experience. Consider the following guiding questions:

- Did the course as previously taught meet its stated objectives for most students?
- If you gathered formative and summative assessment information, did students report that the instructional and assessment methods employed met their needs?
- Are students with disabilities currently using accommodations in the course? Could those needs be met with advanced course design planning?
- Do you think there may be students who have chosen not to disclose a disability to the appropriate institutional office?

- Is there a UDL guideline you might implement that has the potential to improve the course experience and/or academic outcome for students? For example, if students are not demonstrating interest in the initial course meetings and/or assignments, how might you improve engagement early in the course?

Consider that online or hybrid courses tend to rely on watching video, reading texts, and viewing lecture content, and that formative course practice exercises are completed individually or in groups more often than didactic presentation or lengthy class discussions occur (Rao & Tanners, 2011). Behling and Posey (in press) astutely noted, "Ultimately, how UDL is applied will vary—as each context is unique and the resources and individuals involved will differ—but the UDL implementation process and mindset of 'tight goals, flexible pathways' is consistent."

As mentioned, reflecting on the goals for a course and subsequently the objectives of each lesson is an ideal starting point; it allows for the opportunity to distinguish among course goals and how students will attain those goals (Smith, 2012). Considering how students will meet course goals provides the chance for instructors to represent content that employs an array of methods and that affords multiple options for students to engage in and subsequently express knowledge of course content.

**Course Design and Planning**

As faculty, we (the authors) strive to develop course syllabi that reflect UDL concepts, using UDL guidelines. We begin with an explanation highlighting how information will be presented and how students will engage and subsequently be assessed, with a focus on variety. The syllabus explanation can be provided in both written and audio/video format with captions (Guideline 1). The intent is to explicitly describe course goals and their connection to assignment objectives as well as to offer suggestions about how to be successful in the course (Guideline 6). This tactic can prompt an instructor to remove potentially extraneous course material that is not well aligned with stated course goals (Smith, 2012).

Next, we give thought to semester course planning, which can be particularly idiosyncratic. We find introducing a weekly routine and describing how students can be successful within the context of the weekly routine to be beneficial (Guideline 6). Scheduling the days on which assignments are consistently due helps students plan and maintain a routine throughout a term (Guideline 3). For example, an instructor can plan for low-stakes assessments to be due each Wednesday and higher-stakes assessments to be due each Sunday. Additionally, we include an invitation on the course syllabus to meet with the instructor when desired using a preferred meeting method (e.g., online, in person, at the campus coffee shop or the instructor's office) about course-related matters (Guideline 1).

Although the course syllabus is students' first interaction with the instructor and course content, there are other course planning tasks. We consider how overall instructional planning can support student executive functioning. Instructors are often required to record "first-day attendance" for students. First-day attendance can be completed using a low-stakes assessment—in this case, an untimed, open-note quiz on the syllabus content (Guideline 3). The quiz can be prepared to highlight elements of the course that provide student choice and support academic success. For example, students can be oriented to and provided the option of using a hard-copy text or an e-book that supports a text-to-speech application (Guideline 4); additional topical "readings" that are open source, reflecting varied levels of understanding; and relevant video-based topical materials that align with and complement readings, as well as slide-based audio/video/scripted instructor-designed lectures. Finally, long-term course assignments can be structured to provide formative feedback (Guideline 8).

For example, in a teacher education behavior management course, students are expected to complete an eight-part "behavior change project." Each part is completed and submitted weekly over 8 weeks, and weekly instructor feedback ensures mastery. The eight sections are subsequently combined and submitted for a final grade during the last week of the course term, at which time summative feedback is provided as well.

Group work is a common tactic used to complete course projects (Guideline 8); therefore, group composition should be considered at the outset of the term. These groups can also be used as ongoing small discussion groups throughout a course term—for example, when students have questions or concerns about how to complete an assignment or prepare for an exam. When structuring groups, use of a short questionnaire will appraise student diversity; prior experience, including work and technology expertise; previous coursework and study habits; and even whether students have worked together in the past. Guidelines for effective group behavior and assignment completion should be provided, and instructors should schedule time to periodically meet with work groups completing long-term projects.

UDL course delivery and instructional methods set the stage for learning mastery when instructors intentionally and consistently use practices that anticipate the varied learning strengths and preferences of students. All students benefit from the consistent use of teaching practices that allow for the efficient allocation of finite attentional resources to be applied to course task demands.

## Course Delivery and Instruction

Each course lesson, whether delivered in person or virtually, begins with connecting a course objective to the specific lesson topic. Next, students are oriented to the actual content (e.g., reading, video, activity) with which they will engage to achieve the course objective. Course content used in instruction will have been examined to ensure it allows for the use of assistive technology (e.g., screen reader, magnifier), if necessary, and for accessibility purposes (Guidelines 2 and 4). In addition, the evaluation to be used to assess understanding will be explained at the outset of the lesson (see Figure 7.2).

**Figure 7.2**
*Lesson Orientation Process*

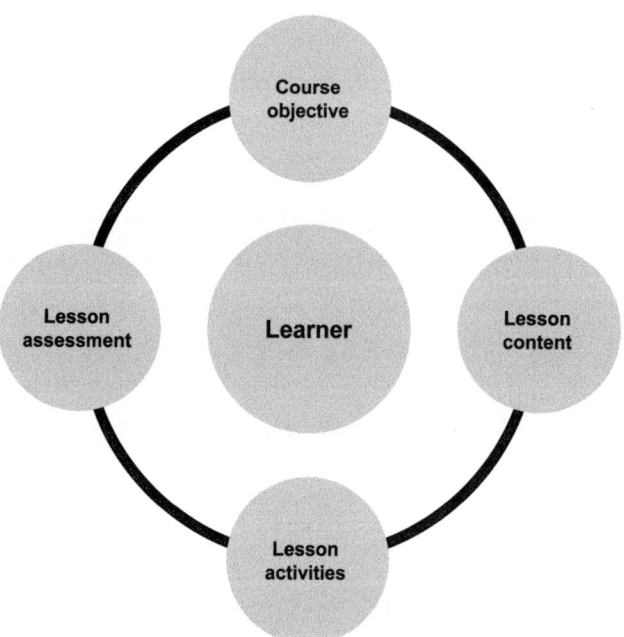

Next, we strive to stimulate interest in the lesson. This step is especially important in establishing an authentic connection between course objectives and activities with learner interests. An emotional connection to an educational activity can enhance both attention to and retention of lesson content (Tyng et al., 2017). Instructors often hear about the importance of reviewing any background knowledge students possess; while this is helpful, there are other beneficial strategies. For example, beginning a course with a case-based activity may be an effective tool for forming long-term interest in course objectives (Guideline 7).

In a special education preservice teacher educator course, we have employed guest speakers with disabilities who have recently graduated from high school or college. The graduates speak about their school, work, and personal experiences, while the preservice teachers have the opportunity to converse with the recent graduate. With permission, the invited speakers can be recorded for use in future courses as well. In an internship-level course for future special educators, a similar approach has been used but has included the use of a small-group activity. In this case, student interns are familiarized with the campus inclusive postsecondary education program for students with an intellectual disability. Next, in three meetings each an hour-long held at the beginning of the term, the small groups of intern teams work with the students to develop their initial semester calendars and talk with the students about their college and adult life goals (Guidelines 7 and 8). The preservice teacher candidates are oriented to notions about expectations that school-based personnel (e.g., teachers, administrators, school counselors) often have about the capacity of students with significant disabilities to participate in further education and to live independently. The teacher candidates prepare a short video, podcast, or written report about their brief interactions with the students and how the experience supports or refutes their preconceived beliefs about the capabilities of young adults with intellectual disabilities (Guideline 5).

A primary instructional practice for presenting course content remains instructor discourse, which is often combined with a slide deck (e.g., PowerPoint) summarizing the teaching content. PowerPoint lessons can be recorded and uploaded to a learning management system course page and can include the use of captions and a slide-by-slide script of the instructor's remarks. The content can subsequently be accessed at any time using an array of multisensory tools and techniques (e.g., listening, reading, script printout; Guideline 4). Such techniques can be designed so the display of captions, for example, may be set to the on or off position in the event users find the text distracting. Recordings of slide deck presentations should be kept short (i.e., ideally less than 10 minutes). Dukes et al. (2019) examined student use of video-based instructor lessons and found that most students were not viewing learning management system–based course video beyond the 10-minute mark. A course lecture is typically longer than 10 minutes, so preparing a lecture made up of multiple recordings is a recommended means of keeping videos short while still addressing all lesson topics. The primary intent of such techniques and the use of varied media formats (e.g., YouTube videos, more and less complex readings) is to increase the probability that all students' academic preferences and strengths are supported (Guideline 5).

When creating a presentation slide there are a range of UDL tools and strategies that can be applied to promote student interest and learning. The first is to bring attention to the primary lesson "takeaways," or objectives. For example, they can be labeled, at the individual-slide level, "Big Idea 1," "Big Idea 2," and so on. After the explanation of a "Big Idea" can be a slide titled "Respond and Review (if needed)," which we use as a built-in low-stakes formative assessment tool (Guideline 3). This slide presents a question, which can be asked via video, about the "Big Idea" content just described. Students are encouraged to review the previous set of slides if they have difficulty successfully responding to the query (Guideline 9). In both in-person and synchronous online classes, we use polling tools (e.g., Google forms, Jamboard) periodically during a lesson. In asynchronous courses, we use the Flipgrid video-based application along with the learning management system discussion board to promote consistent student engagement. Finally, we also include an optional "Want to Know More?" section for each course lesson to encourage curious students to continue to explore the topic beyond typical class expectations (Guideline 7). Table 7.1 presents some of the tools and strategies just described and includes recommendations about additional course design, course assessment, learning evaluation tools, and strategies.

Table 7.1
*CAST UDL Guidelines Applied to Higher Education*

| Guideline | Multiple means of engagement | Multiple means of representation | Multiple means of action and expression |
|---|---|---|---|
| Increase access | Recruiting interest<br>• Provide assignment menus<br>• Peer-to-peer instruction | Perception<br>• Record lectures<br>• Lecture transcripts<br>• Visual supports | Physical action<br>• Use Flipgrid<br>• Audio explanation of video content |
| Build understanding | Sustaining effort and persistence<br>• Use formative assessment<br>• Use lesson storytelling | Language and symbols<br>• Define keywords<br>• Use multimedia lessons | Expression and communication<br>• Use writing prompts<br>• Use exit slips (Nearpod app) |
| Internalize knowledge | Self-regulation<br>• Self- and peer-assessment<br>• Task rubrics and checklists | Comprehension<br>• Activate background knowledge<br>• Promote generalization | Executive functions<br>• Actionable formative feedback<br>• Use review and respond |
| **Goal:** Develop expert learners who are: | Purposeful and motivated | Resourceful and knowledgeable | Strategic and goal-directed |

*Note.* Adapted from *Universal Design for Learning Guidelines Version 2.2*, by CAST, 2018 (http://udlguidelines.cast.org). Copyright © 2018 by CAST, Inc.

## Course Assessment and Learner Evaluation

Assessing student learning is a critical component of instruction, and UD principles can be applied in this area too. Here we must return to and stress a point made earlier: UD techniques do not lessen academic standards. As Scott et al. (2003) stated, "It is our assumption that the role of the college instructor is to teach all students in the classroom as effectively as possible without compromising academic standards and expectations" (p. 42). Or as one college instructor interviewed by Behling and Posey (in press) put it, "The rigor of my graded assignments stayed the same: I had literature reviews, analysis, and citations required. What changed was how students could get there."

Supplying specific details about assignments and projects can be a useful way to allow students to clearly understand the instructor's expectations for various levels of course grades. Instructors can also complete daily or weekly check-ins with students, getting feedback on what pieces of the course they understand and which parts are unclear (Guideline 6). Based on this feedback, instructors can then adjust their instruction—in real time—to meet student needs.

Depending on (and maintaining) the technical requirements of a course or a major, instructors can consider moving away from traditional timed exams (e.g., multiple choice, short answers) and allow students to complete assignments and projects in a format of their choice outside of class. For example, students might write a traditional paper, develop a webpage or a blog, film a short movie, or create a verbal webcast. Such approaches could also be applied to what are typical written papers. One of the authors of this chapter teaches a course addressing key components of special education law. Instead of taking tests or writing papers, students develop an informational flyer describing the major parts of the law, including an outline of school responsibilities and family rights. It is prepared with the intent of sharing it with parents of students they teach, and students design the layout. Such approaches allow students to display mastery of content while providing options for recruiting interest (Guideline 7) and for expression and communication (Guideline 5).

Some of these approaches could also be applied to discussion board posts. For example, students might record and post either visual or audio clips of their responses to the prompt or question (e.g., Flipgrid responses). Likewise, feedback to students could be presented in video or audio format.

There are many ways to incorporate UDL into assessment techniques, and we recognize most of the approaches discussed here relate to social sciences or humanities courses. More examples can be found in Behling and Posey (in press), Poore-Pariseau (2013), and Rao and Tanners (2011).

## Expanding the Use of UDL Through Campus Partnerships

Ideally, UD practices are used in an array of campus settings. Of course, such proliferation means institutional leadership must be part of the discourse about the value of UDL and support its implementation. When engaging administration on UDL (or any other effort, for that matter), first reflect on the values and needs of your campus leadership: What is their mission and vision for the institution? What are their current successes and challenges? What metrics are being used to define institutional successes and challenges? What terminology is being used among leadership when discussing institutional efforts? Once you have carefully considered these and other questions, you will be better positioned to prompt administrators to consider whether they are willing to encourage campus stakeholders to learn about and adopt UDL in their respective settings.

In 2015, one of us approached campus leadership about engaging in a study to examine the use of closed captioning in online courses. The pitch included data on the continuing increase in the institution's online course offerings, the metrics used annually to evaluate public state universities by the state's board of governors (e.g., retention rate, graduation rate, timeliness to graduation), information on the application and value of UDL instructional practices, and statistics on the rising number of colleges and universities facing litigation about online course access for students with disabilities. Ultimately, leadership agreed to fund a study to examine the use of closed-captioning in a set of online campus courses (Kmetz et al., 2016). The study was eventually replicated and expanded in 2018 (Dukes et al., 2019), and in this later iteration both closed-captioning and interactive transcript use by students in online courses were examined.

In summary, numerous important findings came to light. First, student course performance improved in both studies (Dukes et al., 2019; Kmetz et al., 2016), and it is especially important to note that students who used the assistive technology tools at greater rates performed best (regardless of disability status). Second, faculty courses in which the tools were used were rated more highly by students on "respect and concern for students," "facilitation of learning," "communication of ideas and information," and "overall rating of instructor." The study team—made up of campus faculty in the colleges of education, arts and sciences, and business and including campus instructional designers—provided administration with a detailed report describing the positive study outcomes. The team also shared the findings in presentations on campus and at conferences nationally.

## Conclusion

As Behling and Posey (in press) summarized the results of interviews with 12 faculty members from across the United States, "The message was the same: UDL impacts the efficacy of teaching and learning among different populations and across different higher education levels." Universal design for learning offers instructors a pedagogical lens through which they can explore all elements (from planning to instruction to assessment) of their courses. They can consider ways to make a course's instructional methods and strategies more inclusive for students with a range of backgrounds and learning preferences and needs. This includes not only students with disabilities but also individuals who are English-language learners, adult learners, and/or otherwise post-traditional college students. UDL can reduce student anxiety and promote deeper and more consistent course participation. High expectations and academic rigor are maintained while the need for retroactive accommodations decreases.

## References

Behling. K., & Posey, A. (in press). UDL in American colleges & universities: A common pathway to success. In J. W. Madaus & L. L. Dukes III (Eds.), *Handbook of higher education and disability*. Edward Elgar.

Burgstahler, S. (2015). Preface. In S. Burgstahler (Ed.), *Universal design in higher education: Promising practices*. DO-IT, University of Washington. https://www.washington.edu/doit/preface-0

CAST. (2018). *Universal design for learning guidelines version 2.2*. http://udlguidelines.cast.org

Center for Universal Design. (2018). *About UD*. https://bit.ly/about-ud

Dukes L. L., III, Frechette, C., & Kmetz, K. (2019). *How closed captioning and interactive transcripts impact student learning*. University of South Florida St. Petersburg. https://www.3playmedia.com/wp-content/uploads/USFSP_3Play_FinalReport.pdf

Dukes L. L., III, Koorland, M. A., & Scott, S. S. (2009). Making blended instruction better: Integrating the principles of universal design for instruction into course design and delivery. *Action in Teacher Education, 31*(1), 38–48. https://doi.org/10.1080/01626620.2009.10463509

Evans, N. J., Broido, E. M., Brown, K. R., & Wilke, A. K. (2017). *Disability in higher education: A social justice approach*. Jossey Bass.

Higher Education Opportunity Act of 2008, Pub. L. No. 110-315, 122 Stat. 3078 (2008). https://www2.ed.gov/policy/highered/leg/hea08/index.html

Hope, J. (2021). Adopt framework that promotes collaboration for providing disability services. *Disability Compliance for Higher Education, 26*(11), 6–7. https://doi.org/10.1002/dhe.31081

Izzo, M. V., Murray, A., & Novak, J. (2008). The faculty perspective on universal design for learning. *Journal of Postsecondary Education and Disability, 21*(2), 60–72. https://www.ahead.org/professional-resources/publications/jped/archived-jped/jped-volume-21

Kmetz, K., Frechette, C., Dukes L.L., III, Emert, N., & Brodosi, D. (2016). Closed captioning matters: An investigation examining the value of closed captions for all students. *Journal of Postsecondary Education and Disability, 29*(3), 231–238. https://www.ahead.org/professional-resources/publications/jped/archived-jped/jped-volume-29

McGuire, J. M., Scott, S., & Shaw, S. F. (2006). Universal design and its applications in educational environments. *Remedial and Special Education, 27*(3), 166–175. https://doi.org/10.1177/07419325060270030501

Moore, E. J. (2017, November 10). But is it rigorous? *Innospire Education*. http://innospire.org/but-is-it-rigorous

National Center for Education Statistics. (2018, May). Table 311.10: Number and percentage distribution of students enrolled in postsecondary institutions, by level, disability status, and selected student characteristics: 2015–16 [Data table]. In *Digest of Education Statistics*. U.S. Department of Education, Institute of Education Sciences. https://nces.ed.gov/fastfacts/display.asp?id=60

National Center for Education Statistics. (2022, April 26). *A majority of college students with disabilities do not inform school, new NCES data show*. https://nces.ed.gov/whatsnew/press_releases/4_26_2022.asp

Poore-Pariseau, C. (2013). Universal design in assessments. In S. Burgstahler (Ed.), *Universal design in higher education: Promising practices*. DO-IT, University of Washington. https://www.washington.edu/doit/universal-design-assessments

Rao, K. (2013). Universal instructional design of online courses: Strategies to support non-traditional learners in postsecondary environments. In S. Burgstahler (Ed.), *Universal design in higher education: Promising practices*. DO-IT, University of Washington. https://www.washington.edu/doit/universal-instructional-design-online-courses-strategies-support-non-traditional-learners

Rao, K., & Tanners, A. (2011). Curb cuts in cyberspace: Universal instructional design for online courses. *Journal of Postsecondary Education and Disability, 24*(3), 223–247. https://www.ahead.org/professional-resources/publications/jped/archived-jped/jped-volume-24

Scott, S. S., McGuire, J. M., & Foley, T. E. (2003). Universal design for instruction: A framework for anticipating and responding to disability and other diverse needs in the college classroom. *Equity & Excellence in Education, 36*(1), 40–49. https://doi.org/10.1080/10665680303502

Shaewitz, D., & Crandall, J. R. (2020, October 19). Higher education's challenge: Disability inclusion on campus. *Higher Education Today.* https://www.higheredtoday.org/2020/10/19/higher-educations-challenge-disability-inclusion-campus

Silver, P., Bourke, A., & Strehorn, K. C. (1998). Universal instructional design in higher education: An approach for inclusion. *Equity & Excellence in Education, 31*(2), 47–51. https://doi.org/10.1080/1066568980310206

Smith, F. G. (2012). Analyzing a college course that adheres to the universal design for learning (UDL) framework. *Journal of the Scholarship of Teaching and Learning, 12*(3), 31–61. https://eric.ed.gov/?id=EJ992116

Tarconish, E., Taconet, A., Madaus, J., Gelbar, N., Dukes L. L., III, & Faggella-Luby, M. (2021). The spectrum of disability documentation requirements at twelve institutions: A thematic analysis. *Learning Disabilities: A Multidisciplinary Journal, 26*(2), 43–56. https://doi.org/10.18666/LDMJ-2021-V26-I2-11121

Tyng, C. M., Amin, H. U., Saad, M. N. M., & Malik, A. S. (2017). The influences of emotion on learning and memory. *Frontiers in Psychology, 8.* https://doi.org/10.3389/fpsyg.2017.01454

CHAPTER 8

# A Conversation About Disability Law With Paul Grossman and Jamie Axelrod

Michael Berger

***Paul Grossman***, *JD, is an active member of the State Bar of California and the Disability Rights Bar Association. Currently, he is executive counsel for the Association on Higher Education and Disability (AHEAD). Grossman has been a civil rights lawyer for nearly 50 years, participating in the development and growth of civil rights protections based on race, national origin, disability, sex, and sexual orientation. He taught disability law at Hastings College of Law for more than 20 years and remains a guest lecturer and legal advisor on postsecondary student disability law across the country.*

***Jamie Axelrod***, *MS, is the director of disability resources at Northern Arizona University and a former president of AHEAD. He is a sought-after speaker on topics related to disability access and higher education. Axelrod has served as cochair of Northern Arizona University's Commission on Disability Access and Design and AHEAD's board* of directors, as well as on the board of directors for the Coalition for Disability Access in Health Science Education.

**How has the COVID-19 pandemic affected the interpretation and enforcement of disability law by administrators and faculty in colleges and universities?**

**PAUL GROSSMAN (PG):** The COVID-19 pandemic has increased the potential number of persons with disabilities who will need the protections of America's two primary federal disability antidiscrimination laws: the Section 504 of the Rehabilitation Act of 1973 (hereafter Section 504) and the Americans with Disabilities Act of 1990, as amended (hereafter the ADA).

With COVID comes long COVID. Students with that condition, who are experiencing both physical and cognitive impairments, will be coming to campus. Disability advocates are keeping a lookout for any litigation that will address whether long COVID is a disability covered by disability antidiscrimination laws. There is already federal guidance, suggesting that long COVID well may be covered, but how it is diagnosed and documented is much less clear. On a case-by-case basis, some shorter-term but intense forms of COVID or comorbid conditions may also qualify for coverage, but more decisions and agency guidance, likely first from the U.S. Equal Employment Opportunity Commission (EEOC), also will be needed.

Taking a broader look, I think it is reasonable to predict that COVID is likely to alter the mix of disabilities that will typically be present on campus—likely extenuating the existing trend toward more students with an anxiety disorder and/or depression. Most interesting to me, COVID has and will continue to challenge every postsecondary institution to reconsider the range of accommodations it can or should provide: their feasibility, the impact of technology, as well as which new requested accommodations do or do not entail an undue burden or a fundamental alteration.

There will be both new challenges and new opportunities for innovation. As the U.S. Supreme Court has pointed out, the fact that an academic or other practice has been done in one certain way for many years does not mean that it is the only way it may be done in the future (*PGA Tour, Inc. v. Martin*, 2001; *Southeastern Community College v. Davis*, 1979).

Unfortunately, it is rather predictable that, as there are more people—including students with disabilities—who request unprecedented, innovative accommodations, there will be more requests that are denied. Consequently, there will be more disability complaints filed with the EEOC, U.S. Department of Justice (DOJ), and U.S. Department of Education Office for Civil Rights (OCR) and in the federal courts. As a student of U.S. civil rights judicial history, I foresee this uptick leading to opinions and rulings that seek to push back against this trend, making success by persons with disabilities who use the courts less likely and less appealing as a strategy for recompensing disability discrimination. This trend, when combined with recent examples of Supreme Court attacks on use of the courts to secure civil rights, makes for a bad brew. Politics, and not COVID, is the main driver here. But the number of cases COVID will generate, along with the agency and judicial resources it requires, does not help. Consequently, I am coming to a diminished degree of faith in the courts as a tool for civil rights enforcement. The disability community may soon come to learn that the only way to get a disability rights boost from COVID will be to bring our increased numbers to bear as a force for social justice and legislative action, particularly if we can build alliances with other organizations that represent people whose rights are also under attack in the current Supreme Court.

Social justice movements may exert themselves in many ways and settings but almost always include America's colleges and universities. Administrators and leaders should expect diversity, equity, and inclusion (DEI) coalitions that will include students with disabilities seeking new forms of accommodation, raising both pedagogical and legal questions.

***After the COVID-19 pandemic, what questions are access and disability services (ADS) offices dealing with?***

**PG:** As my colleagues and consulting partners Jamie, Mary Lee Vance, and I tour the country teaching postsecondary student disability law, the single most common question raised with us is this: How should postsecondary institutions respond to requests from students with disabilities for accommodations in the form of distance/remote learning? This is a primary example of unprecedented innovation in accommodation. If you look at employment cases and recent OCR letters, it's clear that the courts and the OCR have made a shift. The shift is not so much to favor work-at-home or distance-learning accommodations as it is in favor of individualized, diligent consideration of requests for this form of accommodation. Clearly, colleges and universities can no longer dismiss such a request out of hand (see, e.g., OCR, 2021a, 2021b).

In our classes, we regularly teach the importance of decision-making processes. The first process we emphasize is the interactive process, and the second one is the fundamental alteration process, also referred to as the *Wynne v. Tufts* process (*Wynne v. Tufts University School of Medicine*, 1991/1992).

Let's discuss the interactive process as it might pertain to a request for an accommodation as some form of distance learning. First, the student must have a disability that requires distance learning as a necessary and effective accommodation. There should be a logical nexus between the student's substantial limitations that are owing to a disability and the requested accommodation. Further, during the interactive process, it's quite important to get clarity over what the student means by the phrase *distance or remote learning*. Jamie and I have broken distance learning down into three different models.

Using the legal analytical precepts commonly applied in postsecondary student disability law, each model is sufficiently distinct as to lead to different outcomes whether the accommodation request need or need not be granted.

**Model 1: Some students just want the college to turn on a camera so they can watch a conventional (i.e., brick-and-mortar) class.** Such students don't want or need anything more than that. Raising an undue burden defense to that kind of accommodation is now much less likely to be successful because, throughout the course of the COVID-19 pandemic, colleges were doing this and more. Colleges now know how to do it, and they know what software and hardware to use. As no change in a course offering, course content, or teaching style is contemplated, this model is also least likely to raise a fundamental alteration question. Nonetheless, one may exist for several reasons. Sometimes, remote learning is simply incompatible with the essential objectives of a course, as might occur in a laboratory or clinical setting. If a large percentage of the students wanted this form of accommodation, this model also might require a fundamental alteration review due to concerns over a loss of a critical mass in the number of students engaged in interaction with each other or with the teacher.

I participated in something very similar to Model 1 for over 20 years of teaching as an adjunct professor of disability law. Very little was expected of me to implement this form of accommodation. The law school had the audio hardware and software to make this form of accommodation readily available. The particular software that my college used made available, online, my PowerPoints in sync with the audio recording of my presentation. This feature made the online instruction more effective.

As far as I could tell, the administrative burden on the college was small. I was visited by an audio/visual technician once at the start of each semester. To address privacy expectations, the administration put a sign on the classroom door stating that my class would be recorded, and then they went ahead and did it.

I had several students who were medically fragile wounded warriors who almost never made it to my live class. When I asked the ADS office, I could determine whether they saw my classes online. These veterans came in twice during the semester to meet me in person for office hours. But that was it. Otherwise, they were participating from a veterans affairs facility.

These students did well on their examinations. That and what I learned from them during their office visits was all I needed to know or be concerned with. If all or most of my students were online, there would be other important considerations, but with just a few students attending remotely, their remote attendance did not impact the nature of the class in any material way. Given the nature of my class, I doubt that, today, my college could raise a legitimate undue burden or fundamental alteration objection to the few students who needed to attend it remotely, using Model 1.

**Model 2: A student wants to remotely participate in a traditional class.** Here the considerations seem pretty much the same as for Model 1. As more technology, more attention by the instructor, and possibly more personnel may be involved, there is a slightly more compelling undue administrative or financial burden argument, but one that would likely fail given widespread use of this model during the pandemic. Whether there could exist a legitimate fundamental alteration objection by the college, I would recommend it be addressed as case-by-case determination. The nature and objectives of the class are likely to be key considerations with regard to granting or denying a request for this form of accommodation. Again, a lab or clinical class, a class that necessarily includes fine, detailed personal observation, would certainly raise fundamental alteration considerations. On the other hand, in some instances, where the key objection to Model 1 is the absence of participation by the student, with regard to participation Model 2 may be harder to object to on fundamental alteration grounds. As in the case of Model 1, a critical mass concern may also be pertinent.

**Model 3: A student wants an online class, provided either in real time or asynchronously.** It is only logical that an online course, taught with online technologies with teaching modalities and assignments appropriate to online instruction, will provide the greatest online value. However, this is likely to be a materially different kind of instruction from what takes place in the traditional classroom. Consequently, this accommodation model is more likely to raise an authentic undue burden consideration and even more likely a fundamental alteration question.

Although given the pandemic experiences, it appears that it will be hard for colleges and universities to successfully raise an undue burden objection to Models 1 or 2. Model 3 might require additional equipment and enough additional training, new curricula, and human resources to posit an economic or administrative undue burden argument.

More important, even though this model was widely used during the COVID-19 pandemic, in my opinion, its use now may still raise a legitimate fundamental alteration objection and defense. During the pandemic, medical necessity and the direct threat of COVID contagion forced colleges and universities to go online. The choices were between no instruction and remote instruction. These are no longer the only choices. Use during the pandemic does not mean that, in any particular academic domain, online instruction was as effective as in-person instruction. Though classes such as chemistry and engineering laboratories were adapted to online instruction, putting a lab or clinical class online is logically distinguishable from putting online a large-scale history class. Nor does it mean that all professors/instructors have teaching styles and curricular materials that are readily adaptable to the online environment. Further, there is now evidence that, for postsecondary students, under some circumstances, the effectiveness of online instruction is not the same as instruction in the traditional setting.

Under Model 3, in some instances the difference between a traditional class and an online class may be so great that the college or university could persuasively argue that it is not being asked to make a course accessible to students with disabilities but that it is being asked to create a whole new course. Creating an online class may best serve the needs of some students, but there remains a legitimate argument that under the fundamental alteration doctrine, it may be something beyond what is required by Section 504 or the ADA. Of course, an institution that wishes to best address the needs of most of its students would offer multiple sections of the same subject through both traditional classes and Model 3—a universal design (UD) approach.

So, I return to my theme: The devil is in the details. In response to a request for remote learning as an accommodation, the only sure way to remain in compliance is to give the request an individualized, diligent, and thorough consideration process. Often this will necessitate consideration of the student, the objectives of the course, the nature of the instruction, and more, including what the student means by the term *online instruction*.

**JAMIE AXELROD (JA):** Three years ago, a student might have said, "Hey! I want to participate in my program remotely." ADS would have said, "No, that's not reasonable; that's not what this program is. We have other online programs. This is an in-person program." But then we did do it for 2 years during the COVID-19 pandemic. There are people who will say, "Yes, we have been doing this, but let's look a little bit more closely at where it's appropriate." I think faculty are a little more averse to online teaching, and many didn't like it. If they weren't online instructors, many of them worked at an institution that offered some type of hybrid model in which half the students were in the room and the other half were participating remotely via Zoom—for example, 25 students in class and 25 participating remotely—and it took faculty a while to figure out how to do that. It might happen that with a class of 50, there will be 49 people in front of me and only one person online. I must keep the flow going and make sure that I'm engaging with that one online person. That's not an easy thing to do. I think that bears some real consideration based on the class and whether that hybrid model would be a fundamental alteration or an undue burden. When this issue comes up, administrators may say, "Let's not just dismiss this. Let's think about it. Where and how can hybrid be effective?" There's this idea that we're going to have to look at this on a case-by-case basis and understand the circumstance and the situation.

Different schools are going to use remote participation differently. At Northern Arizona University (NAU), we said that we were going hybrid in 2020. We outfitted every single classroom on campus to be able to do hybrid live-streaming classes. We viewed this initiative as a chance for innovation at our institution. We learned that we could deliver education this way, and we're going to open new programs. I don't know what small, private, elite institutions did; they may have set up only four remote equipped classrooms. Other institutions may say, "This this is not who we are or what we're about, and we're going to go back to in-person."

Remote and hybrid participation is not the only COVID impact. Colleges and universities are seeing many more requests for private residence hall housing for students who are concerned about exposure over the long term. Institutions may be seeing more requests from students, who simply have some substantial anxiety or other mental health conditions, saying they need accommodations for COVID because they're concerned about exposure and with whom they're living and sharing their space. There are questions about masking protocols. If I'm a student and I'm severely immunocompromised, can I ask for an accommodation for my classes that requires everyone to wear a mask versus requesting them to wear a mask?

There are all kinds of big questions, but COVID has opened administrators' eyes to the idea that these more complex questions can't simply be put aside. We need to really think these things through. These issues are just going to continue. The idea that people are willing to sit down and consider them in a rational way and come to a reasoned decision is a good thing because in that process lots of potential approaches or solutions can be identified. They might be something reasonable to do or something to consider in specific circumstances, or, in fact, may enhance the academic experience for the entire campus. The people at the table include folks from campus health services, accessibility services or the ADA coordinator, and facilities. Decisions start at a higher level but are fed by information from the ground. It's not only students who bring forth questions and requests and concerns but faculty and staff as well. My ADS office happens to do employee accommodations as well, so we're not just getting remote requests or safety requests or masking requests from students—we're also getting those requests from faculty and staff.

**PG:** All of Jamie's examples present real conundrums to be resolved. At this very moment, disability law is undergoing a lot of change. Many questions that need addressing have been in the pipeline for a while, but COVID has created additional questions and upped the importance of others that predate the pandemic. I highly anticipate that there are going to be legal challenges, new precedents set, and new guidance forthcoming in the forms of regulation amendments and clarifications by DOJ as well as OCR interpretations and policies. In light of COVID, in the postsecondary context, I am hoping that these changes will address accommodations for persons with immunosuppression, accommodations for anxiety and depression, accommodations that pertain to modification of attendance and midterm disenrollment policies, and accommodations that remove some of the disincentives for students who should be taking a reduced courseload.

As part of this period of change, not too far down the road, the disability community will need to carefully study and respond to proposed amendments to the regulations implementing Section 504 and various provisions of the ADA. It is entirely reasonable to expect that, as a whole, these regulation revisions will be a positive development, expanding, clarifying, making more effective, and updating the current regulations. Of course, some changes may be unwise, inconsistent with what our students need, or simply silent on questions that should be resolved through concrete guidance. In all these circumstances, when the regulations are up for public comment, the post-COVID era's disability community and postsecondary educators must speak up and let their views and comments be known.

COVID has certainly increased the number of people who will need the protections of Section 504 and the ADA. Inevitably, the number of people needing accommodations, including on college campuses, will also increase. Those persons with disabilities who feel they have been denied their rights will be turning to OCR, DOJ, advocacy organizations, and the courts to invoke their rights under Section 504 and the ADA. At the very same time, civil rights protections in general and disability rights in particular are under steady attenuation in the federal courts, including in the U.S. Supreme Court. The issues disposed of by the courts often take place behind a curtain, as subtle, esoteric, and highly legalistic matters. Nonetheless, these precedents must not be allowed to flourish; rather, they need to be explained, exposed, and redressed politically and legislatively.

Unfortunately, there is no shortage of examples of actual and impending attacks on our civil rights. As I seek to expose what the Supreme Court majority is doing, two examples immediately come to my mind. The first example concerns a successful global attack on the regulatory authority of federal government. The second concerns an impending attack on an essential way of addressing in court broad-scale disability discrimination.

**Example 1.** Generally, over time, the federal government has gained an increasingly effective role in protecting civil rights. This is owed in considerable degree to the Chevron Doctrine, which strongly presumes that when Congress delegates to various federal agencies the authority to write regulations implementing a law, those regulations are a legitimate, enforceable interpretation of that law (*Chevron U.S.A., Inc. v. National Resources Defense Council, Inc.*, 1984). The importance of the power of federal regulations has been recognized by the disability rights community from its inception, as reflected in the famous "504 Sit-In at 50 United Nations Plaza" that began on April 5, 1977, when disability rights leaders and advocates occupied a federal building in San Francisco for 26 days to force the Carter administration to issue the first regulations implementing Section 504 (Shapiro, 2002).

In a recent decision, a majority of the Supreme Court created a powerful exception to the Chevron Doctrine, removing it from application whenever the court is faced with a "major question." This exception, one that comes without precedent, will make it much easier for defendants to successfully attack the viability, legitimacy, and enforceability of federal regulations as well as agency interpretations of their own regulations (*West Virginia v. Environmental Protection Agency*, 2022). Thus, for example, a college, rather than having to explain why it denied a deaf student interpreting services, may attack the regulation that requires such services in the first place (e.g., Academic Adjustments, 2000). If such an attack were successful, no deaf students attending college in the United States would be required to receive interpreting services. Of course, Congress could pass, and a president could sign, a new law reinstating an interpreting requirement *if* it could reach a consensus on such a piece of legislation.

**Example 2.** This example concerns disparate impact (see below), a critically important theory of liability for addressing certain forms of disability discrimination. It has also been used regarding race, national origin, and sex. The application of disparate impact theory to disability discrimination has recently come under attack and is almost certainly headed for review in the Supreme Court. Disability discrimination defendant institutions, including CVS drugstores and the Los Angeles Community College District (LACCD), have argued in the 9th Circuit Court of Appeals that disparate impact as a tool for proving disability discrimination is not authorized by Section 504 or the ADA (*CVS Pharmacy, Inc. v. Doe*, 2020, 2021; *Payan v. Los Angeles Community College District*, 2021). In the CVS matter, at least four justices of the Supreme Court have already signaled an interest in resolving this issue. An opinion by the court, addressing this challenge, seems inevitable. As one of those esoteric, legalistic matters that I have mentioned earlier, this very troubling development requires more explanation.

Disparate impact is the primary tool that plaintiffs and advocates use to attack systemic benign discrimination. The term *benign*, in this instance, means without an intent to discriminate. If disability law were simply to be confined to purposeful, individual discrimination, requirements would be of almost no value. Using a current real example, suppose you have a student who is blind and that student complains to the DOJ, OCR, or a private council, such as the National Federation for the Blind (NFB), "I will never meet the math graduation requirement of the college that I am attending because all of the quizzes are online and the quiz website is inaccessible to me" (*Payan v. Los Angeles Community College District*, 2021). Such a plaintiff/student could seek to redress this claim in one of two ways: First, OCR or a court order could decide that the blind student is entitled to an individual accommodation. Maybe the student could be assigned an alternative set of quizzes, formatted in braille. This would be a feasible incremental solution, addressing the immediate needs of the complaining student—albeit even that student will not be provided an identical opportunity or experience compared with that of sighted students.

By contrast, using disparate impact analysis, the student's claims would merit a more effective remedy, one requiring the college, going forward, to ensure that all the courseware it purchases will be accessible to blind students who use commonly available adaptive technology. The college could no longer rely on an ad hoc approach to compliance, waiting to fix problems only when a student complains (*United States v. Regents of the University of California,* 2022).

All of this is by way of explaining why disparate impact, an intent-free form of proof with a potential for yielding high-impact outcomes, is a tool that the disability community cannot afford to lose. And we know it! Here is where the story turns interesting and instructive. You might ask why, if, in 2021, the Supreme Court agreed to hear the CVS matter, the court has not yet issued an opinion. The immediate answer is that, under well-organized and persistent pressure from customers, both CVS and LACCD were persuaded to abandon pursuit of their attacks upon disparate impact before the court.

In the case of LACCD, every type of disability group repeatedly put pressure on the board of trustees, including advocacy organizations, civil rights attorneys, parents, administrators, union officials, faculty, the plaintiffs, student organizations, and so on. Of all the parties who petitioned the board, it was evident to me, as a witness, that the party that really mattered was students, the "customers" of LACCD. Particularly at an entity with an elected board, students with disabilities represented a uniquely legitimate and persuasive voice for change. Students in wheelchairs or students with severe speech impairments showed up and communicated, "You can't do this to me! How can you educate me, award me a diploma, and then destroy my right to be free from discrimination in the workplace?"

The COVID-19 pandemic has not been a quiescent time for the law. America's civil rights protections, including disability rights, sit vulnerable to a slow form of suffocation. I have given two examples, but I can think of at least three more and, not far down the road, it is highly likely that another entity, less vulnerable to customer pressure, will petition the Supreme Court for the opportunity to seek the elimination of disparate impact. Clearly, the disability community, expanded in size and potential influence by COVID, has its work cut out for itself. We must rededicate ourselves to broad alliances across the complete range of disabilities as well as the full spectrum of diverse communities, including those regarding race, sex, sexual orientation, and national origin. We must pay close attention to every chance there may be for others to diminish our rights. We must spend the time and energy necessary to oppose at the ballot box and in the courts those who would diminish our rights.

At the same time, institutions of higher education have their own responsibilities to protect and advance civil rights. Faculty cannot profess to be committed to DEI and fail to understand that students with disabilities are a legitimate element of diversity; as to equity, since adoption of the ADA, little has improved with regard to income, employment, housing, etc. And inclusion remains a historic and continuing key objective of the disability community.

Especially on campus, paternalism for the disability community is no more likely to be a successful tool for gaining equality than it has been for any other community. This is true going all the way back to the 504 sit-in (see, e.g., Carmel, 2020) and forward to what was recently accomplished with CVS and LACCD. The disability community can effectively assert itself to fend off attacks and bring about positive change. But this cannot happen unless individuals with disabilities are admitted to and effectively accommodated in colleges and universities! Members of this community need to become teachers, policy wonks, public servants, politicians, lawyers, judges, etc. As is true for every diverse community in the United States, nothing should be decided without input from community members.

***How can the stakeholders, as outlined in the framework, learn about the legal requirements on disability?***

**JA:** It's not that simple to understand legal obligations, and it is critical to spend some time becoming familiar with the regulations. Training is one approach for students. We could offer a course on campus in one of our departments about the regulations, whether it's through disability studies or disability studies and history cross-listed with "Exploring Civil Rights"—there is a section in that class that covers disability rights, how they came to be, and what legislation and methods are available through the law. In fact, we have developed a new curriculum in which we're doing more of that in our liberal studies requirements. There's a great opportunity for students, parents, and faculty members to learn about the law through our website by posting short modules, and we would make them open to the public.

But I really feel the best way for people to learn is when they have two or three hours of engagement with these ideas, including with the history of the disability rights movement. The disability rights movement owes so much to the other civil rights movements that if there's an interesting and compelling way to tie those connections into the civil rights movements in the United States, then that really attracts people.

**PG:** I am in complete accord with Jamie. I would just add that we have recently contributed to the book *Laws, Policies, and Processes: Tools for Postsecondary Student Accommodation* (Vance & Thompson, 2023). I am confident that for faculty and administrators interested in this topic area, this book would make a worthwhile investment in a solid foundation in this area of the law.

Two other sources to consider are the websites of many of the advocacy organizations and professional associations, like the NFB, the Bazelon Center (mental health), the Disability Rights Education and Defense Fund, Disability Rights Advocates, the National Association of the Deaf, and the Association on Higher Education and Disability. There are many more.

In addition, there are government agencies and sponsored entities like the EEOC, DOJ, and OCR, as well as the ADA Disability and Business Technical Assistance Centers, all of which have websites or "reading rooms." I find all these resources useful. Many of the government organizations will also provide guidance by phone, and some, especially the OCR, will provide free technical assistance training on campus or by webinar.

***Have you seen disabilities included in the diversity discussion?***

**JA:** A critical issue for chief diversity officers and colleges and universities is the inclusion of disability in the institutional definition of *diversity* and what that means for programming on campus. I'm lucky to be at an institution that has had disability as part of its definition of *diversity* for many years. When we apply to the National Science Foundation or other federal agencies for grants, a comment that we regularly get, especially if they're diversity-related grants, is that you are one of the only applicants who includes disability in your application. Including diversity makes your application strong.

**PG:** A confrontation concerning diversity and disabilities took place this last year in Los Angeles, where a group of protesters confronted the chancellor and the board of governors and said, "You're publishing all these data and information and training, and taking so much leadership with regard to DEI without including people with disabilities whatsoever," threw in their face their five top documents about their plans for the future, and said, "Well, disability is not even mentioned here." And then a group of disability advocates including myself went on to point out, "If you want to help these other groups, you had better recognize that within those groups are a lot of people with disabilities, and that's why they're not succeeding—and if you don't start a dialogue with UD solutions, you're going to waste some of the best ways of raising your graduation rates." And so, they changed the theme officially from DEI to DEIA: disability, equity, inclusion, and access. And understand that this is a system of two million students.

Do I think that students with disabilities are getting their fair share of attention now? No, I don't, but I think it's a lot better than it was a year ago. A lot of that pressure was brought by dissolved student services directors in California. They're tenured, they're organized, they're unionized, and they can raise issues like this, and they do. But there's a part to that that I think is really important: disability community members are advocates for inclusion in a campus definition of *diversity*.

Diversity is not a zero-sum game! The disability community needs to highlight the interdependence and intersectionality of all the diverse communities on campus. In the first place, there is no community that does not include individuals with disabilities. For example, an African American female student with ADHD (attention-deficit/hyperactivity disorder) will benefit just as much from accommodations as a White male student. Further, as Jamie and I have pointed out, it is important to make clear that the disability movement has been and is an intersectional movement.

Coming from a different angle, the disability community needs to emphasize the value of UD, where accommodative practices are deployed to the advantage of all students. For example, real-time captioning makes lectures accessible to students with hearing impairments, but it also advantages students whose first language is not English or anyone who just happens to momentarily lose concentration. A deliberate choice to adopt UD practices can be a force for pedagogical innovation, one that "raises all boats" and one whereby everyone becomes invested in a college that reliably delivers those practices.

I've had a lot of experience with faculty training. Over time, I have noticed a large difference in the numbers of administrators, faculty, and staff who show up to hear my presentation. The difference is not the size of the institution but its leadership. How strong of a message is the chancellor, provost, or president sending about disability rights being a legitimate component of civil rights? Are the leaders committed to compliance with Section 504 and the ADA? I always find disconcerting those institutions that make annual attendance at Title IX training a mandatory element of employment but implement no similar requirement with regard to disability, race, or national origin.

**JA:** Here's the other thing that I would offer: training of faculty and staff. About 95% of those folks you train are going to be in complete agreement that this is the right thing to do—that is, that students with disabilities have rights. We should be taking appropriate steps to ensure their equitable access. But when it comes time for faculty to do something to make that a reality, or maybe do something *differently* to make that a reality, there can be pushback: "But it is not consistent with how I teach this class, and I need to make this modification." They're on board and they're in agreement, but when it comes time to take steps to effectuate, some are not interested, or they're too busy, or it's too difficult. Very few faculty are deniers of learning disabilities today, but there is still work required to make materials accessible so that students can access them. We need to have structures available on campus to help faculty meet those requirements and obligations.

*From the standpoint of disability law, what are the best practical ideas and processes that the accessibility office could offer students with disabilities to be successful?*

**JA:** It's really important to ensure that the office is engaging with students to understand the types of experiences and barriers they're having in the classroom and in the campus community. Some of that's going to be highly individualized, and some will also involve engaging with the entire campus community. We have to be thoughtful about programs, the campus community, and the educational, curricular, and cocurricular experiences to make sure we're providing access for as many people as we possibly can from the get-go.

In working with the campus community to develop a culture of inclusion, we must recognize that students with disabilities are part of the student population when we're designing classes, when we're selecting courseware, when we're looking at materials for the course, and when we're designing physical spaces for cocurricular programs. Can we do that with the recognition that these students are part of the community? Are we thinking about them up front as we design these environments, as opposed to trying to retrofit things and make individualized modifications after the fact? The more we create a culture of avoiding that type of "benign neglect" and ensuring that these students get the message that they are part of the population, the more we can plan for and design right from the beginning with students with disabilities and with all students in mind. And then the disability resources office can focus more on the specific circumstances that require more complex modification or intense work to make sure that access is effective. For many of our students, if we just designed thoughtfully, many of their needs would be met.

Joe Madaus and colleagues at the University of Connecticut recently studied predictors of success for students with disabilities (Newman et al., 2020). This study took the data set of students who were in special education in K–12 and then followed them longitudinally as they went to postsecondary institutions. It asked, "Did you go to [the] disability resources [office] and self-disclose? Did you get accommodations? Did you succeed in school? Did you progress? Did you drop out?" The interesting finding was that the best predictor of success for those students was whether they engaged with universally available academic supports on campus—whether they self-identified or didn't self-identify and whether they used accommodations. Students who didn't self-identify, didn't use accommodations, and didn't use academic supports performed poorly. Students who self-identified and got accommodations did better. And those students, regardless of whether they self-identified or got accommodations, who used those universally available academic supports did the best.

For example, if the tutors at our writing center know how to teach a student with dyslexia how to write, that's going to be much more effective. And if the instructors at the math tutoring center know that students with ADHD can put in mental effort for only 15 minutes at a time, then they can break up the math with other activities. Those students are going to be much more effectively served. So, although accommodations are still important, if we can make the universal academic supports usable by students with disabilities, that effort will have the greatest impact.

**PG:** Jamie's comments are another argument for UD and support services. Nonetheless, I am a touch concerned about implementation of Jamie's recommendation. My concern is about whether the tutoring service or the writing center or the math center etc. will have professionals with the skills and training to deal effectively with students with learning disabilities, for example. I've taught writing to those with dyslexia for years. I don't remotely teach it the same way that a writing center would teach it, and so universality here would be really good, but there needs to be recognition of the level of training that it would require, and that, of course, would necessitate a commitment by upper administration to fund. And, by the way, teaching math is a whole separate endeavor.

**JA:** Here's another great example: Our campus uses an add-in for Blackboard and Canvas called Ally, which is a software accessibility checker and tool for faculty but also gives students direct access to alternative-format materials. It's automated, so it's not perfect, but it's right there, and for administrators like me, I can look at the accessibility of our course shells and the usage of the tool. We are an institution of 30,000 students and serve about 2,000 students at the disability resources office. Maybe 150 of those students *require* alternative-format materials to ensure their access to course materials. When I looked at the download usage from the alternative formats in Ally last academic year, there were 119,000 downloads of documents in alternative formats by 19,000 unique individuals on campus. Those high usage numbers say something about the benefits of those types of systems being available. This is an example of widespread self-initiated adoption of an available support and UD.

*Can you share some insight about the enforcement of disability and discrimination law?*

**JA:** The major theme of enforcement actions by the OCR and the DOJ has been process. Are you engaging in appropriate processes? Do you have appropriate processes set up to use to make good decisions? And are you following up with those?

The OCR doesn't often make substantive decisions about accommodation determinations if the school demonstrates due diligence, so they won't say, for example, "You should have approved that accommodation as reasonable." However, they will comment if you didn't give due diligence consideration. If a faculty member contacted your office about a fundamental alteration, and within 30 minutes of that notification the student is told they are denied the accommodation, that's a problem—because it seems that a thoughtful process was not followed. I think these are the types of issues that come up regularly. It's about process.

**PG:** So many colleges take what I would call an ad hoc approach to compliance: Don't think about it, don't worry about it, and don't plan for it until a problem comes up, and then fix it. For example, a student comes in and says, "I can't use this software." If that happens, then the institution will take care of *that* student. The material will be converted, then a reader assigned, or a workaround may be considered. This approach takes too long—in the life of a student, 3 weeks is an eternity. An ad hoc approach to achieving or maintaining compliance treats the accessibility issue on a case-by-case basis rather than systemically.

The opposite of ad hoc is to not purchase any software until you know it's either accessible or it's easily structured for a workaround. By folding accessibility into your acquisition procedures and processes, you may well end up identifying and purchasing a different and more effective software.

Let's look at this question from the 30,000-foot level and address compliance problems globally. I often wonder if administrators and faculty understand that noncompliance with Section 504 and the ADA can easily be an incredibly expensive proposition—certainly as expensive as noncompliance with Title IX. When you don't devote enough attention to compliance, when you try an ad hoc approach to compliance, you can easily find yourself in court or on the wrong side of OCR. Even when colleges settle claims of disability discrimination, they may have to commit to undertaking disruptive and expensive corrective actions as well as pay legal and expert fees running into the millions of dollars. When settlement is not feasible, under Section 504 a college may find all of its millions of dollars in federal financial assistance in jeopardy—even capped, suspended, or terminated. Under the ADA a college may end up with years of federal court monitoring, fines from the DOJ, damages owed to students, and expensive "injunctive" forms of relief—for example, reconstructing most of an inaccessible football stadium.

Explaining all the tools available to prevent this kind of predicament is hard to state succinctly, but a few stand out:

- training for administrators, faculty, and staff on the basics of Section 504 and the ADA, with authoritative, clear guidance as to when and where to turn for help.
- knowing which processes and procedures to use, and when. If a faculty member believes that an accommodation authorized by a disability support services office entails a fundamental alteration, then what should happen next?
- an independent monitor of compliance, such as an ADA director.
- an effective process for receiving feedback from students, including a fair and effective grievance process.

**JA:** Another question that arises is: Did the institution engage with a student in a good-faith effort to try to create access, or did they just push this student to the side? When schools show that they engage with students, interact with students, try to find solutions, work on difficult problems, and make good-faith efforts to address the issues and concerns that arise, then those efforts don't go unappreciated in the end by the courts. But when the institution delays, blow things off, drops the ball, or doesn't follow up, then these would seem to be inconsistent with good faith and engagement with the student.

So here is another interesting consideration for student affairs educators and disability office professionals: My staff and I were recently reviewing a case decided in a U.S. District Court in February 2022. The student is appealing, so I don't know where that sits, but when was the student at the school and in the program? This complaint was filed around 2014 to 2016, and they are still in active litigation.

When students need to take that ultimate step to go to court, their concerns and issues aren't being resolved in the courts until 8 years after they were a student. Whom does that help? Instead, institutions must be intentional along with being responsive in meeting their legal obligations. That intentional piece is really critical, and in so many schools that's the thing that's missing: intentionality.

**PG:** Sometimes, accommodation requirements can be inconvenient or time consuming. They may entail unsettling change and additional expense for a college or university—in particular, institutions that employ an ad hoc attitude toward compliance. *But* federal regulations regarding accommodations do not require lowering academic standards or curtailing academic discretion, nor do they lead to inferior instructional processes.

All those apprehensions that pertain to academic integrity, standards, and discretion are without legal support. The first postsecondary disability case to hit the Supreme Court, *Southeastern Community College v. Davis* (1979), concerned a deaf licensed vocational nurse who sought admission to a registered nurse (RN) program. There was no question that Davis was academically qualified; however, she depended on lipreading, and at the time everyone in the surgical theater wore a mask. The college made a very comprehensive search for how to accommodate Davis in the surgical clinical training. None could be found. As surgical skills were "essential" to the RN program of instruction, the court concluded that Southeastern could refuse to admit Davis to its program without violating Section 504. The court, taking into account all that the college had done to identify a way to accommodate Davis, found the college entitled to its academic judgment about whom to admit. Early on, the Supreme Court made clear that "essential" or "fundamental" program requirements need not give way to the need for an accommodation.

A very similar standard is provided in the 504 regulations. "Academic requirements that the recipient [college] can demonstrate are essential to the instruction being pursued by such student or to any directly related licensing requirement will not be regarded as discriminatory within the meaning of this section" (Academic Adjustments, 2000, § 104.44[a]). I caution, however, that those faculty and colleges that wish to rest on this regulation had best read it carefully. This provision presents an "affirmative defense." It places the burden on the school "to demonstrate" that a refused accommodation would interfere with an "essential" program or "licensing requirement." Jamie and I teach that to meet this burden, the school should follow the steps taken by Tufts University School of Medicine in *Wynne v. Tufts University School of Medicine* (1991/1992).

The case concerned a medical student with an inconsistent academic record. According to a psychoeducational evaluation conducted by Tufts, owing to his learning disability, Wynne did poorly on multiple-choice examinations but better on essay examinations. Quite logically, going forward, as an accommodation, Wynne wanted all of his examinations in essay format.

Wynne did not envision that his request would excuse him from mastering the same knowledge and skills as all the other medical students. Denied his request, Wynne proceeded to federal court, alleging disability discrimination.

Originally, Tufts defended itself by asserting that its decision was academic in nature and the court, based on academic freedom principles, should defer to Tuft's decision. The court did not agree with this argument. Tufts had not met its demonstration burden. Consequently, Tufts was ordered to reconsider or justify its decision in a more careful and diligent, deliberative fashion. Based on the *Wynne* decision and the many judicial and OCR decisions that follow it, I would describe the demonstration duty as met when a school

- convenes a committee of relevant administrators and faculty, possibly including a DSS representative.

- charges the committee to carefully review the student's proposed accommodation to determine whether it is compatible with or defeats one or more of the essential objectives of the program in which the student is enrolled or whether implementing the proposed accommodation would lower an essential academic standard.
- searches for alternative, compatible accommodations, if the student's proposed accommodation defeats an essential program objective.

Tufts, returning to court after it scrupulously followed a similar process, demonstrated that it was now entitled to deference to its decision to deny Wynne his requested accommodation.

I am unaware of any case in which a postsecondary institution lost in court for failing to implement a particular requested accommodation after it had engaged in the interactive process, provided the plaintiff with several alternative accommodations, but denied the contested accommodations on the basis of diligent, thoughtful deliberations by a committee of qualified individuals.

If administrators and faculty want respect, authority, and deference from the courts, the DOJ, or the OCR, they can have it. All they have to do is go through the interactive *Wynne v. Tufts* process in an authentic way. This is why Jamie and I preach "process, process, process."

**JA:** There is a side benefit to following an inclusive process—and in my experience, 99% of the time when you put that group together and everybody sits down, you actually figure out something that works that doesn't alter the standard, that allows the student access and an opportunity, and that maintains the academic integrity of the program. You give a qualified student a chance to meet or not meet that requirement on their own terms, and the institution gets what it needs. Great things come out of that collaboration. And in my experience, maybe only 1% of the time do you find a fundamental alteration. You need faculty as well for the second step.

**PG:** I think the interactive process with faculty is of minimal importance. But in the second step faculty are of premier importance. Jamie's insight, which I completely agree with, is exactly the insight that the courts are willing to trust. I repeat: If you do this process diligently and authentically, and not as a pretext for discrimination, you will get to a good conclusion. In such circumstances, the courts trust academia to reach a good conclusion.

*A few times, the two of you have used the word discrimination. Some of these issues are happening because disability services offices are becoming less staffed and upper administrative director positions are moving to coordinator positions. There is a downsizing. But is litigation the way forward?*

**JA:** That's why the ability of private folks to bring cases is important—because schools get complaints all the time, and their general counsel looks at it and goes, "We don't want this going any further. Let's fix this." By continuing to build a culture of access and inclusivity, things slowly start to shift.

**PG:** I don't think many disability rights lawyers believe that "litigation is the way forward." Litigation is horrifically slow, usually beyond the means of most students, and it's likely to lead to outcomes that are difficult to implement. Acceptance of disability rights as civil rights, a commitment to the success of students with disabilities by campus leaders, and the kind of change in campus climate advocated by Jamie are all preferable strategies. But sometimes litigation is the only tool that will work. For these circumstances, I just hope that the disability and other diverse communities can turn back the attack on civil rights.

*What makes your institution so supportive of disabilities and inclusive in the cocurricular and curricular spheres?*

**JA:** We have always had some pretty good support from the time I got here. For some reason, state educational institutions in Arizona have always had a lot of support for disability access. Perhaps it's because of the makeup of our population and because we have a lot of members of the older population, who understand disability, or they've had experiences in life that are connected to people with disabilities—children with disabilities, grandchildren with disabilities. They themselves understand disability. Maybe it's because Arizona, back in the day, was the place where lots of people went to improve their symptoms from tuberculosis.

The University of Arizona has a staff of 32 at its disability resources center. The disability resources center at Arizona State University has a staff of 30. I have a staff of 12 at NAU. It seems that, within our system, there has always been a commitment, and I think that commitment within the system extends to the board of regents.

**PG:** On disability matters, institutional leadership has always been there at NAU. When you maintain a level of excellence in your staff it makes a huge difference.

**JA:** We have had six presidents of the Association on Higher Education and Disability who have come from one of the institutions in Arizona. We have always had a lot of good, outspoken advocates working hard in that area—fighting to maintain the gains that we see—and we have just been able to keep that consistent effort.

## References

Academic Adjustments, 34 C.F.R. § 104.44 (2000). https://www.ecfr.gov/current/title-34/subtitle-B/chapter-I/part-104/subpart-E/section-104.44

Carmel, J. (2020, July 22). Before the A.D.A., there was Section 504. *The New York Times*. https://www.nytimes.com/2020/07/22/us/504-sit-in-disability-rights.html

Chevron U.S.A., Inc. v. National Resources Defense Council, Inc., 467 U.S. 837 (1984). https://supreme.justia.com/cases/federal/us/467/837

CVS Pharmacy, Inc. v. Doe, 982 F.3d 1204 (9th Cir. 2020); cert. petition granted (July 2, 2021); writ of cert. dismissed (November 12, 2021). https://supreme.justia.com/cases/federal/us/2021/20-1374

Newman, L. A., Madaus, J. W., Lalor, A. R., & Javitz, H. S. (2020). Effect of accessing supports on higher education persistence of students with disabilities. *Journal of Diversity in Higher Education, 14*(3), 353–363. https://doi.org/10.1037/dhe0000170

Office for Civil Rights. (2021a, August 16). *Re: Complaint #04-21-2120* [Letter]. U.S. Department of Education. https://www2.ed.gov/about/offices/list/ocr/docs/investigations/more/04212120-a.pdf

Office for Civil Rights. (2021b, March 26). Re: Missouri Valley College OCR case number 07202255 [Letter]. U.S. Department of Education. https://www2.ed.gov/about/offices/list/ocr/docs/investigations/more/07202255-a.pdf

Payan v. Los Angeles Community College District, 11 F.4$^{th}$ 729 (9th Cir. 2021). https://casetext.com/case/payan-v-l-a-cmty-coll-dist

PGA Tour, Inc. v. Martin, 532 U.S. 661 (2001). https://supreme.justia.com/cases/federal/us/532/661

Shapiro, J. (2002, April 28). *504 sit-in: Winning rights for the disabled* [Radio broadcast]. National Public Radio. https://www.npr.org/2002/04/28/1142484/504-sit-in-winning-rights-for-the-disabled

Southeastern Community College v. Davis, 442 U.S. 397 (1979). https://supreme.justia.com/cases/federal/us/442/397

United States v. Regents of the University of California, No. 22-7345 (N.D. Cal. Dec. 2, 2022). https://www.justice.gov/d9/case-documents/attachments/2022/11/21/consent_decree_-_u.s._v._uc_berkeley.pdf

Vance, M. L., & Thompson, T. L. (Eds.). (2023). *Laws, policies, and processes: Tools for postsecondary student accommodation*. Association on Higher Education and Disability.

West Virginia v. Environmental Protection Agency, 597 U.S. ___ (2022). https://www.supremecourt.gov/opinions/21pdf/20-1530_n758.pdf

Wynne v. Tufts University School of Medicine, 932 F.2d 19 (1st Cir. 1991), *aff'd*, 976 F.2d 791 (1st Cir. 1992). https://law.justia.com/cases/federal/appellate-courts/F2/976/791/47641

CHAPTER 9

# College Experiences of Students With Disabilities Viewed Through a Technology Lens

Sheryl Burgstahler

The COVID-19 pandemic disrupted everyone's life. Imagine, however, enduring a pandemic without the technological innovations that allowed many of us to take and teach classes, offer and use services, make purchases, communicate with relatives and friends, watch movies, shop, and manage our bank accounts. Unfortunately, as ubiquitous as information technology (IT) appears, some people do not have full access to computers, the internet, and the content and activities they support. Even those individuals who have computers, assistive technology (AT), and an Internet connection may encounter barriers because of the inaccessible design of websites, videos, courses, and other digital content. An institution can ensure that it offers digital opportunities for all of its students by procuring, developing, and using technology that is accessible to, usable by, and inclusive of students with disabilities; however, key stakeholders

---

The content of this chapter is based on activities funded by the National Science Foundation (NSF) under grants CNS-2137312 and DRL-1948591. Any opinions, findings, conclusions, or recommendations expressed are those of the author and do not necessarily reflect the views of the NSF.

often lack knowledge and skills for doing so. This chapter reveals the potential of the universal design in higher education (UDHE) guidelines to steer the design of technologies as well as the products and environments they support. The Collaborative Framework is a tool that identifies the roles of and relationships between key stakeholders. Both underpin practices that support positive outcomes for students with disabilities.

## My Journey With Assistive and Accessible Technology

My current role, as director of accessible technology services, is to lead efforts to promote the procurement, development, and use of accessible IT at the University of Washington (UW). My work in providing accessible technology education, consultation, and innovative policy and practices in education started when I heard about a 6-year-old boy named Rodney who was severely physically disabled.

I was chair of the mathematics and computer science department, teaching courses in these fields, at a private college when I learned about Rodney, who had no use of his hands but operated a typewriter by pressing the keys with a mouth wand (a short stick attached to a mouth guard). His teacher shared with me a copy of the first letter Rodney typed. In part, he wrote:

May 3. 1982,

Dear President Reagan,

I want to tell you my name. My name is Rodney and I Am 6 years old . . . I am handicapped bebecause I can't use my legs or my hands because I have little muscles and dbones. I go to Skyline Exceptional School . . . I get to learn to type with my special mouth wand. Someday I will get to use a computer because I am smart even tho handicapped.

# Equity Through Technology

This is my first letter L typed. I Worked hard typing. TThank you for being nice ... Rodney

(Burgstahler, 2020, p. 76)

I wondered if Rodney could control a desktop computer. When we first met, I discovered that he could perform all of the functions of a computer by pressing keys on the keyboard with his mouth wand *except* those that required the suppression of two keys simultaneously; he could not press the Shift, Control, or Repeat keys at the same time as another key. I contacted several technology leaders before I located someone who had a solution and sent me a hand-drawn diagram of a switch box that, once connected to the keyboard, could lock the three keys. I hired an engineering student at the college to build it. Figure 9.1 shows a drawing of me with Rodney as he controlled a computer using his mouth wand, standard keyboard, and "magic switch box." Over several years, he demonstrated to me, his teachers, and other educators that a computer was a major contributor to his success in school and his transition to higher education.

**Figure 9.1**
*Sheryl and Rodney With His Magic Switch Box*

*Note.* From *Line Drawings, Collections, and Stickers*, by Disabilities, Opportunities, Internetworking, and Technology Center (https://www.washington.edu/doit/resources/line-drawings). Reprinted with permission.

This was my first experience in AT, a field that has opened a world of opportunities for people with disabilities. Because of my background, I was hired in 1984 to lead a new unit to support desktop computer users at UW, and I made sure that our mission was to help everyone—explicitly including faculty, students, and staff with disabilities—gain full access to technologies.

By the time Rodney was a college student and worker in our UW Access Technology Center, he did not need an external device to operate a computer because, by that time, a "sticky keys" feature was routinely included in operating systems to lock the three keys that erected a barrier. By then, thousands of types of AT software and hardware were commercially available, and they could be interfaced with mainstream IT to allow access for virtually everyone. Among the software options were those that enhance learning for students who process information differently than a "typical" student (e.g., those who have learning disabilities or are otherwise neurodivergent). As soon as mice were commonplace, students like Rodney could operate software as long as it made features typically accessed with a mouse also fully operable with the keyboard alone, such as by using arrow keys. Other features that used to be AT add-ons only but are now offered to any users include smartphone customization options such as text size, foreground and background colors, and speech output. Today, colleges and universities can expect that some of their students

- use speech recognition, head pointers, mouth sticks, eye-gaze tracking systems, and myriad other assistive technologies because they cannot use their hands;
- rely on captions or transcripts to access audio content;
- benefit from synthesized speech and refreshable braille displays because they cannot see the screen;
- have low vision and use software to increase the size of fonts and zoom into parts of computer screens; and

- use text-to-speech technologies to read aloud digital text because they have a reading-related disability or are English-language learners.

## Achieving Equity Through Technology

To ensure equity for all students, institutions need to provide (1) appropriate AT wherever computer access is available to others and (2) accessibly designed mainstream technologies so that AT users and other students can fully benefit from campus offerings. For example, digital materials delivered in HTML, Microsoft Word, PDF, or other formats must be specifically created to be accessible to people who are blind or who are neurodiverse in ways that affect their reading ability. These students may need written materials offered in a text-based digital format so that their text-to-speech and screen reader AT can read it aloud to them. In addition, blind students need headings, lists, tables, and other elements structured in such a way that their screen readers can adequately describe the format; without such an explanation, the information presented to a blind student may be spoken as a linear stream of text, which can be difficult to parse. Similarly, video and audio content presents challenges for people who are deaf or learning English, unless audio content is available in accurate captions or transcriptions. The potential for erecting IT barriers for students with disabilities has expanded as the complexity of mainstream technologies has increased and their frequency of use has grown. The COVID-19 pandemic made this fact dramatically clear.

Most traditional efforts to address IT accessibility challenges follow a medical view of disability, in which the primary focus is on a medical diagnosis that results in functional limitations of students and how they can be accommodated via inaccessibly designed IT (Loewen & Pollard, 2010). In contrast, social and similar views of disability (DePoy & Gibson, 2008) consider variations in sensory, physical, learning, executive function, and other abilities a natural part of the human experience. A social model focuses on the disabling barriers in the environment whereby disability is socially constructed. The social model encourages a universal design (UD) approach, in which more attention is devoted to proactively designing products, environments, policies, and social systems that are accessible to everyone and thus reducing the need for accommodations.

## Compliance Issues

Unfortunately, studies have repeatedly revealed that most IT used in higher education fails to employ accessibility practices (Burgstahler & Thompson, 2019; Kimmons, 2017; Mune & Agee, 2016; Shaheen & Watulak, 2019). Relevant legislation requiring the provision of accessible IT includes Section 504 of the Rehabilitation Act of 1973 and the Americans with Disabilities Act of 1990 and its 2008 Amendments (ADA). Together these laws mandate that "no otherwise qualified person with a disability shall, solely by reason of their disability, be excluded from the participation in, be denied the benefits of, or be subjected to discrimination in public programs" (University of Washington, 2022, para. 3). This includes programs offered by educational entities. The federal government interprets these civil rights laws, along with many state laws and policies, to require access to IT and the opportunities it supports (see, e.g., EDUCAUSE, 2015; Office for Civil Rights [OCR], 2016).

According to the OCR and Department of Justice, with respect to technology the term

> "Accessible" means a person with a disability is afforded the opportunity to acquire the same information, engage in the same interactions, and enjoy the same services as a person without a disability in an equally effective and equally

integrated manner, with substantially equivalent ease of use. The person with a disability must be able to obtain the information as fully, equally, and independently as a person without a disability. (Burgstahler 2017, para. 3)

Resolving compliance-related conflicts—by the OCR as well as in courts of law—has been costly for hundreds of postsecondary institutions and has made clear that the use of inaccessible websites, documents, video presentations, and other IT resources and tools violates the civil rights of students with disabilities. Simply put, it is the responsibility of the institution to procure, develop, and use accessible IT.

The following sections contain UDHE guidelines that, if combined with the Collaborative Framework presented in this book, can be used to steer the accessible design of computer hardware and software applications, the materials they create, the courses and services they support, and the facilities where such technologies are located. Ideally, stakeholder collaboration can make this accessibility a reality.

## Applying the Universal Design in Higher Education Guidelines to Technology Products and Environments

Universal design practices align with the social interpretations of disability and minimize legal risk. Staff can develop or procure digital documents, videos, courses, and services that consider a broad range of user abilities rather than only abilities of typical users. Of all proactive IT design practices—for example, design for user empowerment, ability-based design, user-centered design, accessible design, usable design, and UD—UD has the most comprehensive and well-established foundation of principles, guidelines, and best practices that can be used to direct the design of accessible, usable, and inclusive technology (Burgstahler & Thompson, 2019). The UDHE guidelines that I developed and applied (Burgstahler, 2020) can inform all aspects of postsecondary education and are underpinned by three sets of existing principles, as described in the following paragraphs.

**Figure 9.2**
*Characteristics of Any UD Strategy: Is It Accessible, Usable, and Inclusive?*

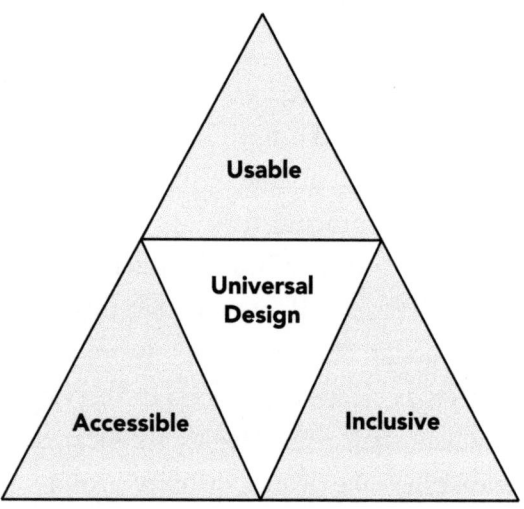

*Note.* From *Creating Inclusive Learning Opportunities in Higher Education: A Universal Design Toolkit* (p. 31), by S. Burgstahler, 2020, Harvard Education Press. Copyright © 2020 by the President and Fellows of Harvard College. Reprinted with permission.

When a product or environment is not accessible to someone, a UD approach requires that all abilities and other characteristics of potential users be considered in design processes. As illustrated in Figure 9.2, universally designed environments and products are calculated to be accessible to, usable by, and inclusive of everyone, including those with disabilities. UD features streamline access for all and minimize or eliminate the time and expense for stakeholders in ad hoc retrofitting efforts to achieve access.

UD is not a new concept; a sidewalk curb cut is an application of UD. Although originally conceived to eliminate physical barriers for people with mobility impairments, the ubiquitous curb cuts today benefit many others, including individuals pushing baby strollers and delivery carts. UD principles have since been used in designing a wide range of products and environments, including IT hardware and software, teaching and learning activities, and student services (Burgstahler, 2020).

**General Principles of UD**

Principles for the UD of any product or environment include the following:

- *equitable use*: The design is useful and marketable to people with diverse abilities.
- *flexibility in use*: The design accommodates a wide range of individual preferences and abilities.
- *simple and intuitive use*: Use of the design is easy to understand, regardless of the user's experience, knowledge, language skills, or current concentration level.
- *perceptible information*: The design communicates necessary information effectively to the user, regardless of ambient conditions or the user's sensory abilities.
- *tolerance for error*: The design minimizes hazards and the adverse consequences of accidental or unintended actions.
- *low physical effort*: The design can be used efficiently, comfortably, and with a minimum of fatigue.
- *size and space for approach and use*: Appropriate size and space are provided for approach, reach, manipulation, and use, regardless of the user's body size, posture, or mobility. (Story et al., 1998, pp. 34–35)

**UD Applied to IT**

UD-inspired principles and guidelines have recently emerged to address IT applications. The international Web Content Accessibility

Guidelines (WCAG; World Wide Web Consortium, 2018) recommend that all IT designs adhere to the following guiding values:

- *perceivable*: Users must be able to perceive the content, regardless of the device or configuration they're using.
- *operable*: Users must be able to operate the controls, buttons, sliders, menus, and other features, regardless of the device they're using.
- *understandable*: Users must be able to understand the content and interface.
- *robust*: Content must be coded in compliance with relevant coding standards to ensure it is accurately and meaningfully interpreted by devices, browsers, and AT.

### Universal Design for Curriculum and Instruction

UD-inspired principles have also been created for the design of curriculum and instruction. Universal design for learning (UDL)—developed by the Center for Applied Special Technology (CAST)—rests on three standards. UDL practitioners recommend that instructors offer their students multiple means of the following (CAST, 2018):

- *engagement:* for purposeful, motivated learners, to stimulate interest and motivation for learning
- *representation:* for resourceful, knowledgeable learners, to present information and content in different ways
- *action and expression:* for strategic, goal-directed learners, to differentiate the ways that students can express what they know

The principles that support UD, WCAG, and UDL form the set of 14 that underpin UDHE and have been found to be suitable for addressing all aspects of higher education (Burgstahler, 2020). UDHE includes the scope of the application, definitions, principles,

# Equity Through Technology

guidelines, practices, and process, as illustrated in Figure 9.3. Each aspect of the UDHE guidelines can be tailored to a specific campus or application area to develop a toolkit of practices.

Postsecondary applications of UDHE include all aspects of technology procurement, development, and use to ensure that everyone has access to information, courses, media, and physical spaces. The UDHE approach reduces the need for IT-related accommodations (e.g., reformatting inaccessible documents, captioning videos); however, in some cases, redesign will be necessary to ensure full access and engagement for a particular student, faculty, or staff member. For example, a student with a learning disability engaging in a universally designed online course will not require remediation of documents but may need extra time on an examination, as determined by a campus access and disability services office.

**Figure 9.3**
*Components of the UDHE Framework*

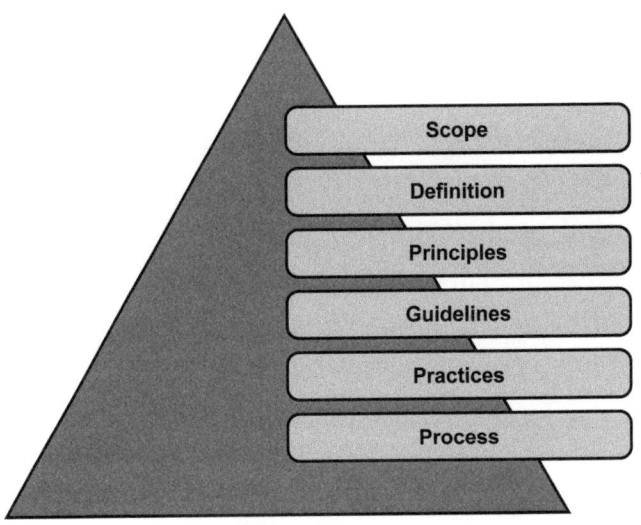

*Note.* From *Creating Inclusive Learning Opportunities in Higher Education: A Universal Design Toolkit* (p. 36), by S. Burgstahler, 2020, Harvard Education Press. Copyright © 2020 by the President and Fellows of Harvard College. Reprinted with permission.

## Applying the Collaborative Framework to Technology Products and Environments

The Collaborative Framework described in this book can help stakeholders apply UDHE to IT products and the environments they support. Widespread implementation requires engagement between key stakeholders toward a common goal (Burgstahler & Thompson, 2019).

### Students With Disabilities

As beneficiaries, students with disabilities can self-advocate for access to both AT and accessibly designed mainstream technology. Some students with disabilities do not ask for accessible technology because of

- concerns about potential discrimination
- limited knowledge of how technologies might benefit them
- limited knowledge of their rights and responsibilities
- an unclear understanding of how the accommodation process in postsecondary education works
- low self-advocacy skills

Ideally, students acquire knowledge and skills in all of these areas by the end of high school, but often that is not the case. Out-of-school programs—such as those supported by the DO-IT (Disabilities, Opportunities, Internetworking, and Technology) Center and its collaborators (e.g., AccessComputing, Neuroscience for Neurodiverse Learners [NNL])—can put students with disabilities in contact with peers and mentors and otherwise help them develop the knowledge and skills they need for successful transitions between academic levels and careers. The DO-IT Center and collaborators employ the student-centered stakeholder model presented in Figure 9.4.

With student success at its core, the framework includes stakeholders who can either promote success or inadvertently erect barriers with respect to the success of students with disabilities. DO-IT staff work with multiple stakeholders and help these groups collaborate to achieve the common goal: success of students with disabilities in academic studies and careers. Most DO-IT projects center on students who have a variety of disabilities (AccessComputing, n.d.). Sometimes projects focus on a subset of students with disabilities, for example in the NNL (n.d.) project. Regardless of the program, students gain self-determination skills; learn how to advocate with the disability services office (DSO), technology staff, and faculty; gain access to empowering technology; acquire strategies for when and how to disclose a disability to an employer; and meet peers, mentors, and IT specialists. DO-IT's programs also create opportunities for students with disabilities to band together, advocate for each other, and promote systemic changes in higher education. Campus-based programs can achieve some of the same goals; for example, the tiered Mentor Program for Students at the College of the Holy Cross (n.d.) employs experienced students to mentor new college students and alumni to mentor experienced students.

**Figure 9.4**
*DO-IT's Student-Centered Stakeholder Model*

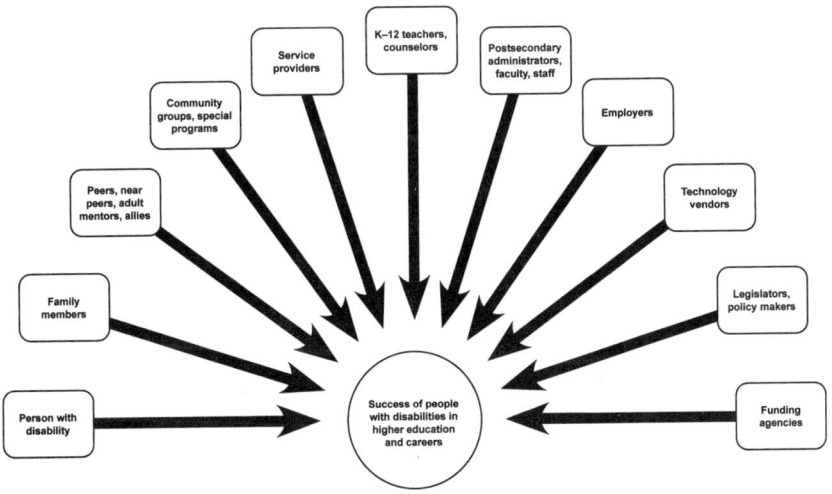

*Note.* From *Creating Inclusive Learning Opportunities in Higher Education: A Universal Design Toolkit* (p. xii), by S. Burgstahler, 2020, Harvard Education Press. Copyright © 2020 by the President and Fellows of Harvard College. Reprinted with permission.

## Disability Services Staff

Disability support staff should work with the central technology unit to determine the specific technology needs of students and to ensure such technology is available on campus. If IT does not have an accessible technology expert on campus, the DSO must identify student access needs and collaborate with relevant administrators to procure training and technologies that secure access. Training for the students or relevant staff should be provided. DSO personnel must provide students with disabilities with access to AT and have information about and access to such AT to keep the institution compliant with relevant laws.

## Administration

Campus leaders set priorities and the culture for an institution in many ways. For example, they can require that all diversity, equity, and inclusion initiatives address accessibility issues. As far as technology, these leaders can establish the expectation that any IT procured, developed, and used at the institution be accessibly designed. They may need others at the institution, such as those in IT, to make them more aware of access issues, the current state of accessibility on campus, legal risks with respect to the use of inaccessible IT, and options for making improvements. Administrators can consider instituting a high-level advisory board and taking other measures to engage all stakeholders about the importance of accessibility.

Administrators must also provide resources to ensure the security and privacy of all software products. Testing products for IT accessibility and remediating inaccessible products (e.g., videos, documents) must take place. At the UW, funding is provided through Accessible Technology Services (ATS) to caption high-visibility videos and remediate widely used PDFs. A high-level IT accessibility task force and volunteer IT accessibility liaisons were established to promote accessible IT campuswide.

### IT Staff

Some colleges and universities have AT professionals focused on ensuring that technologies are accessible to people with disabilities; all institutions should employ such professionals. At UW an ATS unit consults with faculty, students, and staff with disabilities about AT and promotes the procurement, development, and use of accessible mainstream technology and universally designed computing facilities and services. Accessible IT training for IT staff members can be found online and through professional organizations.

### Procurement Staff

Procurement personnel can encourage units to build in accessibility requirements into contracts with technology vendors and work with accessible IT staff on the evaluation of products for accessibility. If most technology purchased on campus is procured directly by departments rather than by a procurement office, then systemic change is difficult to achieve—but it is worth promoting. Ideally, IT staff with knowledge about the design of accessible technology, such as ATS at the UW, can offer training and consulting in this area, including on how to apply WCAG. Institutions should find ways to use their collective purchasing power to increase industry awareness of the importance of accessibility by developing procurement policies and procedures that include accessibility considerations. If all institutions did this, the resulting market pressure could significantly increase the availability of accessible products; however, campuses do not often collaborate in an organized way to make it happen.

### Teaching and Learning Centers

Teaching and learning professionals typically offer training, resources, and learning communities for faculty. Such centers should be encouraged to integrate UDHE into all of their programs and resource collections. Teaching and learning centers need to have specialists familiar with AT, procurement, and accommodations that allow students with disabilities to actually benefit from course offerings. A member of the DSO and/or the IT accessibility team may be able to train existing team members and offer guidance in hiring new staff.

## Technology Companies

The technology industry could make the work of postsecondary institutions easier if they routinely sold and licensed products that are designed to be accessible to individuals with disabilities, including those who use AT; however, for most companies, this is not the case. Usability professionals should test products at all development stages on their accessibility to people with disabilities. Campus units like ATS can help with this effort. Engagement with technology companies can be productive as well because it can encourage them to make their products more accessible and to hire people with disabilities. For example, Microsoft has put together a successful program focused on hiring and supporting individuals on the autism spectrum.

## Researchers

The availability of accessible technology and practices will increase if researchers in technology design routinely include individuals with disabilities and UD considerations in every phase of design, development, and evaluation. Faculty can gain skills in this area through online resources, professional organizations, and campus IT groups, such as ATS.

## Faculty

Some instructors consider addressing course access issues as the the sole responsibility of DSOs and often lack knowledge and skills regarding how they can proactively apply UDHE guidelines to level the playing field for their students—including when technology is used to create curriculum materials and support learning activities.

Training, which could be hosted by staff in a DSO, a teaching and learning center, or an accessible technology unit, should include tips for getting started and be offered in multiple formats to meet individual needs and preferences (e.g., short presentations, asynchronous learning opportunities, online resources, and one-on-one consulting). In addition, faculty who teach technology-related courses should include content that covers the importance and application of UD so that the next generation of professionals in their fields will design more accessible and inclusive products. In this effort, faculty could benefit from training hosted by their academic department. There they can share how they include disability-related content in their courses—for example, engineering faculty can teach future engineers how to design accessible products. Faculty should also consider proposing that their academic unit provide support (e.g., in creating accessible documents, captioning videos).

## Applying UDHE and the Collaborative Framework to Online Learning

Although there is evidence that positive outcomes result from applying proactive, accessible, and inclusive design approaches such as UDHE (Center for Universal Design in Education, n.d.), such practices are not routinely applied (Behling, 2017; Kent, 2015; Massengale & Vasquez, 2016). Typical learning management systems make it possible to create courses accessible to individuals with disabilities; therefore, for the most part, the accessibility of a course depends on the choices course designers and instructors make in creating digital materials (e.g., documents, videos) and pedagogical and assessment methods (AccessComputing, n.d.; Burgstahler & Thompson, 2019). To increase the universal design of online learning, accessible and inclusive practices must be applied and multiple stakeholders must be involved. Online learning is a good example of how the UDHE and the Collaborative Framework can be applied.

### Applying UDHE Guidelines to Online Learning at UW

Most online instructors employ an accommodations-only approach rather than one that is proactive such as UDHE (Barnard-Brak & Sulak, 2010; Fisher & Parsi, 2018; Roscorla, 2016). Common IT-related accommodations for students with disabilities in online environments are remediating inaccessible documents (mostly PDFs) and captioning videos. UDHE can be used to guide the design of online learning activities that are accessible, usable, and inclusive. There is no shortage of guidance for online course instructors and designers who want to make their offerings accessible to, usable by, and inclusive of students with disabilities (see, e.g., AccessCyberlearning 2.0, 2019; Center for Universal Design in Education, n.d.; Chambers et al., 2016; Cifuentes et al., 2016; Dell et al., 2015; Fidalgo & Thormann, 2017; Moorefield-Lang et al., 2016; Rao et al., 2015; Robinson & Wizer, 2016; Rogers-Shaw et al., 2018; Seale, 2014; Thomson et al., 2015). This literature suggests the following UDHE practices, among others:

- multiple ways to learn, demonstrate learning, and engage
- videos captioned and audio transcribed
- clear instructions as well as consistent layouts and organization schemes
- materials that use a text format and structured headings, lists, and tables
- descriptive text used for content in images and hyperlinks
- large sans serif fonts
- plain and high-contrast backgrounds as well as uncluttered pages
- plain English and spelled-out acronyms
- outlines and other scaffolding tools

- adequate time for assignments and tests
- for any on-site components, facilities that can be easily maneuvered with a wheelchair

Many online learning designers and instructors require resources and training to develop UDHE practices. For example, at UW, ATS offers the following resources for online learning designers and instructors:

- an accessible technology website (UW, n.d.) with best practices for the accessible design of online courses as well as websites, documents, and videos
- a 1-hour webinar each month and recorded webinars from past events, each addressing a specific issue such as captioning videos and designing accessible documents
- tailored presentations for faculty groups
- individual appointments for consultation on designing a course, document, etc.

### Applying the Collaborative Framework to Online Learning at UW

If applied widely, UDHE can bring about institutional change toward more accessible and inclusive online learning offerings. The Collaborative Framework can contribute to this change by identifying key stakeholders, their existing knowledge and skills, their training needs, and ways they can most effectively work together. In terms of online learning, UW wrestles with how to institutionalize more accessible and inclusive IT. UW addresses issues for individuals and campus units and helps stakeholders work together. For example, an IT accessibility task force could represent major units on campus to encourage collaboration and jointly report activities and recommendations relevant to the procurement, development, and use of accessible IT. At UW, the Access Technology team in the IT department (ITAT) engages with other stakeholders as it promotes the procurement, development, and use of technologies that are accessible to faculty, students, staff and visitors. ITAT staff members work with

- the central UW-IT staff, other campus units, and the procurement office evaluate the accessibility of IT products being used or that units are planning to use. When possible, ITAT works with the procurement office to include wording in contracts that requires the company to comply with WCAG; when not possible, ITAT attempts to insert wording in contracts that requires vendors to continually indicate the accessibility specifications of their product.
- companies that provide IT the campus currently uses. ITAT staff members share accessibility barriers and suggest ways they might be fixed. They work with other campuses in this regard to put greater pressure on leadership about accessible design and to engage in an online community that shares the results of accessibility tests on digital products commonly used in higher education.
- an IT accessibility liaison group of more that 150 volunteers from units throughout the campus. With leadership from ITAT, these liaisons meet regularly to learn more about how to design accessible IT, share ideas with other campus units, and be encouraged to learn more from ITAT and each other.
- the campuswide e-learning community of practice and the central teaching and learning center and similar groups to share accessible IT information with the faculty and trainers and to link to resources from their websites.

## Conclusion

Since 6-year-old Rodney received his magic switch box, many more forms of AT that benefit students with all types of disabilities have become available However, even though the field of AT has made extraordinary advances since that time, an urgent need exists for mainstream technologies to be more accessible, usable, and inclusive for AT users and other students with disabilities. Although established UDHE principles, guidelines, and practices currently direct the development and use of technologies and their applications, they are not routinely applied in higher education. Why?

Institutions need to apply the framework described in this book to engage in collaborative practices with students with disabilities, DSOs, faculty, and administration to include, enhance, and identify technology access needs that ensure equity and inclusion for students with disabilities and, in the process, all students. It is important that colleges and universities apply accessible and inclusive practices supported by UDHE guidelines to the design of assistive and mainstream technologies and the products and environments they support. For maximum impact, however, key stakeholders must be identified, their specific roles defined, and effective collaboration mechanisms established. The Collaborative Framework can be used to underpin technology-related practices that support positive outcomes for students with disabilities. These combined efforts can lead to a paradigm shift from design for the average, or "typical," student to design for everyone—and from ableism to a celebration of all abilities in higher education.

## References

AccessComputing. (n.d.). *How do learning management systems differ on accessibility?* University of Washington. https://www.washington.edu/accesscomputing/how-do-learning-management-systems-differ-accessibility

AccessCyberlearning 2.0. (2019). *Capacity building institute*. DO-IT, University of Washington. https://www.washington.edu/doit/accesscyberlearning-20-capacity-building-institute-2019

Barnard-Brak, L., & Sulak, T. N. (2010). Online versus face-to-face accommodations among college students with disabilities. *American Journal of Distance Education, 24*(2), 81–91. https://doi.org/10.1080/08923641003604251

Behling, K. (2017). Accessibility considerations for hybrid courses. In K. E. Linder (Ed.), *Hybrid teaching and learning* (New Directions for Teaching and Learning, No. 149, pp. 89–101). https://doi.org/10.1002/tl.20230

Burgstahler, S. (2017, January 30). ADA compliance for online course design. *EDUCAUSE Review*. https://er.educause.edu/articles/2017/1/ada-compliance-for-online-course-design

Burgstahler, S. (2020). *Creating inclusive learning opportunities in higher education: A universal design toolkit*. Harvard Education Press.

Burgstahler, S., & Thompson, T. (Eds). (2019). *Designing accessible cyberlearning: Current state and pathway forward*. DO-IT, University of Washington. https://www.washington.edu/doit/designing-accessible-cyberlearning

Center for Applied Special Technology. (2018). *Universal design for learning guidelines version 2.2*. http://udlguidelines.cast.org/more/research-evidence

Center for Universal Design in Education. (n.d.). *Published books and articles about universal design in higher education*. University of Washington. https://www.washington.edu/doit/programs/center-universal-design-education/resources/published-books-and-articles-about-universal

Chambers, D., Varoglu, Z., & Kasinskaite-Buddeberg, I. (2016). *Learning for all: Guidelines on the inclusion of learners with disabilities in open and distance learning*. United National Educational, Scientific, and Cultural Organization.

Cifuentes, L., Janney, A., Guerra, L., & Weir, J. (2016). A working model for complying with accessibility guidelines for online learning. *TechTrends: Linking Research and Practice to Improve Learning, 60*(6), 557–564. https://www.learntechlib.org/p/175642

College of the Holy Cross. (n.d.). *Mentor program*. https://www.holycross.edu/orientations-information-incoming-students/mentor-program

Dell, C. A., Dell, T. F., & Blackwell, T. L. (2015). Applying universal design for learning in online courses: Pedagogical and practical considerations. *Journal of Educators Online, 13*(2), 166–192. https://www.learntechlib.org/p/161396

DePoy, E., & Gibson, S. (2008). Disability studies: Origins, current conflict, and resolution. *Review of Disability Studies, 4*(4), 33–40. https://www.rdsjournal.org/index.php/journal/article/view/244

EDUCAUSE. (2015). *IT accessibility risk statements and evidence*. https://library.educause.edu/resources/2015/7/it-accessibility-risk-statements-and-evidence

Fidalgo, P., & Thormann, J. (2017). Reaching students in online courses using alternative formats. *International Review of Research in Open and Distributed Learning, 18*(2). http://dx.doi.org/10.19173/irrodl.v18i2.2601

Fisher, J. F., & Parsi, A. (2018). *Why true equity in learning depends on proactive, not reactive, design*. Getting Smart. https://www.gettingsmart.com/2018/02/why-true-equity-in-learning-depends-on-proactive-not-reactive-design/

Kent, M. (2015). Disability and elearning: Opportunities and barriers. *Disability Studies Quarterly, 35*(1). https://doi.org/10.18061/dsq.v35i1.3815

Kimmons, R. (2017). Open to all? Nationwide evaluation of high-priority web accessibility considerations among higher education websites. *Journal of Computing in Higher Education, 29*(3), 434–450. http://dx.doi.org/10.1007/s12528-017-9151-3

Loewen, G., & Pollard, W. (2010). The social justice perspective. *Journal of Postsecondary Education and Disability, 23*(1), 5–18. https://www.ahead.org/professional-resources/publications/jped/archived-jped/jped-volume-23

Massengale, L. R., & Vasquez, E., III. (2016). Assessing accessibility: How accessible are online courses for students with disabilities? *Journal of the Scholarship of Teaching and Learning, 16*(1), 69–79. https://doi.org/10.14434/josotl.v16i1.19101

Moorefield-Lang, H., Copeland, C. A., & Haynes, A. (2016). Accessing abilities: Creating innovative accessible online learning environments and putting quality into practice. *Education for Information, 32*(1), 27–33. http://dx.doi.org/10.3233/EFI-150966

Mune, C., & Agee, A. (2016). Are e-books for everyone? An evaluation of academic e-book platforms' accessibility features. *Journal of Electronic Resources Librarianship, 28*(3), 172–182. https://doi.org/10.1080/1941126X.2016.1200927

Neuroscience for Neurodiverse Learners. (n.d.). *Overview.* DO-IT, University of Washington. https://www.washington.edu/doit/programs/nnl

Office for Civil Rights. (2016). *Securing equal educational opportunity: Report to the president and secretary of education.* U.S. Department of Education. https://www2.ed.gov/about/reports/annual/ocr/report-to-president-and-secretary-of-education-2016.pdf

Rao, K., Edelen-Smith, P., & Wailehua, C. (2015). Universal design for online courses: Applying principles to pedagogy. *Open Learning, 30*(1), 35–52. https://doi.org/10.1080/02680513.2014.991300

Robinson, D. E., & Wizer, D. R. (2016). Universal design for learning and the quality matters guidelines for the design and implementation of online learning events. *Journal of Technology in Teaching and Learning, 12*(1), 17–32.

Rogers-Shaw, C., Carr-Chellman, D. J., & Choi, J. (2018). Universal design for learning: Guidelines for accessible online instruction. *Adult Learning, 29*(1), 20–31. https://doi.org/10.1177/1045159517735530

Roscorla, T. (2016, January 28). *The struggle to make online courses accessible in higher ed.* Government Technology. https://www.govtech.com/education/higher-ed/The-Struggle-to-Make-Online-Courses-Accessible-in-Higher-Ed.html

Seale, J. (2014). *E-learning and disability in higher education: Accessibility theory and practice* (2nd ed.). Routledge.

Shaheen, N., & Watulak, S. L. (2019). Bringing disability into the discussion: Examining technology accessibility as an equity concern in the field of instructional technology. *Journal of Research on Technology in Education,* 1–15. https://doi.org/10.1080/15391523.2019.1566037

Story, M. F., Mueller, J. L., & Mace, R. L. (1998). The principles of universal design and their application. In M. F. Story, M. L. Mueller, & R. L. Mace (Eds.), *The universal design file: Designing for people of all ages and abilities* (pp. 32–36). Center for Universal Design.

Thomson, R., Fichten, C. S., Havel, A., Budd, J., & Asuncion, J. (2015). Blending universal design, e-learning, and information and communication technologies. In S. Burgstahler (Ed.), *Universal design in higher education* (2nd ed., pp. 275–284). Harvard Education Press.

University of Washington. (n.d.). *Accessible technology.* https://www.washington.edu/accessibility

University of Washington. (2022). Equal access: Universal design of your NSF INCLUDES project. https://bit.ly/uw-equal-access

World Wide Web Consortium. (2018). *Web content accessibility guidelines,* 2.1. http://www.w3.org/TR/wcag21

# PART V

# Implementation and Best Practices

## CHAPTER 10

# How to Use the Collaborative Framework

Neal E. Lipsitz, Michael Berger, and Eileen Connell Berger

This chapter reviews the many uses of the Collaborative Framework and offers guidance for implementing those uses. The framework can be used for facilitating student inclusion and socialization, empowering all stakeholders through shared knowledge, and assessing the efficiency and effectiveness of institutional programs for access, inclusion, and equity for students with disabilities.

## Using the Framework to Facilitate Inclusion and Socialization

The framework is an ideal tool for solving complex problems that are most efficiently and effectively resolved through collaboration of stakeholders who have different roles, varying degrees of responsibilities, and often conflicting priorities.

### Getting to Yes: Collaborating to Solve Problems

The following case involves several academic issues—academic rigor, degree completion, questions of fundamental alteration of a course, and precedent setting—as well as social aspects such as inclusion and belonging. It illustrates how the framework can be used to facilitate a collaborative process to solve problems. Access and disability services (ADS) offices often play a major role in facilitating collaboration among stakeholders who disagree about what is and is not a reasonable accommodation.

Here is the case: A sophomore, Brianna, requests a waiver for a foreign language requirement from the faculty of the global studies (GS) department because of her auditory processing disorder and other disabilities. Brianna also alerts her dean, who refers her to ADS. Brianna describes her auditory processing disorder as taking significantly longer to process and remember new words and grammatical structures. Deficits in oral memory, problems distinguishing between similar sounds, mishearing auditory information, and problems processing or comprehending rapid speech make language learning a challenge for her. She has received accommodations such as extended time on tests and course substitutions in the past and found that tutoring, one-on-one instruction, class notes, and visual and interactive presentations in class have been the most effective ways of learning new material. However, even with course accommodations she is concerned that the college would not be able to provide her the level of support she needs for success in an upper-level foreign language course; thus, she insists on pursuing a waiver.

The academic dean explains to ADS that Brianna's case is complicated because she is not only looking to be excused from or to find an alternative to the college common degree requirement for foreign language study but *also* wants a waiver for a required core course in GS—that is, an advanced-level core course in a foreign language. Brianna wants both requirements to be waived. The dean has empathy for her and wants to support her career choice in the GS major, but the dean's overriding responsibility is to uphold academic integrity. This waiver request also raises issues such as a possible fundamental alteration of the degree program, precedent-setting decisions, and changes in long-standing GS degree policy.

ADS meets with Brianna and agrees that ADS would support eligibility for a waiver as an appropriate accommodation, given the functional limitations resulting from auditory processing, executive functioning, and language processing difficulties. However, ADS cannot guarantee that the academic department policy and academic standards would support a waiver for her major, thus presenting a potential conflict with the academic dean and GS faculty.

Without hesitation, the GS department chair informs the academic dean that the foreign language component is central to the major; therefore, a waiver would *not* be reasonable or appropriate. The department is also concerned about adherence to its long-standing academic policy and the possibility of a fundamental alteration of academic standards—and can't see a way around that problem.

The academic dean asks that ADS be consulted on this matter to ensure the college is compliant with disability law and to see if there are ways to accommodate Brianna without a waiver. The academic dean recognizes conflicting priorities between the student and the faculty and wishes to balance them—on one hand supporting the priorities of Brianna and her parents and on the other hand upholding the GS faculty who stress academic integrity and maintaining a well-established policy. The academic dean enlists the academic advising office to assist Brianna in considering a new career path, since the GS department will not endorse a language requirement waiver.

Brianna's parents strongly support her request for a waiver as a legal right because she has followed the school policy and provided proof of her need for a waiver. They are adamant about her remaining in GS as her career choice. Moreover, they are concerned that their financial investment in her education would be wasted if she could not complete her degree.

The framework maps the actions and notes the priorities for each stakeholder in an objective way. The grid shows how the stakeholders see the case through the lenses of their roles, responsibilities, and biases. Table 10.1 summarizes the facts of the case and places into the framework the actions and thoughts of the stakeholders as viewed through the lenses of self-advocacy, individual differences, and life transitions.

Table 10.1

*The Collaborative Framework Considering Self-Advocacy, Individual Differences, and Life Transition*

| Lens | Example of stakeholder focus and priorities | | | | |
|---|---|---|---|---|---|
| | Student | Faculty | Accessibility services | Senior administrators | Parent/ guardian |
| Self-advocacy | Wants global studies language requirement waived. | Advocates for academic integrity and department standards. Fundamental alteration? | Supports student advocacy. | Wants to honor student's entitlements and academic integrity. | Wants their student to have entitlements. |
| Individual differences | Language and auditory processing disorder. Wants alternative to language. | Otherwise qualified? Considers this a technical requirement. | Individual determination. Suggests possible course modifications. | Meets student's needs. | Stays involved in their student's accommodations and needs. |
| Life transition | Took foreign language in high school with extended time. Stressed. Wants to drop foreign language course. | No major role in this case. | Advocates for student. | Class dean approves dropped course. | Advocates for the student and requests alternatives to the requirement. |

The next set of lenses in the framework considers academic rigor, new pedagogies, and technology, as shown in Table 10.2. The framework maps the conflict between the student's request for a waiver and the faculty's insistence on a policy that has been in place and never questioned for many years and that constitutes a critical requirement for the GS major: the successful completion of an advanced language course. The advocacy of ADS in collaboration with the academic dean creates an opening for discussion with the GS faculty about alternative ways of completing the foreign language requirement and, at the same time, is an opportunity for the dean to learn more about learning difference, strategies, and accommodations that could possibly enable Brianna to complete the required course.

ADS proposes cross-cultural courses as a substitute for the advanced language course but is rebuffed by the GS department; those courses are already part of the degree requirement. Brianna's parents complain she is already stressed and suggest a pass/fail metric and translation software as alternatives to the language requirement. The discussion among the stakeholders creates substitutions including adoption of new ways to learn languages. Principles that fall under new pedagogies and universal design for learning broaden the perspective of academic faculty, the dean, and the student. ADS further suggests adding tutoring, personalized instruction, and a summer course so Brianna can have focused study without conflicting courses or assignments. Brianna begins to consider different alternatives. Technology solutions are introduced that offer several new tools to assist her, such as virtual courseware and apps for instant translation from one language to another. The GS faculty, however, are concerned that alternatives to the traditional language requirement might set a new precedent and represent a fundamental alteration in the course learning objectives but are left to consider new instructional approaches that would allow Brianna to remain in their department. ADS works with the GS department and senior administration to consider several alternatives to the traditional language requirement.

Table 10.2

*The Collaborative Framework Considering Academic Rigor, New Pedagogies, and Technology*

| Lens | Example of stakeholder focus and priorities | | | | |
|---|---|---|---|---|---|
| | Student | Faculty | Accessibility services | Senior administrators | Parent/ guardian |
| Academic rigor | Needs tutoring. Wants language requirement waived. | Asserts that advanced foreign language course is central to the major. Other cross-cultural courses are not substitutes. | Proposes course substitutes as a "reasonable" accommodation. | Consults with accessibility services and faculty. | Student is already stressed. Asks about pass/fail. |
| New pedagogies | Remains open to suggestions that could satisfy language requirement. | Expresses concern about setting precedent. Offers tutoring. | Suggests tutoring, summer courses, more personalized instruction. | No major role in this case. | No major role in this case. |
| Technology | Asks about virtual language course and access to translation software. | Expresses concern that use of technology may set a precedent. Fundamental alteration? | Brainstorms various methods of support for satisfying requirement. | Provides funding as needed. | No major role in this case. |

Table 10.3 maps the lenses of stakeholders for disability law, attitudes, and inclusion/socialization. Disability law plays a key role in solving the dilemma posed by this case. Here, initially, Brianna feels entitled to the ADS determination of eligibility for a waiver of the foreign language requirement but is slowly recognizing that competing policies and academic expectations are important to the faculty. ADS, upon the advice of general counsel, has suggested a thoughtful (not ad hoc) and deliberative process to consider alternatives and different ways of learning languages for students with learning differences.

General counsel recommended consideration of the *Wynne v.*

*Tufts University School of Medicine* (1991/1992) case, which outlines a deliberative and transparent process for determining whether an accommodation is a fundamental alteration. This case is based on the court's deference to academics only when a fair and deliberative process is followed. In the event of an Office for Civil Rights (OCR) complaint or a court case brought by a student, the *Wynne v. Tufts* process protects the college from discrimination complaints when the institution can show its sincere efforts in reviewing whether the student's request is compatible with or defeats the essential academic standard. Importantly, the process requires the faculty to consider and research alternative accommodations for students with disabilities that would be compatible with the requirements of the degree program.

As described in Chapter 8 of this volume, Paul Grossman and Jamie Axelrod recommend that colleges employ this process to deal with a claim of fundamental alteration as described by the courts and referred to as *Wynne v. Tufts*. ADS, with the support of general counsel, recommends that the college follow this process with Brianna's request for a waiver and consider the alternatives and strategies for support suggested by ADS.

Based on the *Wynne v. Tufts* decision and the many judicial and OCR decisions that followed, in order to meet the demonstration of duty to engage in a deliberative process, Paul Grossman (Chapter 8) recommends that the college

- convene a committee of relevant administrators and faculty, possibly including an ADS representative.
- charge the committee to carefully review the student's proposed accommodation to determine whether it is compatible with or defeats one or more of the essential objectives of the program in which the student is enrolled or whether implementing the proposed accommodation would lower an essential academic standard.

- search for alternative, compatible accommodations, if the student's proposed accommodation defeats the essential program objective

Note that the *Wynne v. Tufts* process does not guarantee the student will receive the waiver nor that faculty necessarily prevail. In fact, in the *Wynne v. Tufts* case the courts upheld the denial of student accommodation after faculty members completed their in-depth review of the student's request, deciding that the accommodation was a fundamental alteration in the medical school examination policy. The important takeaway from this case is that there must be a measured and open process to consider alternatives that could be adopted. If in the opinion of the faculty there are no alternative accommodations that satisfy the requirements of the program, then the student will still be denied a waiver. In the court's view, the judgment of fundamental alteration is in the purview of academia, but the court insists there be an established, deliberative process to review the alternatives, not an ad hoc reflexive response to a request for an accommodation.

Table 10.3 captures the benefits of a collaborative *Wynne v. Tufts* process. Although Brianna still feels entitled to the waiver, she begins to learn about the faculty's perspectives, expectations, and responsibilities. The framework maps out opportunities for change, for learning new perspectives, and for broadening recognition of differences; it also highlights opportunities for including the faculty perspective to consider learning differences that require alternative supports, use of technology, and ways for students to demonstrate knowledge.

## Table 10.3
*The Collaborative Framework Considering Disability Law, Attitudes, and Inclusion/Socialization*

| Lens | Example of stakeholder focus and priorities | | | | |
|---|---|---|---|---|---|
| | Student | Faculty | Accessibility services | Senior administrators | Parent/ guardian |
| Disability law | Is entitled to approved accommodations for language requirement. | Engage *Wynne v. Tufts* process to address questions of fundamental alteration and academic rigor. | Suggests several alternative ways to achieve the requirement. Participate in *Wynne v. Tufts* process. | Ensures compliance. Supports both student and faculty. Gets general counsel involved. | Advocates for student's rights. |
| Attitudes | Could feel discriminated against. May understand faculty perspective. | Current major has solid requirements. Needs to consider rigidity of language requirements. | Wants to find a satisfactory resolution for all through collaborative process. | Wants to find a satisfactory resolution for all involved. | Expects the institution to provide what they want. |
| Inclusion/ socialization | Is entitled to accommodations. Collaborative process promotes inclusion. | Considers alternatives to current language requirements. | Sustains collaborative discussion of alternative solutions. | Facilitates collaborative discussions among stakeholders. | Hopes for a positive outcome. |

How did Brianna's case end up? The GS faculty consulted with general counsel and ADS and considered alternative ways to satisfy the language requirement. They concluded that the foreign language waiver was a fundamental alteration; however, they were supportive of the accommodations (e.g., extra time on exams), tutorial support, and use of translation technologies that would give Brianna access to completing the foreign language requirement. Their empathy for the student, knowledge of her learning difference, and interest in applying the accommodations and scaffolding that would support Brianna through her degree program allowed her to remain in their department and made the faculty invested in her success. Ensuring fair and equitable access for students with disabilities in educational environments and acknowledging that they belong to a diverse intersectional community can begin to reverse the exclusion and neglect that students with disabilities face in higher education.

Likewise, the faculty may begin to consider alternatives to the long-standing policy requiring an upper-level language course. Changes in technology must be considered when evaluating the academic rigor of academic programs. Parents would welcome the careful consideration of Brianna's request and trust the institution to consider all reasonable requests for alternatives to satisfy the language requirements. ADS working with senior administration, including general counsel, facilitates the discussions of alternative solutions during the *Wynne vs. Tufts* process.

Key lessons learned from Brianna's case include the following:

- This specific case had two areas of conflict: (1) between the GS department and the student, and (2) between the GS faculty and ADS, which found Brianna eligible for a foreign language waiver.
- The framework facilitated a resolution by bringing to the surface all stakeholder perspectives in an objective way by allowing all stakeholders to consider the roles, responsibilities, and priorities of all involved.
- The framework facilitated problem solving and conflict resolution by sharing all stakeholder perspectives of the problem both at a high level and at a detailed, granular level—what the issues were and where there were potential areas of common ground. ADS played a key role as mediator and facilitator.
- The framework supported diversity by helping to implement inclusivity for students with disabilities and inspiring a process that was inclusive of all stakeholders, with specific attention to individual differences.

## Identifying Allies and Collaborators

Because the framework specifies the major stakeholders and their responsibilities, it can help to identify potential allies and collaborators. Pfeifer et al. (2020) found that students with disabilities in science, technology, engineering, and math (STEM) majors who had gained knowledge of self, rights, accommodations, and learning contexts were better able to effectively communicate with accessibility services providers and with their instructors. The framework is a useful tool to include in student consultations with ASD staff or advisors.

For advisors who may not know exactly how to advise students with disabilities with respect to accommodations, Helen Whall, professor emerita of English, recalled how the framework can be helpful to faculty and students.

> The Framework . . . it is a teaching device for teachers and that is something—especially established faculty—we're a hard group to teach. What I love about the framework is that it pulls it together. And I can look at it and say, "Who is responsible for what, and what do these words mean?" If I am responsible for this, and then I look over and look at pedagogical strategies on accommodations, and I say, "What does that mean?" and I look up the framework and say, "Oh! I think I'll call up [administration] and find out." So, I love the coordination of it; I love the fact that it provokes questions like "What does that mean if that is my responsibility?" and the synthesis of it, I think, is really useful.
>
> With faculty advising, I've always said that I do not know all the answers, but I know the people to call with the answers. Then these things develop and you wonder, Do I still know who to call? And on something like disability issues—which is hitting the university level more now—I think it has been

coming from the ground up that students are coming in, [they] are better aware of their rights, better dealt with in high school as far as accommodations and alternative strategies—so now they're my advisee. Well, that becomes a disclosure that we will have this accommodation that will help them locate assistance. Who do you talk to about this? The self-advocacy model—then I can become a collaborator with my advisee as to how they can continue to develop and self-advocate. (Lipsitz et al., 2018)

## Using the Framework to Empower Through Shared Knowledge

The framework informs all stakeholders of potential allies, collaborators, and resources for meeting the needs of students with disabilities. It also reveals potential conflicts so that through a collaborative process common ground can be identified.

### Enhancing Student Advocacy and Self-Determination

Chapter 1 describes the research showing that the knowledge of the specific process and the right connections in the hierarchy of the institution are key to successful student advocacy, especially in student–faculty relationships (Bruce & Aylward, 2021). The framework acts as a road map for a student's search for allies and provides some context for resistance to requests.

> Meeting the needs of students with disabilities requires disability services providers to work with other stakeholders to be effective. And while the traditional model requires students to reach out to disability services providers, faculty members, and others for the support they need, many students don't realize what services are available and don't understand who does what on campus. (Hope, 2021, p. 6)

The framework clarifies who does what and why. As students better understand how the system works, they become more effective in their self-advocacy.

Students with disabilities, such as Jenny, a former graduate student of education, have highlighted why the framework is useful for self-advocacy and understanding one's rights:

> Looking back on my experience as a student, I definitely wish that I had a tool like the framework. When I used the framework, I was able to reflect on my experience with disability services in a more comprehensive way than I would have without it. It was my first time seeking accommodations, so I would have found something like the framework especially useful in understanding and contextualizing my rights and role as a student with a disability. In this way, I was new to everything about disability services, so having extra support in understanding not only my rights, but different parts about the accommodation process, would have been helpful. Another thing is that I see this framework as potentially useful in the evaluation realm. And as a student, I could have tracked my own progress in building my skills as a self-advocate by looking at differences in myself from semester to semester. (Lipsitz et al., 2018)

### Facilitating Onboarding and Training of New ADS Staff and Other Employees

The framework can be used as a training tool for any of the stakeholders or, for that matter, anyone interested in how students with disabilities should be served within an academic environment. Currently, generally inadequate training exists to aid faculty members in helping students with disabilities succeed in their classes (Wizikowski, 2013). By reviewing cases or even legal proceedings using the framework, appropriate and effective roles and responsibilities of each stakeholder can be demonstrated through each lens. The matrix can provide a range of perspectives, from the very detailed view (for those working in ADS) to the broader view (for those collaborating with ADS) to the high-level view (for senior administrators). Moreover, court cases often result in mandatory training for college and university personnel. The framework could be employed as part of a comprehensive training model to meet such requirements.

In fact, Robert T. Jones, a former associate director of multicultural education, explains why the framework would be beneficial for organizational development and change:

> What really appeals to me is the fact that any particular issue or problem is seen through different lenses, and everyone has a part to play, but all those parts are not the same. I can see my role in relation to that of all of the other stakeholder roles. I envision having the participants break into groups and talk about the framework to break it down and come up with the best plan to support that student. Looking at something holistically, not just from a medical point of view, or a clinical point of view, or a counseling point of view, is needed to guarantee the success for a particular student. This is not reinventing the wheel. I think this is making the wheel better. (Lipsitz et al., 2018)

## Using the Framework to Assess and Analyze

### Analyzing Ongoing Cases

The framework can be used within ADS, potentially on a regular basis, for case review. ADS staff can note where things are going well, where there is potential for improvement, or where there may be risk of potential complaints. For example, any case review could reveal roles or responsibilities not being fulfilled for certain stakeholders or any number of lenses not being clearly attended to. Ongoing case conferencing with the framework could uncover areas of service provision or needs for further training (e.g., a better understanding of one's roles and responsibilities or of the lenses). For example, specialized training for ADS providers can be limited (Ofiesh & McAfee, 2000). Madaus et al. (2009) indicated that 9% reported no training in reading documentation, and only 27% received such training from their academic program.

Overall, case conferencing with the framework could provide for a detailed analysis of the workings of a case or a more general overview of how the campus environment is responding. A detailed analysis might reveal that a particular student is not receiving all the accommodations to which they are entitled. A more general analysis might reveal where collaboration among specific stakeholders is not working well. The beauty of a broader audience for case conferencing is that larger systemic issues can be identified and subsequently addressed. For example, the outcome of a broadly based case conference could be better working relationships among the stakeholders.

**Conducting Internal and External Reviews**

As colleges and universities conduct internal and external reviews for accreditation, assessment, and other purposes, the framework can be employed by ADS and others involved in providing services to students with disabilities. Moreover, there are likely ways to adapt the framework for use with other departments. ADS (and potentially other offices) may find the framework useful when conducting student learning outcomes assessment within their office or area; this could be part of a larger assessment project or a stand-alone assessment effort. For example, self-advocacy skills training is important for the success of students with disabilities (Wizikowski, 2013). Disability self-awareness education is a part of self-advocacy skills training and could easily be assessed as a student-learning outcome at the postsecondary level. The framework could function as an outline within which specific outcomes would have to be defined. The power of the framework in this regard is its capacity to provide a structure that could guide the assessment process. One could track the stakeholders contributing to a particular student learning outcome in conjunction with the specific lens through which they may be looking.

## Assessing Campus Attitudes Toward Students With Disabilities and Disability as Diversity

How well is the college or university responding to ADA requests? How is the institution treating students with disabilities? Where might any biases, misunderstandings, or need for further training be located? Trammel and Hathaway (2007) concluded that although the decision to seek help is complex and multilayered, a student's acceptance of accommodations is partly a function of the "disability environment" on campus. Marshak et al. (2010) suggested that campuswide awareness efforts be made so that the campus climate among students, staff, and faculty values students with disabilities and is as educated and understanding as possible about disability and accommodation issues. By looking at an amalgam of cases, the framework can indicate how well the various stakeholders are meeting the needs of students with disabilities and offer a snapshot of the campus climate vis-à-vis disability.

## Assessing Liability Risk and Gaps in Service Delivery

The framework is a powerful tool for assessing the effectiveness of service delivery for students with disabilities, evaluating the strengths and weaknesses of the ADS office, and identifying areas in need of improvement. For example, the framework could reveal different interpretations of policy between different stakeholders, insufficient onboarding and faculty/staff training, and duplicative efforts leading to inefficiencies. Regular review of the framework with members of ADS with the administration (e.g., general counsel, upper administration) could ensure a review of updates in disability law and that ADS has adequate resources and staff. Such review offers a window into where an institution may be at risk for liability, where gaps in service delivery may exist, and which practices, policies, and/or attitudes might require improvement to lessen potential gaps in compliance.

### Analyzing a Decision or Process in the Past: What Went Right, What Went Wrong, and What Was Learned

One useful application of the framework is to facilitate the analysis of case studies involving students with disabilities to improve the service delivery that meets the expectations of all stakeholders and the law. The framework provides a readily used structure to collect, organize, and analyze the most significant information about a particular case. It is also useful for comparing best practices and benchmarks against the specific details of a particular case study. The example that follows shows how the framework can facilitate the analysis of a case that ended up in the courts.

The following case (*Grabin v. Marymount Manhattan College*, 2014) highlights the importance of clear communication among stakeholders; collaborative practices among academic and student services administrators; and the importance of sharing and respecting distinct roles, responsibilities, and knowledge when providing accommodations for a disability. Heather Grabin was a transfer student majoring in communications at Marymount, primarily a women's college, in Manhattan, New York. Grabin had a history of a variety of illnesses. While Grabin displayed effective communication to most stakeholders, she especially inspired trust that allowed several faculty members to support her. However, her self-advocacy failed with one adjunct professor who taught a core course for her major. When this professor followed neither his own course absence policies nor the college's rules, Grabin contacted the academic and student services office for help in securing fair and equitable treatment, requesting adjustments after several absences and missed assignments due to urgent care visits and a hospitalization. After several appeals during and after the course, Grabin independently completed the assignment for the course; however, the professor refused to accept it. The academic dean finally told Grabin that she had no power to interfere with or change a faculty decision about grades or accommodations. The dean of students remained unmoved after Grabin's many appeals.

This case demonstrated strong student self-advocacy and a divided college administration that acted with an inconsistent and uncoordinated policy. In 2012, Grabin initiated legal action, alleging that Marymount discriminated against her on the basis of disability and claiming the school discriminately failed to accommodate her disability after she had provided medical documentation to administrators. Marymount moved for summary judgment, arguing that Grabin was not disabled, that the college was unaware of her disability, and that the college did not fail to offer her appropriate accommodations. The judge considered the significance of the student narrative and required an in-depth investigation of the facts, denying summary judgment for the college. While several depositions were obtained, the case was eventually dismissed for a lack of documentation, because records were kept by neither Grabin nor the college. However, the case was extremely stressful for Grabin: It marginalized her and prevented her from getting her degree. This case was also a drain on the college's resources.

The case analysis detailed in Table 10.4 shows how the framework can be used to parse the intertwined responsibilities of stakeholders. Duplication and omissions are made apparent.

## Table 10.4
### Completed Collaborative Framework for Grabin v. Marymount Manhattan College Case

| Lens | Stakeholder | | | | |
|---|---|---|---|---|---|
| | Student | Faculty | Accessibility services | Senior administrators | Parent/ guardian |
| Self-advocacy | Grabin did not provide documentation to ADS but did to admissions and housing officers. Informal agreements made with faculty. | Made informal agreements on deadlines. | Had no involvement, no record of request for accommodations, and no written diagnosis from a qualified clinician. | One dean assured Grabin of flexible deadlines; the other did not believe she had a disability. | Self-supporting adult. No parental/ guardian role in this case. |
| Individual differences | Grabin notified associate dean of absences due to her illness and requested "reasonable accommodations." | While some faculty made ad hoc accommodations for absences, adjunct faculty was not clear on course policy. | Student affairs did not refer Grabin to accessibility services office or inform her of the policy. | Student services dean was notified by Grabin about her Thalassemia but did not believe she deserved accommodations. | No parental/ guardian role in this case. |
| Life transition | Grabin was managing her health and communicating with administrators and faculty on her own in order to complete her degree in communication arts and move on to employment. | Many but not all faculty were sympathetic and supportive. | Unaware of her documentation, ADS told Grabin they couldn't help her. | Did not help Grabin satisfy her graduation requirements. | No parental/ guardian role in this case. |
| Academic rigor | Grabin testified that she completed each project assigned and was assured of credit. Received unclear messages from faculty. | Adjunct professor did not actually give her credit for late assignments, so Grabin received a failing grade and was denied graduation. | Was not involved in the uncertainty of the case. | Student affairs administrators were unable to help Grabin. Upheld faculty decision in academic questions. | No parental/ guardian role in this case. |

Table 10.4 (Continued)

| Lens | Stakeholder | | | | |
| --- | --- | --- | --- | --- | --- |
| | Student | Faculty | Accessibility services | Senior administrators | Parent/ guardian |
| New pedagogies | Created alternative assignment deadline and format for final project and could not work with other students. | Adjunct professor denied access to submission portal because the deadline had passed and insisted on group project work. | Not involved. | Not involved. | No parental/ guardian role in this case. |
| Technology | Adequate technology skills in other courses. | Adjunct professor taught technology course but did not use alternative technologies or means of expression to satisfy requirements. | Not involved. | Not involved. | No parental/ guardian role in this case. |
| Disability law | Depended on her deans for support and information. | No knowledge. | Had no involvement, no record of request for accommodations, and no written diagnosis from a qualified clinician. | Did not consider compliance and the law. | No parental/ guardian role in this case. |
| Attitudes | Received confusing messages about policy for late assignments. Lax policy for students with disabilities. | Most faculty were supportive with ad hoc accommodations, but adjunct instructor was not supportive. | Not involved. | Conflicting messages between student services and academic affairs confused the student. | No parental/ guardian role in this case. |
| Inclusion/ socialization | No information pertinent to this case. | No information pertinent to this case. | ADS provided access for inclusion based on physical disability only, such as facilities access and physical accessibility. | Did not refer Grabin to ADS, denying her access to rights for students with disabilities. | No parental/ guardian role in this case. |

This case study is a classic example of stakeholders not performing their appropriate roles or fulfilling their responsibilities. In this case, each stakeholder decided on their own what would be the proper policy regarding accommodations. The analysis of this case reveals the following:

- There was no consistent institutional policy for accommodations that would have ensured compliance with the law.
- There was no collaborative and cooperative process for accommodations.
- Faculty, adjunct faculty, and senior administrators were apparently untrained in disability law and best practices.
- Stakeholders did not refer the student to ADS.

One recommendation is clear: ADS and other student service offices should partner with the faculty and administration to provide a pathway to access support (e.g., access services, mental health counseling, health services, academic services). This case demonstrates that better collaboration upfront will drive consistency and clarity for students as well as for other stakeholders, including faculty and administrators. Training all stakeholders on accommodation policies, mandated access, and the role of ADS is also an important action item.

## Conclusion

Ensuring access, equity, and inclusion for students with disabilities is complex, because the law and practice together demand individualized determinations and decisions. With its emphasis on collaboration, the framework is a practical and useful tool for all stakeholders to navigate the complexities inherent in providing services to students with disabilities. Throughout this book, the authors share their personal and professional experiences that animate and operationalize the framework. Their scholarship and insights highlight the importance of collaboration as well as inclusive and transparent processes that promote openness to achieve equity for those who may otherwise be marginalized or excluded.

## References

Bruce, C., & Aylward, M. (2021). Disability and self-advocacy experiences in university learning contexts. *Scandinavian Journal of Disability Research, 23*(1), 14–26. https://doi.org/10.16993/sjdr.741

Grabin v. Marymount Manhattan College, No. 12 Civ. 3591, 2014 WL 2592416 (S.D.N.Y. June 10, 2014). https://www.leagle.com/decision/infdco20140611e99

Hope, J. (2021). Adopt framework that promotes collaboration for providing disability services. *Disability Compliance for Higher Education, 26*(11), 6–7. https://doi.org/10.1002/dhe.31081

Lipsitz, N., Berger, M., & Berger, E. (2018, June 12–15). *Collaborative solutions for complex problems: Preventing disability complaints on your campus* [Conference presentation video]. Postsecondary Training Institute, Baltimore, MD, United States.

Madaus, J. W., Banerjee, M., & McGuire, J. M. (2009, April 2–4). *Preparing postsecondary learning disability documentation: Suggestions for practice* [Paper presentation]. Conference of the Council for Exceptional Children, Seattle, WA, United States.

Marshak, L., Van Wieren, T., Ferrell, D. R., Swiss, L., & Dugan, C. (2010). Exploring barriers to college student use of disability services and accommodations. *Journal of Postsecondary Education and Disability, 22*(3), 151–165. https://www.ahead.org/professional-resources/publications/jped/archived-jped/jped-volume-22

Ofiesh, N. S., & McAfee, J. K. (2000). Evaluation practices for college students with LD. *Journal of Learning Disabilities, 33*(1), 14–25. https://doi.org/10.1177/002221940003300105

Pfeifer, M. A., Reiter, E. M., Hendrickson, M., & Stanton, J. D. (2020). Speaking up: A model of self-advocacy for STEM undergraduates with ADHD and/or specific learning disabilities. *International Journal of STEM Education, 7*, Article 33. https://doi.org/10.1186/s40594-020-00233-4

Trammell, J., & Hathaway, M. (2007). Help-seeking patterns in college students with disabilities. *Journal of Postsecondary Education and Disability, 20*(1), 5–15. https://www.ahead.org/professional-resources/publications/jped/archived-jped/jped-volume-20

Wizikowski, H. T. (2013). *Academic support experiences and perceptions of postsecondary students with disabilities: A public and private university comparison* (Publication No. ED552851) [Doctoral dissertation, Claremont Graduate University School of Educational Studies]. ProQuest Dissertations and Theses Global.

Wynne v. Tufts University School of Medicine, 932 F.2d 19 (1st Cir. 1991), *aff'd*, 976 F.2d 791 (1st Cir. 1992). https://law.justia.com/cases/federal/appellate-courts/F2/976/791/47641

# Appendix

## The Collaborative Framework

| Lens | Stakeholder | | | | |
|---|---|---|---|---|---|
| | Student | Faculty | Accessibility services | Senior administrators | Parent/ guardian |
| Self-advocacy | | | | | |
| Individual differences | | | | | |
| Life transition | | | | | |
| Academic rigor | | | | | |
| New pedagogies | | | | | |
| Technology | | | | | |
| Disability law | | | | | |
| Attitudes | | | | | |
| Inclusion/ socialization | | | | | |

*Note.* Copyright © 2023 by Neal E. Lipsitz, Michael Berger, and Eileen Connell Berger.

# Index

*Figures and tables are indicated by "f" and "t" following the page numbers.*

## A

Abes, E., 127, 128–129
Ableism
    as barrier to registering for accommodations, 127
    disability disclosure and, 128, 129
    discrimination and, 107–108
    in higher education, 125–126
    inclusion of students and, 62
    job descriptions and, 118
    in language and policies of institutions, 8
Academic experiences and sense of belonging, 64–65
Academic performance and success
    access and disability services' impact on, 126–127, 178–180
    inclusion of students and, 25–26
    life transition and, 10
    peer support and, 9–10
    predictors of, 178–179
    self-advocacy and accommodations, 4, 10
    students' responsibility for, 110, 113, 115–116
Academic rigor
    Collaborative Framework, 12–14
        discrimination example using, 232, 233*t*
        problem-solving example using, 218–219, 220*t*
    defined, 12
    faculty and, 12–13, 23–24, 142
    stakeholder roles and responsibilities, 31, 33*t*, 34, 36*t*
    universal design for learning and, 144, 153
    waivers of required courses and, 216–217
Access and disability services (ADS)
    academic outcomes, impact on, 126–127, 178–180
    academic rigor and, 12–13
    accommodation plans, 77
    accommodation types, 7, 11
    assistive technology and, 18–20, 202–203
    Collaborative Framework
        discrimination example using, 231–235, 233–234*t*
        lenses mapped to, 28–30, 29*t*
        roles and responsibilities in, 31, 33*t*, 34, 35–37*t*
        used in training for, 227–228
    COVID-19 pandemic and impact on, 162–168
    denial of accommodations and, 113–114
    downsizing of, 186
    empowerment from, 50
    faculty training and, 19, 129
    FERPA rights of students and, 109–110
    funding for, 117
    grievances and complaints, 116
    inclusion of students and, 28, 78
    life transition and, 11
    outreach initiatives of, 25
    problem-solving and dialogue on changing needs, 127–128
    service delivery effectiveness and, 230–231
    stakeholder collaborations, 114–115, 216
    student awareness of, 10, 226–227
    student success and, 126–127, 178–180
    technology companies, engagement with, 204
    waivers of required courses, case example, 215–224, 218*t*, 220*t*, 223*t*
AccessComputing, 200

Accessible, defined, 194–195
Accommodation letters, 95–98
Accommodations, xviii, 89–104. *See also*
  Access and disability services; Assistive
  technology; Disability law; Self-advocacy
  case reviews for, 228–229
  collaborations with stakeholders for, 216
  confidentiality and, 110
  for coursework, 75–77
  COVID-19 pandemic and, 160–161
  denial of, 113–114, 132, 161, 162–167,
    180–181, 183–185, 222, 231–235
  disability rights and, 112–114
  disclosing disability and, 127–129,
    143–144
  faculty and, 7–8, 25, 93, 95–98, 113
  funding for, 117
  graduate school and, 94–98
  inconsistencies in, 108
  individual differences and, 7–8
  introduction to disability services and,
    90–92
  online learning and, 162–166
  parental advocacy for, 7, 10, 91, 92,
    109–111, 217
  personal account of, 51
  PhD programs and, 98–102
  predictors of student success and use of, 179
  recommendations from ADS offices for, 11
  requesting, 111–112, 125–126
  stigma and, 24
  UDHE approach and reduced need for, 199
  undergraduate years and, 92–93
ADA (1990). *See* Americans with Disabilities Act
ADHD (attention-deficit/hyperactivity
  disorder), 131, 132, 179. *See also*
  Neurodiversity
Administration
  academic rigor and, 13
  assistive technology and, 202
  attitudes about students with disabilities, 24
  Collaborative Framework
    lenses mapped to, 28–30, 29t, 30f
    roles and responsibilities in, 31, 33t, 34,
      35–37t
  disability rights and, 117, 177
  inclusion of students and, 77–78
  new pedagogies and, 17
  student support services, training for
    faculty on, 21–22
  training for, 25
  universal design for learning and, 155

ADS. *See* Access and disability services
Advisors, 14, 93, 129, 225–226
Advocacy. *See* Self-advocacy
Advocacy organizations, 175
AHEAD (Association on Higher Education
  and Disability), 78, 187
Ahn, M. Y., 64
Allies and collaborators, 225–226
Alternative-format materials, 180
Americans with Disabilities Act (ADA, 1990)
  accommodation denials and, 113
  accommodation requests and, 111–112
  on assistive technology, 18, 194
  COVID-19 pandemic and, 169
  disability rights provided by, 107–109, 113
  enforcement of, 181–182
  individual differences among students and
    accommodations for, 7
  revisions to, 169
Anxiety, 125, 160, 167
Aquino, Katherine C., xviii, 26, 27, 61, 66
Ashmore, J., 121
Assessments
  accommodations for, 97, 100, 110
  Collaborative Framework for preparing, 4
  internal and external reviews, 229–230
  new pedagogies and, 14–17
  universal design for learning and, 18, 146,
    148, 152–155
Assistive technology (AT), xix, 189–211
  Collaborative Framework, 17–20,
    200–205, 201f, 207–208
    discrimination example using, 232, 234t
    problem-solving example using,
      218–219, 220t
  compliance issues with, 194–195
  course delivery and instruction, 149–150
  disability law on, 18, 194
  equity through, 193–194
  funding for, 18, 202
  inclusion and access through, 19
  personal experience with, 190–193, 191f
  self-advocacy for, 200–201
  short- and long-term planning for, 18–19
  stakeholder roles and responsibilities, 31,
    33t, 34, 36t
  training in, 19, 204–205
  universal design for higher education and,
    195–199, 196f, 199f, 206–207
Assistive Technology Act (2004), 18
Association on Higher Education and
  Disability (AHEAD), 78, 187

# Index

Attention-deficit/hyperactivity disorder (ADHD), 131, 132, 179. *See also* Neurodiversity
Attitudes toward students with disabilities
   barriers to higher education and, 142
   Collaborative Framework, 22–25
      assessment of, 230
      discrimination example using, 232, 234*t*
      problem-solving example using, 220–222, 223*t*
   disability law implementation and, 23
   implicit bias and, 97
   personal account of, 48–49
   stakeholder roles and responsibilities, 31, 33*t*, 34, 37*t*
Auditory processing disorder, 216
Autism spectrum disorder, 66, 135, 204. *See also* Neurodiversity
Autonomy, 57–58
Axelrod, Jamie, xix, 159–160, 166–168, 174, 177–183, 185–187, 221
Aylward, M., 6

## B

Background knowledge, 150
*2012/2017 Beginning Postsecondary Students Longitudinal Study (BPS:12/17)*, 68–71, 69–70*t*
Behling, K., 145, 147, 153, 156
Belonging, 63–66. *See also* Inclusion and socialization
Berger, Eileen Connell, xvii, 3, 45, 215
Berger, Michael, 3, 15, 159, 215
Bettencourt, G. M., 64
Bias. *See also* Ableism; Attitudes toward students with disabilities
   Collaborative Framework, 218
   perceived rates of, 66
   visible disabilities and, 97
Blind students, 171–172, 193
Bruce, C., 6
Burgstahler, Sheryl, xix, 16, 21, 189
Burnout, neurodiversity and, 124–125

## C

Campus culture. *See* Attitudes toward students with disabilities
Campus leaders. *See* Administration

Case-based activities, 150
Case reviews and analyses, 228–229
Cawthon, S. W., 11
Center for Applied Special Technology (CAST), 144, 145, 153*t*, 198
Chevron Doctrine, 170
Chiu, Y.-C. J., 126–127
*The Chronicle of Higher Education*, on extra time for exams, 97
Chukwuma, E., 25
Civil rights. *See also* Disability law; Disability rights
   self-advocacy and, 5
   U.S. Department of Education. *See* Office for Civil Rights
   using courts to secure, 161
Closed captioning
   as assistive technology, 193, 202
   course delivery and instruction, 151–152
   for online courses, 155–156, 206
   universal design for higher education and, 206
   universal design for learning and, 147, 176–177
Coburn, K. L., 9
Cognitive development, 13
Cole, E., 11
Collaborative Framework, xvii, 3–42
   academic rigor, 12–14
   assistive technology, 17–20, 200–205, 201*f*, 207–208
   attitudes toward students with disabilities, 22–25
   blank grid of lenses and stakeholders, 32*t*, 237
   disability law, 20–22
   inclusion and socialization, 25–28
   individual differences, 7–8
   lenses of, 3, 4–28
   life transition, 9–12
   new pedagogies, 14–17
   online learning and, 207–208
   personal account of, 56–57
   purpose of, 3–4
   self-advocacy, 4–7, 226–227
   stakeholders in, 3, 28–37, 29*t*, 30*f*, 33*t*, 35–37*t*
Collaborative Framework, how to use, xix–xx, 215–237
   allies and collaborators, identification of, 225–226
   attitudes toward students with disabilities, assessment of, 230

empowerment through shared knowledge, 226–228
internal and external reviews, 229–230
liability risk and gaps in service delivery, assessment of, 230–231
ongoing cases, analysis of, 228–229
past decisions or processes, analysis of, 231–235, 233–234*t*
problem-solving example, 215–224, 218*t*, 220*t*, 223*t*
College of the Holy Cross, 201
Community-based learning, 17
Community colleges, 113
Confidentiality, 110. *See also* Privacy
Cook, B. G. (2000), 24
Cook, L., 21
Coping skills, 6, 132
COVID-19 pandemic
ADS offices and, 162–168
campus housing and, 167
disability law and, 160–170
employment for people with disabilities and, 118
MOOCs, rise in popularity of, 16
Crip theory (Abes & Darkow), 127
Cultural model of disability, 121–122
Culture of campuses. *See* Attitudes toward students with disabilities
Culver, K. C., 13–14
Curriculum. *See also* Universal design for learning
ableism and, 107–108
universal design for higher education and, 198–199, 199*f*
CVS drugstores, 171–172

# D

Danso-Danquash, Teresa, 23
Darkow, D., 127, 128–129
Davis, H. H., 64
Deaf students, 176–177, 193
Deil-Amen, R., 62
de Klerk, E. D., 19
Department of Education, U.S. (DOE), 143, 161. *See also* Office for Civil Rights
Depression, 125, 160
De Sisto, M., 74
Developmental disabilities. *See* Neurodiversity
Dining halls, 93, 113–114

Disability identity development model (Gibson), 8
Disability Knowledge Community, 78
Disability law, xix, 159–188. *See also specific laws and court cases*
on assistive technology, 194–195
attitudes toward students with disabilities, changes in, 23
Collaborative Framework, 20–22
discrimination example using, 232, 234*t*
problem-solving example using, 220–222, 223*t*
COVID-19 pandemic and, 160–170
disparate impact and, 171–174
diversity discussion, disability included in, 175–176
enforcement of, 20, 180–186, 194–195
federal government protection of civil rights, 170
mandated training and, 228
self-advocacy and, 6
stakeholder roles and responsibilities, 31, 33*t*, 34, 37*t*, 174–175
student success and ADS offices, 178–180
updates to, reviewing, 230
Disability resource offices and professionals. *See* Access and disability services
Disability rights, xviii, 105–120
accommodation process and, 112–114
collaborations for, 114–115
fight for, 107–108, 112, 170
grievances, 115–116
human resources and, 117–118
life transition and, 108–112
senior-level administration and, 117, 177
student awareness of, 226–227
Disability services office. *See* Access and disability services
Disclosure of disabilities. *See* Self-disclosure of disabilities
Discrimination. *See also* Ableism; Disability law
disparate impact theory and, 171–174
medical model of disability and, 121
perceived rates of, 66
Discussion board posts, 154
Discussion groups, 149
Disparate impact theory, 171–174
Distance learning. *See* Online learning
Diversity. *See* Individual differences
Diversity, equity, and inclusion (DEI) initiatives, 26–27, 142, 161–162, 173, 175–176

# Index

DOE (United States Department of Education), 143, 161. *See also* Office for Civil Rights
DO-IT (Disabilities, Opportunities, Internetworking, and Technology) Center, University of Washington, 21, 200–201, 201*f*
DOJ (United States Department of Justice), 20, 161, 182, 194–195
Dukes, Lyman L., III, xviii, 141, 152

## E

Educational records, 109. *See also* FERPA
Employment, 117–118
Empowerment
　of ADS offices, 50
　Collaborative Framework for, 226–235
　diversity, equity, and inclusion initiatives, 26–27
　new pedagogies and, 14
　universal design for higher education and, 195
English language learners, 176–177, 193
Equal Employment Opportunity Commission (EEOC), 20, 160, 161
Equity, 58, 133. *See also* Assistive technology; Diversity, equity, and inclusion initiatives
Escher, Jill, 123
Evans, N. J., 141
Exams, 97, 100, 110. *See also* Assessments
Executive functioning, 148
External reviews, 229–230

## F

Faculty
　academic rigor and, 12–13, 23–24, 142
　accommodations and, 7–8, 25, 93, 95–98, 113
　as advisors, 14, 93, 129, 225–226
　as allies, 114
　assistive technology training for, 19, 204–205
　attitudes about students with disabilities, 23–25
　Collaborative Framework
　　discrimination example using, 231–235, 233–234*t*
　lenses mapped to, 28–30, 29*t*, 30*f*
　roles and responsibilities in, 31, 33*t*, 34, 35–37*t*
　use of, 225–226
　competing accessibility needs in classes, 128
　disability law training for, 21–22, 24–25, 177, 182
　disclosure of disability to, 95–98, 128–129, 143–144
　inclusion and socialization of students, 27–28, 64–65, 72, 72–73*t*, 75–77
　as mentors, 129
　new pedagogies and, 16–17
　online classes and, 166–167, 207
　student support services, training on, 21–22
Family support. *See* Parents and guardians
FERPA (Family Educational Rights and Privacy Act, 1974), 27, 109–110, 111, 116
Flexible learning, 15–16
Flipgrid, 152
Forber-Pratt, A. J., 8
Free and Appropriate Public Education (FAPE), 110
Friendships. *See* Social supports and friendships
Fullan, M., 14
Fundamental alteration claims
　COVID-19 pandemic and, 160
　denial of accommodations and, 113, 180–181
　online learning and, 162–167
　problem-solving example using Collaborative Framework, 215–224

## G

Gething, L., 22
Gibson, Clara, 122
Gibson, J., 8
Gillen-O'Neel, C., 64
Grabin, Heather, 231–232
*Grabin v. Marymount Manhattan College* (S.D.N.Y. 2014), 231–235, 233–234*t*
Graduate school, 94–98, 102–103
Graduation rates, 62
Grossman, Paul, xix, 159, 160–166, 168–177, 179–187, 221
Group work, 149

Guardians. *See* Parents and guardians
Guest speakers, 151

## H

Hadley, W. M., 10
Hafner, D., 25–26
Harper, D. C., 25
Hathaway, M., 229–230
Hehir, T., 49
Helming, Carl, 112
Heumann, Judy, 27
Hidden disabilities, 97, 127. *See also* Neurodiversity
Higher Education Academy, 15
Higher Education Opportunity Act (2008), 144
HIPAA (Health Insurance Portability and Accountability Act, 1996), 27, 110
Homesickness, 65
Hope, J., 142
Housing, 90–92, 94, 100–101, 113–114, 167
Human resources, 117–118
Hutcheon, E. J., 8
Hybrid classes, 167

## I

IDEA (Individuals with Disabilities Education Act, 2004), 21, 110–111
Identity development, 8–9
IEPs (Individualized Education Programs), 111
Implicit bias, 97
Inclusion and socialization, xviii, 61–85. *See also* Diversity, equity, and inclusion initiatives; Social supports and friendships
    accommodations for, 7
    assistive technology and, 18–19
    campus culture and, 22
    Collaborative Framework, 25–28
        discrimination example using, 232, 234*t*
        problem-solving example using, 220–222, 223*t*
    disability resource professionals and, 78
    discussion and implications of study, 73–74
    life transition and, 9–11
    literature review, 64–67
    methods of study, 68–71, 69–70*t*
    personal account of, 52–53
    positionality of researcher, 67
    results of study, 71–72, 72–73*t*
    sense of belonging, defined, 63
    stakeholder roles and responsibilities, 31, 33*t*, 34, 37*t*, 74–78
    technology and, 18–19
Individual differences
    Collaborative Framework, 7–8
        discrimination example using, 232, 233*t*
        problem-solving example using, 218, 218*t*
    diversity concepts and, 23
    life transition and, 10–11
    personal account of, 54–56
    stakeholder roles and responsibilities, 31, 33*t*, 34, 35*t*
Individualized attention, 134
Individualized Education Programs (IEPs), 111
Individuals with Disabilities Education Act (IDEA, 2004), 21, 110–111
Interactive process of decision making, 162–163
Internal reviews, 229–230
Internships, 151
Isolation
    neurodiversity and, 124–125, 134–135
    social experiences and sense of belonging, 66
    student involvement on campus and, 10

## J

Jones, Robert T., 228

## K

Kampsen, A., 9, 10
Kasnitz, D., 121
Kim, E., 26
Knight, A., 127

## L

Lalor, A. R., 24
Langworthy, M., 14
*Laws, Policies, and Processes: Tools for Postsecondary Student Accommodation* (Vance & Thompson), 174
Leadership. *See* Administration

# Index

Leake, D. W., 75
Learning disabilities, 143, 179, 199. *See also* Neurodiversity
Learning management systems, 151–152, 180, 205
Leyser, Y., 23
Liability risks, 77, 230–231
Life transition
    Collaborative Framework, 9–12
        discrimination example using, 232, 233*t*
        problem-solving example using, 218, 218*t*
    defined, 9
    disability rights and, 108–112
    neurodivergence and, 133
    new pedagogies and, 16
    personal account of, 46–47
    stakeholder roles and responsibilities, 31, 33*t*, 34, 35*t*
Light, R. J., 11
Lipsitz, Neal E., xviii, 3, 121, 142, 215
Lombardi, A. R., 24
Los Angeles Community College District (LACCD), 171–172

## M

Mace, Ron, 143
Madaus, Joseph W., xviii, 141, 178–179, 229
Mandated reporters, 110
Marchetti, C., 78
Marshak, L., 229–230
Massive open online courses (MOOCs), 16
McGraw, Phil, 124
Meal plans, 113–114
Medical model of disability, 121, 125–126, 135, 193
Medical records and diagnoses, 109–111
Mentoring, 15, 52–53, 129, 201
Mentor Program for Students of College of the Holy Cross, 201
Metacognition, 14
Microsoft, 204
Miller, A. L., 64
Mingus, M., 127
Mintz, Kevin T., xvii–xviii, 45
Mission of institutions, 22
MOOCs (massive open online courses), 16
*Music* (2021), 123

## N

NASPA–Student Affairs Administrators in Higher Education, 78
National Center for Education Statistics (NCES), 141
National Council on Severe Autism (NCSA), 123
National Institutes of Health (NIH), 56
National Science Foundation, 21
National Survey of Student Engagement, 64
Neurodiversity, xviii, 121–137
    assistive technology and, 193
    how to think about, 122–129
    personal experience on college campus, 130–135
Neurodiversity movement, 121–122
Neuroscience for Neurodiverse Learners (NNL), 200–201
*New Directions in Special Education* (Hehir), 49
Newman, L. A., 77–78
New pedagogies. *See also* Universal design for learning
    Collaborative Framework, 14–17
        discrimination example using, 232, 234*t*
        problem-solving example using, 218–219, 220*t*
    defined, 14
    stakeholder roles and responsibilities, 31, 33*t*, 34, 36*t*
NIH (National Institutes of Health), 56
NNL (Neuroscience for Neurodiverse Learners), 200–201
Northern Arizona University (NAU), 167, 187
Noyens, D., 65

## O

Obsessive-compulsive disorder (OCD), 131, 134
ODL (open distance learning), 19
Office for Civil Rights (OCR, U.S. Department of Education)
    on accommodations for online learning, 162
    on assistive technology, 194–195
    complaints filed with, 116, 161
    enforcement of disability laws, 20, 49, 180
    fundamental alteration determinations and, 221
Office of Student Accessibility Services. *See* Access and disability services

Online learning
  accommodations for, 162–166
  Collaborative Framework, 207–208
  effectiveness of, 165–166
  live-streaming lectures, 163–164, 167
  massive open online courses, 16
  new pedagogies and, 15, 17
  open distance learning, 19
  remote employment and, 118
  remote participation in traditional classes, 164–165
  universal design for higher education, 205–208
  universal design for learning, 147, 152, 155–156
Open distance learning (ODL), 19
Organizational development, 228
Organizational skills, 132

## P

Palmer, J. M., 19
Parents and guardians
  accommodations, advocacy for, 7, 10, 91, 92, 109–111, 217
  Collaborative Framework, roles and responsibilities in, 31, 33*t*, 34, 35–37*t*
  FERPA rights of students and, 109, 116
  inclusion and socialization of students and, 27
  life transition and, 11–12
Past decisions, analyses of, 231–235, 233–234*t*
Peer support, 9–10. *See also* Social supports and friendships
Pesonen, H. V., 66
Pfeifer, M. A., 6, 225
PhD programs, 98–102, 103
Piro, Valerie, xviii, 89
Polling tools, 152
Posey, A., 145, 147, 153, 156
PowerPoint lessons, 151–152
Privacy, 110, 163–164, 202
Problem solving, 215–224, 218*t*, 220*t*, 223*t*
Procurement policies and procedures, 203
Psychosocial disability identity development model (Forber-Pratt & Zape), 8

## R

Racism, 107
Rao, K., 145
Reed, D. S., 10
Rehabilitation Act (1973). *See also* Section 504 of Rehabilitation Act
  accommodations under, 110–111
  on assistive technology, 18
  increase in students with disabilities and, 23
Remote learning. *See* Online learning
Remote participation in traditional classes, 164–165
Research projects for students, 15, 64
Residence halls, 90–92, 94, 112–113
Retention rates, 64–66

## S

Scaffolding, 15–16
Scott, S. S., 78, 153
Screen readers, 193
Section 504 of Rehabilitation Act
  on assistive technology, 18, 194
  COVID-19 pandemic and, 169
  enforcement of, 181, 183–184
  on IEPs, 110–111
  implementation of, 23, 107–108
  protesters fighting for, 112, 170
  revisions to, 169
Self-advocacy, xvii–xviii, 45–60
  academic success and, 4, 10
  assistive technology and, 200–201
  Collaborative Framework, 4–7, 226–227
    discrimination example using, 232, 233*t*
    problem-solving example using, 218, 218*t*
  defined, 4
  knowledge of disability and accommodations, 6–7
  personal accounts of, 46, 53–54, 57–59, 109, 227
  skills training in, 6, 10, 229–230
  stakeholder roles and responsibilities, 34, 35*t*
Self-assessment, 14
Self-awareness, 6, 11, 229
Self-determination
  Collaborative Framework, 226–227
  gaining skills in, 201
  life transition and, 10
  personal account of, 57–59
  self-advocacy and, 5

# Index

Self-directed learning, 15–16
Self-disclosure of disabilities
    academic outcomes and, 126–127
    to access accommodations, 10, 127–129, 143–144
    barriers to, 127, 129
    disability law and, 21
    employment and, 117–118
    to faculty, 95–98
    rates of, 76, 141
Self-reflection, 7, 15, 58
Sense of belonging, 63–66. *See also* Inclusion and socialization
Service delivery effectiveness, 230–231
Service-learning, 14–15
Shepler, D. K., 66
Shore, Stephen, 135
Sia (musical star), 123
Silver, P., 143
Smith, Terrence, 130
Social cues, 130–131
Socialization. *See* Inclusion and socialization
Social justice, 22, 141
Social or sociocultural model of disability, 121–122, 126, 136, 193–194
Social supports and friendships
    academic outcomes and, 9–10
    academic rigor and, 12–13
    inclusion and socialization of students, 27, 53, 65–66, 72, 72–73*t*
    life transition and, 9–10
    neurodiversity and, 124–125, 130–131, 134–135
    self-advocacy and, 5–6
*Southeastern Community College v. Davis* (1979), 183
Stakeholders. *See also* Access and disability services; Administration; Faculty; Parents and guardians; Students with disabilities
    accommodations, collaborations for, 216
    case reviews and analyses, 228–229, 235
    Collaborative Framework, 28–32, 29*t*, 30*f*, 32–33*t*
        discrimination example using, 231–235, 233–234*t*
        problem-solving example using, 215–224, 218*t*, 220*t*, 223*t*
        roles and responsibilities in, 34, 35–37*t*, 174–175
    disability law and, 174–175
    inclusion and socialization of students, 27–28
    personal account of experiences with, 49–52, 55
Stapleton, Issy, 123–124
Stapleton, Kelli, 124
STEM (science, technology, engineering, and math) majors, 6, 225
Stereotypes. *See* Attitudes toward students with disabilities
Stigma
    attitudes about students with disabilities, 24
    disclosure of disability and, 128, 143–144
    inclusion of students and, 62, 66
    isolation and withdraw of students with disabilities, 10
    neurodiversity and, 125
    self-advocacy and, 5, 6
Stodden, R. A., 75
Strayhorn, T. L., 61, 63
Stress. *See* Life transition
Student advisory groups, 114, 115
Student affairs administrators, 77–78
Student-centered stakeholder model, 200–201, 201*f*
Student engagement
    academic rigor and, 13
    inclusion and socialization, 62
    massive open online courses and, 16
    online learning and, 164–165
    self-efficacy and, 17
    universal design for higher education, 198–199
    universal design for learning, 144, 150, 152
Student involvement on campus. *See* Inclusion and socialization
Student learning outcomes assessments, 229–230
Student research, 15, 64
Students. *See also* Academic performance and success; Academic rigor; Assessments
    attitudes toward students with disabilities, 25
    diversity exposure as learning experience for, 23
    responsibility for success, 110, 113, 115–116
    self-directed learning, 15–16
Students with disabilities. *See also* Academic performance and success; Self-advocacy; Self-determination; Self-disclosure of disabilities
    Collaborative Framework
        lenses mapped to, 28–30, 29*t*, 30*f*
        roles and responsibilities in, 31, 33*t*, 34, 35–37*t*

predictors of success, 178–179
statistics on number of, 25, 141
Syllabi, 77, 147–148

## T

Teaching and learning centers, 203–204
Technology. *See* Assistive technology; Online learning
Technology companies, 204, 208
Test, D. W., 4, 5–6
Text-to-speech software, 193
Time management skills, 14, 131–132, 148
Tinto, V., 9, 62–63
Toxic positivity, 126
Training
  on assistive technology, 19, 203–205
  Collaborative Framework used in, 227–228
  on disability law, 21–22, 24–25, 177, 182
  mandatory, 228
  on reading documentation, 229
  on student support services, 21–22, 25
Trammel, J., 229–230
Transition to college. *See* Life transition
Treeger, M. L., 9
Tufts University School of Medicine, 184–185, 220–222, 223*t*
Tutoring centers, 179

## U

Undue burden
  COVID-19 pandemic and, 160
  denial of accommodations and, 113
  online learning and, 163–167
United States Department of Justice (DOJ), 20, 161, 182, 194–195
Universal design for higher education (UDHE)
  assistive technology and, 195–199, 196*f*, 199*f*, 206–207
  characteristics of, 195–197, 196*f*
  curriculum and instruction, 198–199, 199*f*
  IT designs, 197–198
  online learning and, 205–208
  principles of, 197
  in teaching and learning centers, 203–204

Universal design for learning (UDL), xviii–xix, 141–158
  advantages for all students, 176–177
  assistive technology and, 150
  campus partnerships and, 155–156
  course assessment and learner evaluation, 153–155
  course delivery and instruction, 149–153, 150*f*, 153*t*
  course design and planning, 147–149
  defined, 76, 142
  faculty training on, 22
  Higher Education Opportunity Act on, 144
  inclusion of students and, 27–28, 76
  new pedagogies and, 16
  online learning and, 147, 152, 155–156
  origins of, 143
  principles of, 144
  social or sociocultural model of disability and, 194
  UDL circle, 145–147, 146*f*
University of Arizona, 187
University of Washington, 21, 190–192, 200–202, 201*f*, 206–208
Upton, T. D., 25
U.S. Department of Education (DOE), 143, 161. *See also* Office for Civil Rights

## V

Vance, Mary Lee, xviii, 105
Veterans, 164
Video-based lessons, 152
Vision impairment, 171–172, 193
Vision or mission of institutions, 22

## W

Waivers of required courses, case example, 215–224, 218*t*, 220*t*, 223*t*
Walstra, R., 25
Web Content Accessibility Guidelines (WCAG), 197–198, 203
Whall, Helen, 225–226
Wheelchair accessibility, 90–91, 93–94, 99–101, 112
Wheeler, B., 22
Wolbring, G., 8
Woosley, S. A., 66

Wraga, W. G., 12
*Wynne v. Tufts University School of Medicine* (1st Cir. 1991/1992), 184–185, 220–222, 223*t*

# Y

Yeager, K., 5

# Z

Zape, M. P., 8